THE ORDERING MIRROR

The
Ordering Mirror

Readers and Contexts

THE BEN BELITT LECTURES AT BENNINGTON COLLEGE

Introduction by
PHILLIP LOPATE

FORDHAM UNIVERSITY PRESS
New York
1993

Library of Congress Cataloging-in-Publication Data

The Ordering mirror: readers and contexts / introduction by Phillip Lopate.
    p. cm.
Fifteen essays previously published. 1977–1992. in the Ben Belitt lecture series.
ISBN 0-8232-1515-6 : $30.00
    1. American literature—History and criticism. 2. English literature—History and criticism.
PS121.073 1993
810.9—dc20

To Edith Barbour Andrews
(Bennington '41)
"And now it is my turn!"

Contents

FOREWORD

"The Ben Belitt Lectureship Series is a pageant of minds, named
for a poet whose mind is a pageant."

John W. Barr
Chairman, Board of Trustees
Bennington College

When Bennington College alumna Edith Barbour Andrews (1941)
established the Ben Belitt Lectureship Series in 1977, she called it
"a thanks for the past and support for the future," citing the
"enchantment, devotion, and love for the written word" she experienced as a student at Bennington. Her passion, generosity, and
foresight resulted in a series of lectures—now a collection of
essays—by some of the keenest, most eloquent critics and writers
of our time.

In establishing the series, Andrews specified that the lectureship
be named in honor of her teacher Ben Belitt, and that publication
of the lecture chapbooks honor another Bennington teacher,
William Troy.

Troy, who taught at Bennington College for eight years
beginning in 1938, was a highly regarded critic during the 1930s
and 40s. Among the contemporaries with whom he ranks are
Edmund Wilson, Kenneth Burke, and R. P. Blackmur. In the
preface to the 1976 publication of William Troy: Selected Essays,
edited by Stanley Edgar Hyman, Allen Tate placed Troy "among
the handful of the best critics of this century." For his teaching at
Bennington and elsewhere, Hyman cited Troy as "the greatest of
lecturers in literature."

The year 1938 marked Ben Belitt's arrival on the Bennington
campus as well as the start of a teaching career that would span
more than five decades. Over that time, Belitt gained international
recognition as a poet, critic, and translator, garnering prizes and
honors for his six volumes of poetry, culminating in a collection of

"new and selected poems" published in 1986 under the many-faceted title of *Possessions*. His extensive translations of Borges, Alberti, Neruda, Lorca, and others, and his collection of essays dealing with the theory and practice of translations are also well known. His creative work, however, was always integral to his teaching creatively; and, for Bennington, it is as a teacher that he is held in such profound esteem.

At the 1977 inauguration of the series, Ben Belitt noted that "the Lectureship broadens the whole base of the College's continuing quest for a meeting of the best minds available for the implementing of the study of imaginative letters. . . . Though the Lectureship specifies my name, along with that of William Troy, my former colleague and mentor, I consider the real custodian to be the total intellectual fellowship which I have shared since 1938 in the service of a collective vision involving a community of letters, sciences, and arts, and embracing all modes of study and inquiry at Bennington."

The community of Bennington College welcomes the chance to share that collective vision through this remarkable series of essays.

ELIZABETH COLEMAN
President
Bennington College

INTRODUCTION: THE MONOLOGUE AS CONVERSATION

PHILLIP LOPATE

THIS ESSAY COLLECTION, by some of the best literary minds of our time, took over fifteen years to distill into book form. Originally, each essay was delivered as a formal lecture to the Bennington College community, and was issued shortly afterward as a chapbook, in handsome isolation. The latecoming reader has a different, time-collapsed experience of these annual events, as though a slow, stately academic procession were suddenly speeded up and crunched together. Also missing is the erotics of a formal lecture, as the audience, Leda-like, waits with resignation and receptivity for its Zeus to descend and take hold, while the speaker mayhap suffers performance anxiety. In return, however, the reader gains the cumulative opportunity to distinguish, at leisure, patterns of thought, rhetorical strategies, and common themes as they pass from one speaker to another, to participate in the call-and-response of intellectual life at this historical period. For what began as a series of monologues has become a conversation.

It may seem odd that a school like Bennington, renowned for informality and a spirit of improvisation, has chosen to sponsor a blue-chip parade of veteran intellects. Indeed, I must confess that I approached this almost too-respectable enterprise at first with skepticism, so often do such celebrations of intellectual eminence disappoint. I am happy to testify, though, that the Belitt Lectures provide a feast of thinking; collectively, they represent a state-of-the-art demonstration of the contemporary literary essay.

What unifies these fifteen singular voices is their passion for literature and their ability to bring language to life through a mode of witty and provocative discourse, at once magisterial and epigrammatic. The panache of the *mot juste* is often memorable: "He went at full tilt into the sump of his teenage self, filling notebooks with druggy, bewildering lines that would be a kind of fossil fuel to him for years to come" (Seamus Heaney on the young Dylan Thomas). "Dying cultures make the best cultures" (Richard Ellmann on Decadence). "The most authentic of literary Sublimes has the Epicurean purpose of rendering us discontented with easier pleasures in order to prepare us for the ordeal of more difficult pleasures" (Harold Bloom on Whitman and Stevens). "In particular, you cannot create a character without thereby making a suggestion about how your reader should act" (Richard Rorty on the inextricable bonds of aesthetics and ethics).

It would seem that the formal circumstance of public address has called forth, in our fifteen critics, a highly developed exchange of ironic courtesies. That they have been summoned to deliver a Belitt Lecture is clearly an honor, acknowledging as it does a publicly successful literary career; and yet the scale of the event—an hour-long talk—limits the range of possibilities, inspires modesty, compression, doubt. That ironic play between modesty and ambition is, in fact, part and parcel of the essay form, as Georg Lukács pointed out. It

> is at the root of that humor and that irony which we find in the writings of every truly great essayist. . . . And the irony I mean consists in the critic always speaking about the ultimate problems of life, but in a tone which implies that he is only discussing pictures and books, only the inessential and petty elements of real life—and even then not the innermost substance but only their beautiful and useless surface. . . . The essayist dismisses his own proud hopes which sometimes lead him to believe that he has come close to the ultimate: he has, after all, no more to offer than the explanations of the poems of others, or at best of his own ideas. But he ironically adapts himself to this smallness—the eternal smallness of the most profound work of the intellect in face of life—and even emphasizes it with ironic modesty.

Alongside the "ironic modesty" in these talks is a sort of pull toward the nobility of belief. Here we must remember that the literary address is not merely synonymous with the literary essay: because it is delivered orally, in this case before an assembled academic community, it must take into consideration expectations that might not affect the purely written literary essay. The specific circumstances seem to invite one to assert conviction—a credo of sorts—and also to leave the youthful listener in an expectant, or at least not too lugubrious, mood. Indeed, many of the Belitt Lectures follow a "plot" of working from darkness and gnarled doubt toward something a bit more hopeful.

What is even more striking, in our secular age, is the frequency of religious, sacred-ceremonial, or even necromantic references peppering these essays. George Steiner, who delivered the first address, perhaps set the tone with his very moving invocation of the old-fashioned ritual of reading, presenting the "ceremonious encounter between reader and book" as a kind of sacrament. Denis Donoghue, citing the Book of John, discusses the divinity of the Word. Frank Kermode titles his playful essay "Divination," and analyzes the impact of variant readings on theology in Revelation 1:5. Hugh Kenner devotes his whole talk to "Magics and Spells," concluding thunderously that "only triviality can pretend that by its analytic habits magic has at last been superseded." Cynthia Ozick invokes the supernatural, "sacred terror" and Swedenborgian metaphysics in Henry James's background. Bernard Malamud calmly testifies like a professional alchemist: "In writing I had to say what had happened to me, yet present it as though it had been magically revealed." Ben Belitt, the self-described "pre-humous" eponym of the series, caps the matter with his brilliant investigation of three spiritual texts, asking "how is praise possible for the modern spirit, in a time of techniques, methodologies, and sciences which invite the skeptical manipulation of all the categories of thought and matter, and substitute cunning for awe?" Seamus Heaney is introduced as one for whom poetry is "priestly, the most sacred vocation."

Why this insistence on awe, priestliness, and magic in a series of literary talks? Is it a compliment to the host, Mr. Belitt, whose course at Bennington "Literature and Belief" is still legendary, and who, as one student testified, "taught us to conceive of all literature as a sacred endeavor"? Can it be that the formal academic lecture is itself a kind of religious rite, focusing the attention in a way akin to liturgical service? Or is learning seen as such endangered arcana in a post-literate age that the literary scholar finds himself identifying with the scholar-monk? The critic as Magus? Clearly, sacredness and literary vocation are somehow intertwined. As Irving Howe, in his meaty essay, "The Making of a Critic," remarks: "in a secular age literary criticism carries a heavy burden of intention, becoming a surrogate mode of speech for people blocked in public life."

It is not surprising that the summons to give the Belitt Lecture would occasion some retrospection about the mission of a literary career. Irving Howe is perhaps the most frankly personal in his assessment of how he became a literary critic (first, he says, by copying the styles of Orwell, Wilson, Rahv, and Trilling!), and the most candid about questions of status and competition in the literary life. He sees himself as part of a "rude" generation of insurgent Jewish intellectuals who punctured the decorum of literary discourse. "All you needed to be called a literary critic, it seemed, was a determination to read with charged attention and a pencil in the clutch of your fingers." Of course, Howe testifies, it did not prove so easy; but his image of the pencil-clutching *arriviste* irresistibly calls to mind George Steiner's gentler vocational definition: "The intellectual is, quite simply, a human being who has a pencil in his or her hand when reading a book."

The role of the intellectual, his or her obligations toward and questionable utility to modern society, are problems much vexed in these pages. Saul Bellow, one of a trio of practicing "creative writers" or, in any case, "non-literary" critics, tries to slip the noose by arguing emphatically that "artists cannot be described as intellectuals. The divergence first manifests itself in differences of language, for the language of intellectuals is the common language of the cog-

nitions, whereas the languages of art are individual. Their uniqueness is a guarantee that they are genuine." The cerebral cognitions
put forward in this passage, and in the essay as a whole, appear to
contradict Bellow's point; here, at least, artist and intellectual would
seem to be one and the same beast. But Bellow wryly apologizes
for his penchant for ideas, saying "nobody wants to be a birdbrain."

If we look dispassionately at the particular group of critics and
writers assembled here, we find they have much in common,
which may help explain the intellectually coherent tone of the collection. They are men, with two exceptions (an imbalance we
hope and suspect will be corrected in future years); and moreover,
what used to be called "men of letters"—that is, free-ranging gen-
eralists and humanists, rather than the narrow academic specialist
umbilically attached to one theory or another, who proliferates
today in the study of literature. Half the Belitt lecturers are Jewish;
a third, Irish. They are for the most part over sixty, and, in a sense,
represent the end of a most eminent line of public intellectuals.
That there is, for the moment, no guarantee that their ranks will be
replenished by literary thinkers of equal stature and range may
account for a note of melancholy valediction that creeps from time
to time into these addresses. George Steiner mourns the loss of a
middle ground between illiteracy and over-specialization; Bernard
Malamud eyes "the resurgence of ignorance in our culture"; Saul
Bellow warns that "Only the purest human consciousness, art consciousness, can see us through this time of nihilism."

Some of this pessimism undoubtedly reflects the personal circumstances of aging individuals staring into their own mortality.
Here we might also cite what the storywriter Max Apple calls "the
style of middle age," or biology at the level of syntax. In Apple's
words: "The style of middle age is a style of reappraisal, a style characterized by hesitation, by uncertainty, by the objects of the world
rather than the passions that transported us from this world. . . .
When copulation loses her rough hold, when we have come near
to the end of our reproductive lives, we hesitate. When we look
past the body, we don't know what we'll find."

Nowhere is the style of middle age more sensitively probed than in Cynthia Ozick's analysis of the turning, in Henry James's art, from the entertaining Victorian lucidities of the early period to the murkier modernist quandaries and gravities of the middle and late James. Ozick shows that "the awkward age" is as much a reference to the menopausal male as the adolescent female.

There is another reason for the reflective hesitancy in these essays. Are the fifteen essayists not, for the most part, spokesmen for the infamous DWEMs (dead white European males)? Besieged on the one hand by multiculturalists and feminists who would revolutionize the syllabus, and on the other hand by deconstructionists who would jettison the very notion of great literary texts and authorship, no wonder they express an occasionally embattled sense of aristocratic isolation. But this isolation generously includes us, somehow. Perhaps it is in the nature of giving an important literary address to invite the audience under the canopy of quality: "we," the privileged few, surrounded by the howling barbarians of popular culture who disdain our intellectual activity.

Politics and its troubled relations with aesthetics is another recurrent theme in these essays. Denis Donoghue lays out the ground of the age-old argument between word and deed, formalism and social activism. Showing how writers of both the Right and the Left have inveighed against the dominant bourgeois culture, Donoghue concludes: "It is time to say that the bourgeois liberal has a strong case, if he would make it." And he makes it. Nadine Gordimer—who has given so much to the struggle against racism in her country—argues that fiction's only morality is to "explore and examine" with "unafraid honesty," as she threads her way gracefully through the snares of fiction, morals, and politics. From the other end, the perils of excessive aestheticism are taken up by Richard Ellmann and Richard Rorty. Ellmann explores "decadence" as both cul-de-sac and escape route. Rorty reads sensitively past Nabokov's own mandarin pronouncements on aesthetic bliss, to uncover the caring, cruelty-hating, disappointed liberal-humanist underneath. Indeed, the liberal re-emerges in these essays as an heroic, if battered, proponent of political principles that have much in common with a sympathetically belle-lettristic approach to literary study.

René Girard takes apart Shakespeare's consummate political play, *Julius Caesar*, to demonstrate that Brutus is not so much Caesar's principled antagonist as his mimic, and that "the characters disagree because they agree too much." Girard also challenges the familiar, political reading of the play that says Shakespeare showed a "conservative" bias in his treatment of the mob: "The crisis turns not only the lower classes into a mob but the aristocrats as well. . . . Our preoccupation with class struggle distorts our appreciation not only of Shakespeare but of tragic literature in general. Our virtuous defenders of the proletariat see only the symptoms that affect their protegés."

Ultimately, one of the greatest pleasures this collection affords is its strong, surprising readings of individual texts. I have already mentioned the Rorty, Girard, and Belitt analyses; I would like to add to the list the candor of Seamus Heaney's masterfully judicious reassessment of Dylan Thomas. In phrasing for us our own inner doubts about this sometimes bombastic and mechanically sentimental poet, then going on to show where and in which poems his genius lies, he performs an act of reclamation much more generous and effective than hagiographic criticism. Then there is Harold Bloom's powerful reading of Whitman's "When Lilacs Last in the Dooryard Bloom'd." Initially it seems outrageous and far-fetched, his premise that Whitman was masturbating as he wrote this great work. But a second reading of this essay has convinced me that Bloom is uncannily right about some of this material, and in any case has entered more deeply into Whitman's consciousness than most of Walt's explicators.

Irving Howe's essay includes an affectionately savvy dissection of Lionel Trilling's rhetorical strategy: "Trilling would begin with a simulated hesitation but soon plant a hint that just ahead lay some revelation about the ways in which 'we'—'the educated classes'— were misconstruing 'the cultural situation.'" Just so; it is interesting to figure out how each of the contributors to this collection adapts an essay strategy. Harold Bloom, who meanders through Bryant, Emerson, Hart Crane, and Stevens before tackling his main subject, lets us in on the joke: "Yet I am sneaking up on him, always the best way for any critic to skulk near the Sublime Walt." René Girard comes roaring out of the chute, demanding with rhetorical questions that we come quickly to the heart of the matter. Ben Belitt, alluding to Pascal's wager, lays down several preconditions for his argument, including the mischievously straight-faced "let us be somber." George Steiner begins with a painting, thereby triangulating his discourse between image, text, and listener. And so on. I would not want to spoil the reader's fun by giving away each maneuver in advance. It is enough to appreciate that we are watching masters of the game of essay-writing, who, even as they comment on the masterpieces of other writers, practice their own literary wizardry.

THE ORDERING MIRROR

Le Philosophe lisant, by Jean–Siméon Chardin.
Musée du Louvre, Paris

THE UNCOMMON READER

GEORGE STEINER

CHARDIN'S *Le Philosophe lisant* was completed on 4th December
1734. It is thought to be a portrait of the painter Aved, a friend of
Chardin's. The subject and the pose, a man or a woman reading a
book open on a table, are frequent. They form almost a sub-genre
of domestic interiors. Chardin's composition has antecedents in
medieval illuminations where the figure of St. Jerome or some
other reader is itself illustrative of the text which it illumines. The
theme remains popular until well into the nineteenth century
(witness Courbet's celebrated study of Baudelaire reading or the
various readers depicted by Daumier). But the motif of *le lecteur* or
la lectrice seems to have enjoyed particular prevalence during the
seventeenth and eighteenth centuries and constitutes a link, of
which Chardin's whole output was representative, between the
great age of Dutch interiors and the treatment of domestic subjects
in the French classical manner. Of itself, therefore, and in its historical context, *Le Philosophe lisant* embodies a common topic conventionally handled (though by a master). Considered in respect of
our own time and codes of feeling, however, this "ordinary"
statement points, in almost every detail and principle of meaning,
to a revolution of values.

Consider first the reader's garb. It is unmistakably formal, even
ceremonious. The furred cloak and hat suggest brocade, a suggestion borne out by the matte but aureate sheen of the coloration.
Though clearly at home, the reader is "coiffed"—an archaic word
which does convey the requisite note of almost heraldic ceremony
(that the shape and treatment of the furred bonnet most likely
derive from Rembrandt is a point of mainly art-historical interest).
What matters is the emphatic elegance, the sartorial deliberation of
the moment. The reader does not meet the book casually or in

disarray. He is dressed for the occasion, a proceeding which directs our attention to the construct of values and sensibility which includes both "vestment" and "investment." The primary quality of the act, of the reader's self-investiture before the act of reading, is one of *cortesia*, a term rendered only imperfectly by "courtesy." Reading, here, is no haphazard, unpremeditated motion. It is a courteous, almost a courtly encounter, between a private person and one of those "high guests" whose entrance into mortal houses is evoked by Hölderlin in his hymn "As on a festive day" and by Coleridge in one of the most enigmatic glosses he appended to *The Rime of the Ancient Mariner*. The reader meets the book with a courtliness of heart (this is what *cortesia* signifies), with a courtliness, a scruple of welcome and entertainment of which the russet sleeve, possibly of velvet or velveteen, and the furred cloak and bonnet are the external symbols.

The fact that the reader is wearing a hat is of distinct resonance. Ethnographers have yet to tell us what general meanings apply to the distinction between those religious and ritual practices which demand that the participant be covered, and those in which he is bare-headed. In both the Hebraic and the Graeco-Roman traditions, the worshiper, the consultant of the oracle, the initiate when he approaches the sacred text or augury, is covered. So is Chardin's reader, as if to make evident the numinous character of his access to, of his encounter with, the book. Discreetly—and it is at this point that the echo of Rembrandt may be pertinent—the furred bonnet suggests the headdress of the Kabbalist or Talmudic scholar when he seeks the flame of the spirit in the momentary fixity of the letter. Taken together with the furred robe, the reader's bonnet implies precisely those connotations of ceremony of intellect, of the mind's tensed apprehension of meaning, which induce Prospero to put on courtly raiment before he opens his magic books.

Observe next the hourglass beside the reader's right elbow. Again, we are looking at a conventional motif, but one so charged with meaning that an exhaustive commentary would nearly comprise a history of the Western sense of invention and of death. As

Chardin places it, the hourglass declares the relationship of time and the book. The sand sifts rapidly through the narrow of the hourglass (a sifting whose tranquil finality Hopkins invokes at a key point in the mortal turbulence of *The Wreck of the "'Deutschland'"*). But at the same time, the text endures. The reader's life is measured in hours; that of the book, in millennia. This is the triumphant scandal first proclaimed by Pindar: "when the city I celebrate shall have perished, when the men to whom I sing shall have vanished into oblivion, my words shall endure." It is the conceit to which Horace's *exegi monumentum* gave canonic expression and which culminates in Mallarmé's hyperbolic supposition that the object of the universe is *le Livre,* the final book, the text that transcends time. Marble crumbles, bronze decays, but written words— seemingly the most fragile of media—survive. They survive their begetters—Flaubert cried out against the paradox whereby he lay dying like a dog whereas that "whore" Emma Bovary, his creature, sprung of lifeless letters scratched on a piece of paper, continued alive. So far, only books have circumvented death and have fulfilled what Paul Eluard defined as the artist's central compulsion: *le dure désir de durer* (indeed, books can even survive themselves, leapfrogging out of the shadow of their own initial being: there are vital translations of languages long extinct). In Chardin's painting, the hourglass, itself a twofold form with its iconic suggestion of the torus or figure eight of infinity, modulates exactly and ironically between the *vita brevis* of the reader and the *ars longa* of his book. As he reads, his own existence ebbs. His reading is a link in the chain of performative continuity which underwrites—a term worth returning to—the survivance of the read text.

But even as the shape of the hourglass is a binary one, its import is dialectical. The sand falling through the glass tells both of the time-defying nature of the written word and of how little time there is in which to read. Even the most obsessed of bookmen can read only a minute fraction of the world's totality of texts. He is no true reader, no *philosophe lisant,* who has not experienced the reproachful fascination of the great shelves of unread books, of the libraries at night of which Borges is the fabulist. He is no reader who has not heard, in his inward ear, the call of the hundreds of thousands, of the millions of volumes which stand in the stacks of the British Library or of Widener asking to be read. For there is in each book a gamble against oblivion, a wager against silence, which can be won only when the book is opened again (but in contrast to man, the book can wait centuries for the hazard of resurrection). Every authentic reader, in the sense of Chardin's delineation, carries within him a nagging weight of omission, of the shelves he has hurried past, of the books whose spine his fingers have brushed across in blind haste. I have, a dozen times, slunk by Sarpi's leviathan history of the Council of Trent (one of the pivotal works in the development of Western religious-political argument); or the *opera omnia* of Nikolai Hartmann in their stately binding; I shall never manage the sixteen thousand pages of Amiel's (profoundly interesting) journal currently being published. There is so little time in "the library that is the universe" (Borges's Mallarméen phrase). But the unopened books call to us none the less, in a summoning as noiseless but insistent as is the sift of the sand in the hourglass. That the hourglass is a traditional prop of Death in Western art and allegory points up the twofold signification of Chardin's composition: the afterlife of the book, the brevity of the life of man without whom the book lies buried. To repeat: the interactions of meaning between hourglass and book are such as to comprehend much of our inner history.

Note next the three metal discs in front of the book. Almost certainly these are bronze medals or medallions used to weigh down, to keep smooth the page (in folios, pages tend to wrinkle and lift at their corners). It is not, I think, fanciful to think of these medallions as bearing portraits or heraldic devices or mottoes, this being the natural function of the numismatic arts from antiquity to the commemorative coin age or medallions struck today. In the eighteenth century, as in the Renaissance, the sculptor or engraver used these small circumferences to concentrate, to make incisive in the literal sense, a celebration of civic or military renown, to give

to a moral-mythological allegory lapidary, enduring pronounce-
ment. Thus we find, in Chardin's painting, the presentment of a
second major semantic code. The medallion also is a text. It may
date from or recompose words and images of high antiquity.
Bronze relief or engraving defies the mordant envy of time. It is
stamped with meaning as is the book. It may have returned to the
light, as do inscriptions, papyri, Dead Sea scrolls, from a long
sojourn in the dark. This lapidary textuality is perfectly rendered in
the eleventh of Geoffrey Hill's *Mercian Hymns*:

> Coins Handsome as Nero's; of good substance and weight. *Offa
> Rex* resonant in silver, and the names of his moneyers. They
> struck with accountable tact. They could alter the king's face.
>
> Exactness of design was to deter imitation; mutilation if that
> failed. Exemplary metal, ripe for commerce. Value from a sparse
> people, scrapers of salt-pans and byres.

But the "exemplary metal," whose weight, whose literal gravity,
keeps down the crinkling, fragile page, is itself, as Ovid said,
ephemeral, of brief durance, as compared with the words on the
page. *Exegi monumentum*: "I have reared a monument more lasting
than bronze" says the poet (remember Pushkin's matchless *reprise* of
Horace's tag), and by placing the medals before the book Chardin
exactly invokes the antique wonder and paradox of the longevity
of the word.

This longevity is affirmed by the book itself, which provides
the painting with its compositional center and light-focus. It is a
bound folio, in a garb which subtly counterpoints that of the reader. Its format and physique are those of stateliness (in Chardin's
period, it is more than likely that a folio-volume would have been
bound *for* its proprietor, that it would have carried his device). It is
no object for the pocket or the airport lounge. The posture of the
other folio behind the hourglass suggests that the reader is perusing
a multi-volume work. Serious work may well run to several tomes
(the eight volumes, unread, of Sorel's great diplomatic history of
Europe and the French Revolution haunt me). Another folio

looms behind the *lecteur's* right shoulder. The constituent values and
habits of sensibility are patent: they entail massiveness of format, a
private library, the commissioning and subsequent conservation of
binding, the life of the letter in a canonic guise.

Immediately in front of the medals and hourglass, we observe
the reader's quill. Verticality and the play of light on the feathers
emphasize the compositional and substantive role of the object.
The quill crystallizes the primary obligation of response. It defines
reading as action. To read well is to answer the text, to be answerable to the text, "answerability" comprising the crucial elements of
response and of responsibility. To read well is to enter into answerable reciprocity with the book being read; it is to embark on total
exchange ("ripe for commerce" says Geoffrey Hill). The dual
compaction of light on the page and on the reader's cheek enacts
Chardin's perception of the primal fact: to read well is to be read
by that which we read. It is to be answerable to it. The obsolete
word "responsion," signifying, as it still does at Oxford, the process
of examination and reply, may be used to shorthand the several and
complex stages of active reading inherent in the quill.

The quill is used to set down marginalia. Marginalia are the
immediate indices of the reader's response to the text, of the dialogue between the book and himself. They are the active tracers of
the inner speech-current—laudatory, ironic, negative, augmenta-
tive—which accompanies the process of reading. Marginalia may,
in extent and density of organization, come to rival the text itself,
crowding not only the margin proper but the top and bottom of
the page and the interlinear spaces. In our great libraries, there are
counter libraries constituted by the marginalia and marginalia on
marginalia which successive generations of true readers
stenographed, coded, scribbled, or set down with elaborate flourishes alongside, above, below, and between the horizontals of the
printed text. Often, marginalia are the hinges of aesthetic doctrine
and intellectual history (look at Racine's copy of Euripides).
Indeed, they may embody a major act of authorship, as do
Coleridge's marginalia, soon to be published.

Annotation may well occur in the margin, but it is of a different cast. Marginalia pursue an impulsive, perhaps querulous discourse or disputation with the text. Annotations, often numbered, will tend to be of a more formal, collaborative character. They will, where possible, be made at the bottom of the page. They will elucidate this or that point in the text; they will cite parallel or subsequent authorities. The writer of marginalia is, incipiently, the rival of his text; the annotator is its servant.

This service finds its most exacting and necessary expression in the use of the reader's quill to correct and emend. He who passes over printing errors without correcting them is no mere philistine: he is a perjurer of spirit and sense. It may well be that in a secular culture the best way to define a condition of grace is to say that it is one in which one leaves uncorrected neither literal nor substantive *errata* in the texts one reads and hands on to those who come after us. If God, as Aby Warburg affirmed, "lies in the detail," faith lies in the correction of misprints. Emendation, the epigraphical, prosodic, stylistic reconstitution of a valid text in the place of a spurious one, is an infinitely more taxing craft. As A. E. Housman professed in his paper on "The Application of Thought to Textual Criticism" of 1922, "this science and this art require more in the learner than a simply receptive mind; and indeed the truth is that they cannot be taught at all: *criticus nascitur, non fit.*" The conjunction of learning and sensitivity, of empathy with the original and imaginative scruple which produce a just emendation is, as Housman went on to say, of the rarest order. The stakes are high and ambiguous: Theobald may have won immortality when he suggested that Falstaff died "babbling of green fields"—but is the emendation correct? The twentieth century textual editor who has substituted "brightness fell from her hair" for Thomas Nashe's "brightness falls from the air" may be correct, but he is, surely, of the damned.

With his quill *le philosophe lisant* will transcribe from the book he is reading. The excerpts he makes can vary from the briefest of quotations to voluminous transcriptions. The multiplication and dissemination of written material after Gutenberg in fact increases the extent and variousness of personal transcription. The sixteenth- and seventeenth-century clerk or gentleman takes down in his hornbook, commonplace book, personal *florilegium* or breviary the maxims, "taffeta phrases," *sententiae*, exemplary turns of elocution, and tropes from classical and contemporary masters. Montaigne's essays are a living weave of echoes and citations. Until late into the nineteenth century—a fact borne witness to by the recollections of men and women as diverse as John Henry Newman, Abraham Lincoln, George Eliot, or Carlyle—it is customary for the young and for committed readers throughout their lives to transcribe lengthy political orations, sermons, pages of verse and prose, encyclopedia articles, and chapters of historical narration. Such recopying had manifold purposes: the improvement of one's own style, the deliberate storage in the mind of ready examples of argument or persuasion, the buttressing of exact memory (a cardinal issue). But, above all, transcription comports a full engagement with the text, a dynamic reciprocity between reader and book.

It is this full engagement which is the sum of the varying modes of response: marginalia, annotation, textual correction and emendation, transcription. Together these generate a continuation of the book being read. The reader's active quill sets down "a book in answer to" (the root-links between "reply" and "replication" are pertinent). This response will range from facsimile—which is total acquiescence—and affirmative development all the way to nega- tion and counter-statement (many books are anti-bodies to other books). But the principal truth is this: latent in every act of com- plete reading is the compulsion to write a book in reply. The intel- lectual is, quite simply, a human being who has a pencil in his or her hand when reading a book.

Enveloping Chardin's reader, his folio, his hour-glass, his incised medallions, his ready quill, is silence. Like his predecessors and contemporaries in the schools of interior, nocturnal, and still-life painting, particularly in northern and eastern France, Chardin is a virtuoso of silence. He makes it present to us, he gives it tactile weight, in the quality of light and fabric. In this particular painting, silence is palpable: in the thick stuff of the table-cloth and curtain, in the lapidary poise of the background wall, in the muffling fur of the reader's gown and bonnet. Genuine reading demands silence (Augustine, in a famous passage, records that his master, Ambrose, was the first man able to read without moving his lips). Reading, as Chardin portrays it, is silent and solitary. It is a vibrant silence and a solitude crowded by the life of the word. But the curtain is drawn between the reader and the world (the key but eroded term is "mundanity").

There would be many other elements in the painting to comment on: the alembic or retort, with its implications of scientific inquiry and its obvious compositional thrust; the skull on the shelf, at once a conventional prop in scholars' or philosophers' studies and, perhaps, an additional icon in the articulation of human mortality and textual survival; the possible interplay (I am not at all certain here) between the quill and the sand in the hourglass, sand being used to dry ink on the written page. But even a cursory look at the major components of Chardin's *Le Philosophe lisant* tells us of the classical vision of the act of reading—a vision we can document and detail in Western art from medieval representations of St. Jerome to the late nineteenth century, from Erasmus at his lectern to Mallarmé's apotheosis of *le Livre*.

What of the act of reading now? How does it relate to the proceedings and values inherent in Chardin's painting of 1734?

The motif of *cortesia*, of ceremonious encounter between reader and book, implicit in the costume worn by Chardin's *philosophe*, is now so remote as to be almost unrecapturable. If we come across it at all, it is in such ritualized, unavoidably archaic functions as the reading of the lesson in church or the solemn access to the Torah, head covered, in the synagogue. Informality is our password—though there is a poignant bite to Mencken's quip that many who think themselves emancipated are merely unbuttoned.

Far more radical and so far-reaching as to inhibit adequate summary are the changes in the values of temporality as these figure in Chardin's placement of hourglass, folio, and death's head. The whole relationship between time and word, between mortality and the paradox of literary survivance, crucial to Western high culture from Pindar to Mallarmé and self-evidently central to Chardin's painting, has altered. This alteration affects the two essential strands of the classic relation between the author and time on the one hand, and between the reader and the text on the other.

It may well be that contemporary writers continue to harbor the scandalous hope of immortality, that they continue to set down words in the hope that these will last not only beyond their own personal decease but for centuries to come. The conceit—in both its common and its technical sense—echoes still, though with characteristic wryness, in Auden's elegy on Yeats. But if such hopes persist, they are not professed publicly, let alone clarioned to the winds. The Pindaric-Horatian-Ovidian manifesto of literary immortality, with its innumerable repeats in the Western syllabus, now grates. The very notion of *fama*, of literary glory achieved in defiance of and as rebuttal to death, embarrasses. There is no greater distance than that between the *exegi monumentum* trope and Kafka's reiterated finding that writing is a leprosy, an opaque and cancerous infirmity which is to be hidden from men of ordinary daylight and good sense. Yet it is Kafka's proposal, ambivalent and strategic as it may have been, which qualifies our apprehension of the unstable, perhaps pathological provenance and status of the modern work of art. When Sartre insists that even the most vital of literary personages is no more than an assemblage of semantic markers, of arbitrary letters on the page, he is seeking to demythologize, once for all, Flaubert's hurt fantasy about the autonomous life, about the life after his death, of Emma Bovary. *Monumentum*: the concept and its connotations ("the monumental") have passed into irony. This passage is marked, with masterly sadness, in Ben Belitt's "This Scribe, My Hand"—with its reflection on the graves of Keats and Shelley in Rome, by Cestius Pyramid:

I write, in the posthumous way,
on the flat of a headstone
with a quarrier's ink, like yourself;

an anthologist's date and an asterisk,
a parenthetical mark in the gas
of the pyramid-builders,

an obelisk whirling with Vespas
in a poisonous motorcade.

Note the exactness of "the posthumous way"; not the *voie sacrée* to
Parnassus which the classic poet maps for his works and, by exalted
inference, for himself. "The gas of the pyramid-builders'"allows,
indeed invites, vulgar interpretation: "the hot air of the pyramid-
builders," their vacant grandiloquence. It is not Plato's bees, carriers
of divine rhetoric, that attend the poet, but loud, polluting Vespas
("wasps"), their acid sting decomposing the poet's monument even
as the mass-technological values they incarnate decompose the aura
of his work. We no longer look to texts, except in mandarin artifice, as negating personal death. "All is precarious," says Belitt,

A maniac
waits on the streets. Nobody listens. What
must I do? I am writing on water. . . .

The desolate phrase is, of course, Keats's. But it was denied, at
once, in Shelley's assurance of immortality in "Adonais," a denial
Keats hoped for and, somehow, anticipated. Today such denials
ring hollow ("the gas of the pyramid-builders").

The reader reciprocates this ironic declension. For him, as
well, the notion that the book in front of him shall outlast his own
life, that it prevails against the hourglass and the *caput mortuum* on
the shelf, has lost immediacy. This loss involves the entire theme
of *auctoritas*, of the normative, prescriptive status of the written
word. It is no over-simplification to identify the classic ideal of
culture, of civility, with that of the transmission of a syllabus, with
that of the study of sybilline or canonic texts by whose authority
successive generations test and validate their conduct of life

(Matthew Arnold's "touchstones"). The Greek *polis* saw itself as the organic medium of the principles, of the felt pressures of heroic-political precedent derived from Homer. At no juncture is the sinew of English culture and history separable from the ubiquity in that culture and history of the King James Bible, of the Book of Common Prayer, and of Shakespeare. Collective and individual experience found an ordering mirror in a garland of texts; their self-realization was, in the full sense of the word, "bookish" (in Chardin's painting the light is drawn to and projected from the open book).

Current literacies are diffuse and irreverent. It is no longer a natural motion to turn to a book for oracular guidance. We distrust *auctoritas*—the commanding script or scripture, the core of the authoritarian in classic authorship—precisely because it aspires to immutability. We did not write the book. Even our most intense, penetrative encounter with it is experience at second-hand. This is the crux. The legacy of Romanticism is one of strenuous solipsism, of the development of self out of immediacy. A single credo of vitalist spontaneity leads from Wordsworth's assertion that "one impulse from a vernal wood" outweighs the dusty sum of libraries to the slogan of radical students at the University of Frankfurt in 1968: "Let there be no more quotations." In both cases the polemic is that of the "life of life" against the "life of the letter," of the primacy of personal experience against the derivativeness of even the most deeply felt of literary emotions. To us, the phrase "the book of life" is a sophistic antinomy or cliché. To Luther, who used it at a decisive point in his version of Revelation and, one suspects, to Chardin's reader, it was a concrete verity.

As object, the book itself has changed. Except in academic or antiquarian circumstances, few of us will have come across, let alone made use of, the sort of tome being pondered by Chardin's *lecteur*. Who, today, has books privately bound? Implicit in the format and atmosphere of the folio, as we see it in the picture, is the private library, the wall of book-lined shelves, library-steps, lecterns, which is the functional space of the inner lives of Montaigne, of Evelyn, of Montesquieu, of Thomas Jefferson. This space, in turn, entails distinct economic and social relations: as between domestics who dust and oil the books and the master who reads them, as between the sanctified privacy of the scholar and the more vulgar terrain on which the family and outside world conduct their noisy, philistine lives. Few of us know such libraries, fewer still possess them. The entire economy, the architecture of privilege, in which the classic act of reading took place, has become remote (we visit the Morgan Library in New York or one of the great English country houses to view, albeit on a magnified scale, what was once the effective cadre of high bookishness). The modern apartment, notably for the young, simply has no space, no wall-surfaces for rows of books, for the folios, the quartos, the multi-volume *opera omnia* from which Chardin's reader has selected his text. Indeed, it is striking to what extent the cabinet for long-playing records and the record-shelf now occupy spaces formerly reserved for books (the substitution of music for reading is one of the major, most complex factors in the current changes of Western feeling). Where there are books, moreover, they will, to a greater or lesser degree, be paperbacks. Now there can be no doubt that the "paperback revolution" has been a liberating, a creative piece of technology, that it has widened the reach of literature and restored to availability whole areas of material, some of it even esoteric. But there is another side to the coin. The paperback is, physically, ephemeral. To accumulate paperbacks is not to assemble a library. By its very nature, the paperback pre-selects and anthologizes from the totality of literature and thought. We do not get, or get only very rarely, the complete works of an author. We do not get what current fashion regards as his inferior products. Yet it is only when we know a writer integrally, when we turn with special if querulous solicitude to his "failures" and thus construe our own vision of his presentness, that the act of reading is authentic. Dog-eared in our pocket, discarded in the airport lounge, lurching between *ad hoc* brick bookends, the paperback is both a marvel of packaging and a denial of the largesse of form and spirit expressly stated in Chardin's scene. "And I saw in the right hand of him that sat on the throne a book written within and on the back side, sealed with seven seals." Can a paperback have seven seals?

We underline (particularly if we are students or harried book-reviewers). Sometimes we scribble a note in the margin. But how few of us write marginalia in Erasmus' or Coleridge's sense, how few of us annotate with copious rigor. Today it is only the trained epigrapher or bibliographer or textual scholar who emends, this is to say: who encounters the text as a living presence whose contin-ued vitality, whose quick and radiance of being, depend on collab-orative engagement with the reader. How many of us are equipped to correct even the crassest blunder in a classical quotation, to spot and emend even the most puerile error in accent or measure, though such blunders and *errata* abound in even the most reputed of modern editions? And who among us bothers to transcribe, to set down for personal content and commission to memory, the pages that have spoken to him most directly, that have "read him" most searchingly?

Memory is, of course, the pivot. "Answerability to" the text, the understanding and critical response to *auctoritas*, as they inform the classic act of reading and the depiction of this act by Chardin, depend strictly on the "arts of memory." *Le philosophe lisant*, like the cultured men around him in a tradition which runs from classi-cal antiquity to, roughly, the First World War, will know texts *by heart* (an idiom worth thinking about closely). They will know by heart considerable segments of Scripture, of the liturgy, of epic and lyric verse. Macaulay's formidable accomplishments in this respect—even as a schoolboy he had committed to memory a fair measure of Latin and English poetry—were only a heightened instance of a general practice. The ability to cite Scripture, to recite from memory large stretches of Homer, Virgil, Horace, or Ovid, to cap on the instant a quotation from Shakespeare, Milton, or Pope, generated the shared texture of echoes, of intellectual and emotive recognition and reciprocity, on which the language of

British politics, law, and letters was founded. Knowledge by heart of the Latin sources, of La Fontaine, of Racine, of the trumpet-calls in Victor Hugo, has given to the entire fabric of French public life its rhetorical stress. The classic reader, Chardin's *lisant*, locates the text he is reading inside a resonant manifold. Echo answers echo, analogy is precise and contiguous, correction and emendation carry the justification of accurately remembered precedent. The reader replies to the text out of the articulate density of his own store of reference and remembrance. It is an ancient, formidable suggestion that the Muses of memory and of invention are one.

The atrophy of memory is the commanding trait in mid and later twentieth-century education and culture. The great majority of us can no longer identify, let alone quote, even the central Biblical or classical passages which not only are the underlying script of Western literature (from Caxton to Robert Lowell, poetry in English has carried inside it the implicit echo of previous poetry), but have been the alphabet of our laws and public institutions. The most elementary allusions to Greek mythology, to the Old and the New Testament, to the classics, to ancient and to European history, have become hermetic. Short bits of text now lead precarious lives on great stilts of footnotes. The identification of fauna and flora, of the principal constellations, of the liturgical hours and seasons on which, as C. S. Lewis showed, the barest understanding of Western poetry, drama, and romance from Boccacio to Tennyson intimately depends, is now specialized knowledge. We no longer learn by heart. The inner spaces are mute or jammed with raucous trivia. (Do not ask even a relatively well-prepared student to respond to the title of "Lycidas," to tell you what an eclogue is, to recognize even one of the Horatian allusions and echoes from Virgil and Spenser which give to the four opening lines of the poem their meaning, their meaning of meaning. Schooling today, notably in the United States, is planned amnesia.)

The sinews of memory can only be made taut where there is silence, the silence so explicit in Chardin's portrait. To learn by heart, to transcribe faithfully, to read fully is to be silent and within silence. This order of silence is, at this point in Western society, tending to become a luxury. It will require future historians of consciousness (*historiens des mentalités*) to gauge the abridgments in our attention span, the dilutions of concentration, brought on by the simple fact that we may be interrupted by the ring of the telephone, by the ancillary fact that most of us will, except under constraints of stoic resolve, answer the telephone, whatever else we may be doing. We need a history of noise-levels, of the diminution in those natural masses of silence, not only nocturnal, which still enfolded the daily lives of Chardin and his reader. Recent studies suggest that some seventy-five per cent of adolescents in the United States read against a background of sound (a radio, a record-player, a television set at one's back or in the next room). More and more young people and adults confess to being unable to read a serious text without a background of organized sound. We know too little about the ways in which the brain processes and integrates competing simultaneous stimuli to be able to say just what this electronic input does to the centers of attention and conceptualization involved in reading. But it is, at the least, plausible to suppose that the capacities for exact comprehension, for retention, and for energetic response which knit our being to that of the book are drastically eroded. We tend to be, as Chardin's *philosophe lisant* was not, part-time readers, readers by half.

It would be fatuous to hope for the restoration of the complex of attitudes and disciplines instrumental in what I have called "the classic act of reading." The power relations (*auctoritas*), the economics of leisure and domestic service, the architectonics of private space and guarded silence which sustain and surround this act are largely unacceptable to the egalitarian-populist aims of Western consumer societies. This, in point of fact, leads to a troubling anomaly. There is a society or social order in which many of the values and habits of sensibility implicit in Chardin's canvas are still operative; in which the classics are read with passionate attention; in which there are few mass media to compete with the primacy of literature; in which secondary education and the blackmail of censorship induce constant memorization and the transmission of texts from remembrance to remembrance. There is a society which is bookish in the root sense, which argues its destiny by perpetual reference to canonic texts, and whose sense of historical record is at once so compulsive and so vulnerable that it employs a veritable industry of exegetic falsification. I am, of course, alluding to the Soviet Union. And this example alone would suffice to keep before our minds perplexities as old as Plato's dialogues about the affinities between great art and centralized power, between high literacy and political absolutism.

But in the democratic-technological West, so far as one can tell, the die is cast. The folio, the private library, at homeness in classical tongues, the arts of memory, will belong, increasingly, to the specialized few. The price of silence and of solitude will rise. (Part of the ubiquity and prestige of music derives precisely from the fact that one can listen to it while being with others. Serious reading excludes even one's intimates.) Already, the dispositions and techniques symbolized by *Le Philosophe lisant* are, in the proper sense of the term, academic. They occur in university libraries, in archives, in professors' studies.

The dangers are obvious. Not only much of Greek and Latin literature, but substantial portions of European letters, from the *Commedia* to *Sweeney Agonistes* (a poem which, like so many of T. S. Eliot's, is a palimpsest of echoes) have passed out of natural reach. Subject to the scholar's conservation and to occasional, fragmentary visitation by university students, works which were once immediate to literate recall now lead the dreary half-life of those Stradivari fiddles mute behind glass in the Coolidge collection in Washington. Large tracts of once-fertile ground are already beyond reclaim. Who but the specialist reads Boiardo, Tasso, and Ariosto, that meshed lineage of the Italian epic without which neither the notion of Renaissance nor that of Romanticism makes much sense? Is Spenser still a cardinal presence in our repertoire of feeling, as he was to Milton, to Keats, to Tennyson? Voltaire's tragedies

are, literally, a closed book; only the scholar may remember that
these plays dominated European taste and styles of public utterance
for nearly a century, that it is Voltaire, not Shakespeare or Racine,
who holds the serious stage from Madrid to St. Petersburg, from
Naples to Weimar.

But the loss is not only ours. The essence of the full act of
reading is, we have seen, one of dynamic reciprocity, of responsion to the life of the text. The text, however inspired, cannot
have significant being if it is unread (what quick of life is there in
an unplayed Stradivarius?). The relation of the true reader to the
book is creative. The book has need of him as he has need of it—
a parity of trust exactly rendered in the composition of Chardin's
painting. It is in this perfectly concrete sense that every genuine
act of reading, that every *lecture bien faite*, is collaborative with the
text. *Lecture bien faite* is a term defined by Charles Péguy in his
incomparable analysis of true literacy (in the *Dialogue de l'histoire et
de l'âme païenne* of 1909):

> Une lecture bien faite . . . n'est pas moins que le vrai, que le
> véritable et même et surtout que le réel achèvement du texte,
> que le réel achèvement de l'œuvre; comme un couronnement,
> comme une grâce particulière et coronale. . . . Elle est ainsi
> littéralement une coopération, une collaboration intime,
> intérieure . . . aussi, une haute, une suprême et singulière, une
> déconcertante responsabilité. C'est une destinée merveilleuse, et
> presqu'effrayante, que tant de grandes œuvres, tant d'œuvres de
> grands hommes et de si grands hommes puissent recevoir encore
> un accomplissement, un achèvement, un couronnement de nous
> . . . de notre lecture. Quelle effrayante responsabilité, pour nous.

As Péguy says: "what a terrifying responsibility," but also what a
measureless privilege; to know that the survival of even the greatest
literature depends on *une lecture bien faite, une lecture honnête*. And to
know that this act of reading cannot be left in the sole custody of
mandarin specialists.

But where are we to find true readers, *des lecteurs qui sachent lire?*
We shall, I expect, have to train them.

I carry with me a vision of "schools of creative reading" ("schools" is far too pretentious a word; a quiet room and table will do). We shall have to begin at the simplest, and therefore most exacting, level of material integrity. We must learn to parse sentences and to analyze the grammar of our text, for, as Roman Jakobson has taught us, there is no access to the grammar of poetry, to the nerve and sinew of the poem, if one is blind to the poetry of grammar. We shall have to re-learn metrics and those rules of scansion familiar to every literate schoolboy in the Victorian age. We shall have to do so not out of pedantry, but because of the overwhelming fact that in all poetry, and in a fair proportion of prose, meter is the controlling music of thought and of feeling. We shall have to wake the numbed muscles of memory, to rediscover in our quite ordinary selves the enormous resources of precise recollection, and the delight that comes of the texts which have secure lodging within us. We would seek to acquire those rudiments of mythological and scriptural recognition, of shared historical remembrance, without which it is hardly possible, except by constant resort to more and more labored footnotes, to read adequately a line of Chaucer, of Milton, of Goethe, or, to give a deliberately modernist instance, of Mandelstam (who turns out to be one of the masters of echo).

A class in "creative reading" would proceed step by step. It would begin with the near-dyslexia of current reading habits. It would hope to attain the level of informed competence prevalent among the well-educated in Europe and the United States at, say, the end of the nineteenth century. It would aspire, ideally, to that *achèvement*, to that fulfilling and crowning involvement in the text of which Péguy speaks and of which such complete acts of reading as Mandelstam on Dante or Heidegger on Sophocles are exemplary.

The alternatives are not reassuring: vulgarization and loud vacancies of intellect on the one hand, and the retreat of literature into museum cabinets on the other. The tawdry "plot outline" or predigested and trivialized version of the classic on the one hand,

and the illegible variorum on the other. Literacy must strive to regain the middle ground. If it fails to do so, if *une lecture bien faite* becomes a dated artifice, a great emptiness will enter our lives, and we shall experience no more the quiet and the light in Chardin's painting.

(1978)

DIVINATION

FRANK KERMODE

MY SUBJECT IS DIVINATION, and I'd better give a hint as to what it means. *The Oxford English Dictionary,* I'm afraid, is unhelpful, concerning itself largely with the primary sense (prophecy and augury) and coming close to me only in treating what it calls the "weaker sense"—"guessing by happy instinct or unusual insight; successful conjecture. . . ." Now that everybody finds literary theory so much more interesting than literature, we must expect a certain amount of imperialist rapine. *Critical Inquiry* had an article on information-processing in reading poetry, dealing with "variant readings" of a poem, always an absorbing subject. But I soon saw that "variant readings" now means not what it used to mean, namely, *variae lectiones,* conflicts of textual testimony, but rather the different ways in which various people read the same poem. My complaint is not that this matter is not worth the writer's time, or mine, merely that a new interest, supported by all the modern armaments of phenomenology, Gestalt psychology, information theory, and so forth, has usurped an expression that has had for centuries a perfectly plain and very different meaning. Let us, while we may, use the old sense of *varia lectio*; it reminds us of an old, yet still current, sense of the word "divination." It may be weaker, but it is strong enough for me. For divination, *divinatio,* is a power traditionally required by those who wish to distinguish between variant readings, and to purge corrupt texts.

I'll add at once that nobody can suppose divination is *merely* inspired guesswork. Freedom to divine, in this sense, has been restricted since the Renaissance, and especially since the early eighteenth century, by the advance of what might be called science. Philology has always claimed to be so called, and especially in the nineteenth century aspired to the rigor of even more fashionable sciences. Indeed, in its modern forms it still does so. And the truth is that much knowledge has been progressively acquired. How texts are transmitted through time, what are the habits and failings of scribes and compositors, the paradoxes of history which make it possible that the earliest is not the best manuscript or edition—all this lore is now quite well understood. The liberty to divine is reduced by this understanding of the possibilities, and even geniuses are no longer allowed the freedom enjoyed by, say, the great Bentley.

All the same, it would be wrong to think of science as the enemy of divination. All it does is to define its limits. I doubt if you could find a Shakespearean who would deny the proposition that Charlton Hinman's vast book on the printing of the First Folio[1] is one of the essential contributions to the study of Shakespeare's text; yet as far as I can tell Hinman never so much as proposed an emendation. What he did was to define more precisely than had been thought possible where and how the text is likely to have gone wrong. The way of the editor is by this means made clearer and narrower. But he will still have to divine.

Some great diviners like to affirm that divination is a gift you are born with, that it cannot be taught. When he gave this lecture,[2] George Steiner quoted A. E. Housman's famous words to this effect. I doubt if they are wholly right, but they're not wholly wrong, either; history supports them, up to a point. For, as L. D. Reynolds and N. G. Wilson observe in their book *Scribes and Scholars*, "while general principles are of great use, specific problems have a habit of being *sui generis*."[3] And we need to remember also that some, perhaps most, of the most impressive emendations made in texts of every sort were provided by scholars who had never heard of stemmatics, or of Hinman's ingenious optical machine—who were ignorant of principles and information now available to everybody—what went on in scriptoria, what were the habits of Elizabethan compositors, and lots of other things.

However, we mustn't suppose that divination is something only textual scholars do. In the early years of the last century

Friedrich Schleiermacher, generally remembered as the founder of modern hermeneutics—the science of understanding texts—took over the term *divinatio* for something rather different. Schleiermacher needed a word for a moment of intuition which was necessary to his theory, and also, probably, to any common-sense view of what it is we accomplish when we interpret a text. We understand a whole by means of its parts, and the parts by means of the whole. But this "circle" seems to imply that we can understand nothing—the whole is made up of parts we cannot understand until it exists, and we cannot see the whole without understanding the parts. Something, therefore, must happen, some intuition by which we break out of this situation—a leap, a *divination*, he called it, whereby we are enabled to understand both part and whole.

Much has happened since Schleiermacher's day. In our own time we hear a lot about the "reader's share" in the production of sense. For every act of reading calls for some (perhaps minute) act of divination. We may content ourselves with obeying clear suggestions and indications in the text—as, for example, to setting, character, what we ought to be thinking about the action described or enacted. Every competent reader can do that much, and there is in consequence what is called an "intersubjective consensus" about the meaning of the text. But we may have to do rather more; there are works, especially modern books, which may frustrate such responses, or at least suggest a need for going beyond them. And it is quite usual to attach more value to such complex works, and to feel that our relating of part to part and parts to whole is the only means by which anything like the sense of the whole can be achieved. In other words, our power of divination is necessary to the whole operation—without it there will be no sense, or not enough.

It follows, I think, that we can distinguish between normal and abnormal divinations. The first kind we refer to the "intersubjective consensus"—we expect the agreement, without fuss, of competent, similarly educated people. Then there is the second kind, which we also submit to our peers. But this time they will not simply nod agreement, but either reject it as preposterous or hail it as brilliantly unexpected, a feat of genius. For although there is no guarantee whatever that the institutional consensus will always be right, it knows the difference between the valuable normal and the abnormally valuable. Though it will condemn divinations that run counter to its own intuition, the institution will tend to admire most those divinations which cannot be made by the mechanical application of learnable rules. Divination, in other words, still has the respect of the bosses.

What I've been doing so far is this. I've been suggesting that divination as the whole concept applied to the correction of texts is a special form of a more general art or skill, which we all employ, at one level or another, in the interpretation of poems and novels. The difference is merely one of degree; for in *all* cases divination requires, in its treatment of the part, an intuition of the whole. It would be possible here to introduce a related topic of much interest and difficulty: the relation between the reader's act of divination and the process by which authors compose the texts in the first place. The poet's drafts may show him preferring one word to another, even sometimes substituting a word of which the sense is the opposite of the original, as better in relation to the yet undetermined whole of the poem. The novelist, who may or may not have a Jamesian scenario, but who will have some probably indistinct intuition of the whole as he labors through the parts, can be found making the most drastic changes to the part as that intuition fluctuates, or discovers itself. But that would be another lecture, and a harder one as well. I shall stick to lower forms of divination, using examples.

The devil answers even in engines.

The first example, as a matter of fact, is a sort of warning. A word once favored among critics was "sagacity." Dr. Johnson had a great respect for "critical sagacity," and we may take it as representing, under another guise, the power to make acceptable divination.

Johnson admired one emendation made by Bishop Warburton in the text of *Hamlet* so much that he said it almost set "the critic on the level of the author." One day he gave Boswell a test. He pointed to a paragraph in a book by Sir George Mackenzie, and asked Boswell whether he could spot what was wrong with it. "I hit it at once," says Boswell. "It stands that the devil answers *even* in *engines*. I corrected it to '*ever* in *enigmas*.' 'Sir,' said he, 'you're a good critic. This would have been a great thing to do in the text of an ancient author.' " But James Thorpe, from whose learned and amusing book[4] I borrow the example, is inclined to think that Boswell is wrong, at any rate about *engines,* which can be held to make perfectly good sense." It can mean "snares, devices, tricks." "If so: poor over-clever Boswell; alas, poor over-knowing Johnson," says Mr. Thorpe. To be truly sagacious you have to know when divination is not called for.

Diviners had best be prepared to be called over-clever, over-knowing. In the days of Richard Bentley, the "modern" skill in emending ancient text met with a lot of opposition of this nature from people who favored this "ancient" side of the quarrel. Bentley's self-assurance was assaulted by Swift and ridiculed by Pope. The notes to the *Dunciad* are full of such mockery.

> lo! a Sage appears
> By his broad shoulders known, and length of ears

says the text, and the notes call "ears" a sophisticated (that is, a corrupt) reading. "I have always stumbled at it," says the annotator Scriblerus, "and wonder'd how an error so manifest could escape such accurate persons as the critics being ridiculed. A very little Sagacity . . . will restore to us the true sense of the Poet, thus,

> By his broad shoulders known, and length of *years*.

See how easy a change! of one single letter! That Mr. Settle [the Sage] was old is most certain. . . ."[5] Such unkind responses to divination not only remind us of the risk it involves, but also cause us to reflect that the task of the diviner may often be very difficult. Indeed, there are problems for the solution of which it is safe to assert that nobody has ever had, or will ever have, sufficient sagacity. All one can do is to award them what is known as a *crux desperationis*, a cross of despair, a sign that they are beyond human ingenuity.

(a) a nellthu night more
(b) a nelthu night Moore
(c) come on bee true
(d) come on

My second example offers a sample pair of hopeless cases: (a) is from the 1608 Quarto of *King Lear*, (b) from the second Quarto of 1619. It is obvious that nobody could have made head or tail of them had not the true reading survived in the corrected state of Q1 and in the Folio text of 1623: "He met the night-mare." (c) and (d) come from the same scene (III.iv), the first from the uncorrected Q1, the second from the corrected Q1. So if Heminge and Condell hadn't put together the First Folio in 1623 we should not have known that Lear, tearing off his clothes in the storm, says "Come, unbutton heere." He is raving, and might have said either or neither of the things preserved in the Quarto; and no diviner could have done anything about it.

Then the stars hang like lamps from the immense vault. The distance between the vault and them is as nothing to the distance behind them. . . .

However, the diviner's problem may arise from difficulties less obvious than those, for example when he has first to divine that, contrary to appearances, there is a need for his services. The third passage is from the beautifully composed opening chapter of E. M. Forster's *A Passage to India*. Let me play Johnson to your Boswell: what's wrong with it? Well—isn't the distance between the vault and the stars the same thing as the distance behind the stars? Could it be that a typist or compositor has accidentally repeated the word *vault* instead of what the author wrote? (This is called *dittography* by the experts.) Yet the fact is that between 1924 and 1978 nobody noticed there was anything wrong. Now we know that the manuscript reads not the second *vault* but *earth;* and the typescript also survives, so we know it was the typist who made the mistake, and that Forster set a good precedent for all who study him by not noticing it for the remaining half-century of his life. Perhaps some genius a thousand years hence might have been smart enough to see that somebody had gone wrong, and bold enough to risk the conjecture *earth*. Perhaps not. Anyway, he was forestalled. The moral may be: don't burn your manuscripts, diviners can't be trusted in every case.

> **She was praising God without attributes—
> thus did she apprehend Him.
> Others praised Him without attributes,
> seeing Him in this or that organ of the
> body or manifestation of the sky.**

The fourth extract is also from *A Passage to India*. Boswell should find this easier; obviously the second *without* should be *with*. Forster's editor, the late Oliver Stallybrass, who loved his job, once went through my copy checking conjectures against the manuscript, and this one was right. But although the balance of the sentences ("Some . . . Others"), to say nothing of the fact that the second *without attributes* is followed by a catalogue of attributes, makes it obvious to the meanest diviner that something has gone wrong, the right reading appeared in no edition before Stallybrass's, in 1978, more than fifty years late.

We must conclude from this that attentiveness is necessary to divination; reading novels, we are all too ready to skip over interruptions in the flow of words, and in so doing miss many opportunities; for the texts of many standard novelists are much worse than Forster's. Our laziness has important implications; if we miss such manifest errors, we may also miss less manifest subtleties. By underreading we fail to divine the larger sense of a novel. But I'll come a little later to that kind of divination.

In the offing the sea and the sky were welded together without a joint, and in the luminous space the tanned sails of the barges drifted up with the tide and seemed to stand still in red clusters of canvas sharply peaked, with gleams of vanished spirits.

Here I'll give one more instance of a famous text with an obvious corruption. The fifth extract is, as you must well know, from the opening paragraph of *Heart of Darkness*. There is something odd about *vanished spirits*; everything else has to do with the shapes and colors of the natural world. You can argue that Conrad, who was anyway rather keen on ghosts and spirits, is preparing us for the talk about the London river centuries ago, when the Romans used it, and you can supply other explanations of that sort—indeed there are ingenious explanations on record. If you are more skeptical you may look at other versions of the text, and find *varnished spirits,* which doesn't help much. What Conrad himself wrote was *varnished sprits;* I've only to say it for you to think it obvious. Yet if some Boswell had guessed it, that would, as Johnson said, have been something; and there would have been no doubt that he was right. But the answer was got by looking back to the first edition. The other readings are progressively corrupt, as the texts of all novels are, for the next edition repeats the mistakes of the previous one, and adds more.

Heart of Darkness is more or less intensively studied in the classroom by hundreds of experts and thousands of students every year. Unless they use the Signet edition, they all meet this corrupt reading instantly. (The Signet is the only popular text I can lay my hands on that has it right. The *Oxford Anthology*, I regret to say, has it wrong; but there is a new edition on the way.) Nobody, so far as I know, ever divined the true reading. This tells us among other things that there may be something wrong with the way we focus our attention on texts. Of course it doesn't amount to much: "one single letter, as Scriblerus remarked, and *vanished* replaced *varnished;* then somebody thought *vanished sprits* looked queer, and added another single letter to *sprits.*

You are a Counsellor if you can command these elements to silence, and worke the peace of the present, wee will not hand a rope more . . .

Sometimes it seems that we will do almost anything rather than get the right answer. The sixth extract is from the opening scene of *The Tempest*. The Boatswain wants to get rid of the courtiers, who are getting in the way of the sailors as they cope with the storm. "The peace of the present" is an unusual expression, but it might just pass—"bring the present moment into a peaceful state," or something of that kind. Still, it is odd; and if you read *presence* (supposing that Shakespeare wrote *presenc* and the scribe mistook the *c* for a *t*) you have a known expression. It means the area occupied by the king and his court; within it peace is kept or pre-served or "worked" by his officers. This conjecture, by the late J. C. Maxwell, seemed right to me, and I put it in the text of my edition of the play,[6] where it has been on view for over twenty years without attracting the slightest notice. It makes sense; the explanation in terms of graphic error came after the divination, as Housman says it should; but the world remains content with *present*. There are some interesting implications. First of all, there is in all guardians of sacred texts a profound conservatism. Erasmus edited the Greek New Testament, not very well; in fact by later standards very badly. But it became the received text, and for three hundred years scholars who knew perfectly well that it had many obvious mistakes did not dare to change it, and smuggled the right readings into the footnotes. So with Shakespeare, whose texts are riddled with error. In the eighteenth century there was much liberty; but in spite of an occasional plea for boldness, it is now normal to give sage approval to the claim that a text is very conservative. The diviner is not a popular person; he is con-strained by professional skepticism and by our veneration for the received text (as if the merits of the Bible and Shakespeare rubbed off onto scribes and printers) as much as he is by the formidable growth of editorial "science."

Oh Sunne, thy uprise shall I see no more,
Fortune and Anthony part heere, even heere
Do we shake hands? All come to this? The hearts
That pannelled me at heels, to whom I gave
Their wishes do dis-Candie, melt their sweets
On blossoming Caesar: and this pine is barkt
That over-top'd them all.

That is why I have to look back to the eighteenth century for an example of divinatory genius at work on Shakespeare. Look at extract the seventh, which is from the original text of *Antony and Cleopatra*. Antony is nearing the end; he has lost, his followers have left him. Something's wrong, though, and it must be the word *pannelled*. Thomas Hanmer, in 1744, said it should be *spanielled*; and we have most of us accepted this (or *spannelled*) ever since. It is one of the finest emendations in the whole text of Shakespeare and one of the most certain, though Hanmer didn't know the first thing about Shakespearean bibliography. If we ask ourselves why it is so admirable, we shall have to start using words like intuition or divination. Another matter of which Hanmer probably had no conscious knowledge, though it is now well known, is Shakespeare's tendency to associate dogs, melting candy, and flattery. Of course he must in a sense have known about it, to see what was needed in place of *pannelled* was a doggy sort of word; it also had to be a verb in the past tense.

The importance of this point is that such divinations depend on knowledge (of course you can have the knowledge without the power to divine). Hanmer's familiarity with the whole body of Shakespeare's work gave him a place to jump from. He would not be alarmed that if his conjecture gained acceptance we should have to admit that Shakespeare makes hearts turn into dogs, then melt (*discandy*—a word used, for example, of ice melting in a brook or a lake); that the intransitive *discandy* generates the transitive *melt* and the noun *sweets*; that *melt* becomes *melt on*, with its strange suggestion of the erstwhile cold hearts dropping slobbered sweetmeats on a tree (dogs and trees go together) but a tree called Caesar, which is in turn contrasted with a less lucky though originally more upstanding and attractive tree called Antony. Even *barkt*—referring to the manner in which this tree was spoilt—reminds us of the dogs. Hanmer must have known this strange piece of language was perfectly Shakespearean; he knew the manner of his poet.

Also, of course, he knew *Antony and Cleopatra,* at that moment, with the peculiar intimacy of an editor. A little earlier in the play there is a scene in which Antony, smarting under defeat, is enraged to find Cleopatra treating a messenger from Caesar with what he thinks to be rather more than due civility. He who had, at the outset, dismissed with magnanimous impatience the superstitious notion that a messenger should suffer because he bears bad news now has this messenger whipped, rather in the style of Cleopatra herself. He then turns on Cleopatra in a fury of disgust; then there's a sort of detumescence of rage, while Cleopatra waits patiently for him to finish. ("Have you done yet?") His reproaches grow more pathetic, and there follows this remarkable dialogue:

> ANTONY: Cold-hearted toward me?
> CLEOPATRA: Ah (Deere) if I be so,
> From my cold heart let Heaven ingender haile,
> And poyson it in the sourse, and the first stone
> Drop in my necke: as it determines so
> Dissolve my life, the next Caesarian smite,
> Till by degrees the memory of my wombe,
> Together with my brave Egyptians all,
> By the discandering of this pelleted storme,
> Lye gravelesse, till the Flies and Gnats of Nyle
> Have buried them for prey.

Cleopatra speaks in a very elaborate figure of which the basis is Antony's word *cold-hearted.* Let her heart be thought cold; let it also be thought poisoned, so that the heart's hail will be lethal when it melts. Let these deadly hailstones kill first her; then her son; then all her posterity ("the memory of my womb"), until all the Egyptians are dead and consumed by the insects of the Nile, "melted" by them. We cannot help noticing all the synonyms for "melt:" *determine, dissolve, discandy.* There is a contrast between Egyptian heat and the supposed unnatural cold of Cleopatra's heart, with the words for rapid melting mediating between them in such a way as to enforce the absurdity of the whole hypothesis ("*If* I be so . . ."). The play has made us familiar with the notions of Cleopatra's fecundity and sexual warmth, and related the same qualities in the Nile. This great lover cannot have a cold heart; coldness belongs to Rome. The Nile floods annually, and melts its banks; and when Antony says, "Let Rome in Tiber melt!" he is invoking the impossible for merely rhetorical purposes.

I couldn't help making a few of the many possible comments on this wonderful passage; but my real purpose, as you'll have guessed, is to draw attention to its connections with Hanmer's emendation. For Antony's "cold-hearted" here develops into very elaborate figures of melting, and the word *discandy* is used among others. The cold hearts and the melting pass magically over into the later speech, this time attended by a dog. Noting that the melting cold hearts seemed for some reason to be at Antony's heels, Hanmer put the spaniel in. This part called for a very active knowledge of the whole of the play, and perhaps of the greater whole, all the plays.

After all that, we are in a better position, I hope, to see how the addition of "a single letter" may truly be called an extraordinary act of interpretation, and how it calls for knowledge, knowledge which must be drawn from a greater whole yet bear down with all its weight on the smallest part, a word or a phrase. I will now try, with the aid of the eighth extract, to drive home the point that the rightness or wrongness of a particular reading may be a matter of truly enormous consequence; and that a preference for one reading over another may inescapably involve great decisions about the whole text in which the crux occurs. Divining is often a matter of choosing, as it is in this brief sentence from St. Mark's Gospel.

(i) Egō eimi
(ii) Su eipas hoti egō eimi

We have here two versions of the words spoken by Jesus at the
Sanhedrin trial, when the Priest asks him, "Are you the Christ, the
son of the Blessed?" The first means "I am," and the second,
"Thou hast said that I am." The first is positive, the second is non-
committal. The Jesus of Mark is nowhere else positive in his reply
to similar questions, and only a short time afterward declines to
make a straight answer to Pilate when he asks, "Are you the king
of the Jews?" *Su legeis,* says Jesus, which amounts to the same thing
as *su eipas.* And such a reply would in this case be much closer to
the run of the reader's expectations; for Jesus, in Mark's Gospel, has
consistently refused to make public any Messianic claim. Which
reading is the right one?

Now, it often happens that editors of the New Testament
have to choose between a shorter and a longer version of the
same passage. Has something dropped out of one version, or has
something been inserted in the other? Long experience has
evolved a rule: *brevior lectio potior,* the shorter reading is the
stronger; all else being equal, scribes are more likely to miss things
out than put things in. On the other hand, texts could be altered
for doctrinal reasons; and scribes, looking at other manuscripts
than the ones they are copying, sometimes reintroduce errors previously corrected. Also, copying Mark, they may alter him to
conform to Matthew, who was thought to be more authoritative.
Anyway, there is no rule of thumb strong enough to enforce the
shorter version. We have to consider many other matters, some of
them of very great importance.

For example: if the shorter version is right, we have to allow
that its effect is to confound rather than comply with our expectations. Is Mark the kind of text in which the unexpected ought to
be expected? In other words, what *kind* of book is it? Mark inserts
into his account of the Sanhedrin trial the story of Peter in the
courtyard denying Jesus. Peter was the man who first named Jesus
as the Messiah, and here he is denying him at the very moment

when for the first time Jesus himself is making the claim. If we read it that way we are virtually saying that this is a text so subtle that we can read none of it without expectations of similar subtlety. Our reading of the whole is profoundly affected. Matthew, whether he had the choice or not, used the longer version; the problem does not arise in that Gospel, which is not concerned with what is called "the Messianic secret." We have to choose— and not between these two different versions merely, but between two different *books*.

You'll remember that the difference between *homoousia* and *homoiousia*, "of the same substance" and "of like substance," divid- ed the fourth-century church; one iota; "but a single letter," as Scriblerus remarked. The choice involves a whole theology, the pressure of a whole institution rejecting heresy. Christians who declare every Sunday that they believe in Jesus Christ, being of one substance with the Father, do so because of a learned controversy sixteen hundred years ago. A single letter can make a difference.

Tōi agapōnti hēmas kai { lusanti / lousanti hēmas ek tōn hamartiōn hēmōn en tō haimati autou.

That's why I included the ninth extract, another curious instance of a choice, this time purely editorial, that has had endless repercussions upon people's behavior and beliefs. It is from Revelation 1:5, and it means either (a) "unto him who loved us and freed us from our sin in his own blood," or (b) "unto him who loved us and washed us from our sin in his own blood." There are defenses available for the second version, which is the one preferred in the King James Bible. Allusions to regeneration by washing are common enough in the Jewish Bible, and so, of course, are blood sacrifices; but the idea of washing in blood is not. All the evangelical tropes about being washed in the blood of the Lamb depend on this reading of this verse. However, *lusanti,* loosing or freeing, is now almost universally preferred, not only, I think, because it is the reading of the better manuscripts, but also because the washing in blood is un-Jewish and un-Greek. Thus a whole strain of evangelical imagery depends on scribal lapse; those who preferred *lousanti* divined wrong, though with interesting results.

Let us return for a moment to Mark. We have there, I think, a clear demonstration that when we attend to a minute particular of interpretation, we must do so with a lively sense of the whole text in which it occurs. The consequences of our choice may not always be so momentous, of course. And here I want to introduce a new notion, namely, that it may sometimes be necessary to good divination that the practitioner should decide to *minimize* the relation between the part and the whole.

Whose yonder,
That doe's appear as he were Flead? Oh Gods,
He has the stamp of Martius, and I have
Before time seen him thus.

Look at the tenth extract, which is from the first act of *Coriolanus*. There is nothing wrong with the text, so far as I know—which gives us another new notion, namely, that divination is not merely a matter of correcting texts. In the swirl of battle Cominius has some difficulty in recognizing Coriolanus, or rather Caius Martius, as he emerges from the enemy city; he is wounded and covered in blood. He appears "as he were flayed. . . . He has the stamp of Martius. . . ." Is Cominius merely recognizing Martius at last, or is he also saying that the hero looks like Marsyas? Marsyas was a satyr who stole a divine flute, challenged Apollo to a musical contest, lost, and was flayed alive. Though only a satyr, he tried to behave like a god. Coriolanus is sometimes thought of as a beast-god, his conduct depending upon a particularly bleak form of presumption; he behaves toward them as if he were "a God, to punish; not a man of their Infirmity." "He wants nothing of a God but Eternity and a Heaven to Throne in." Shall we, having divined the presence of Marsyas in Martius, collect all the figures which speak of

Coriolanus as a beast, remember that he tried to behave like a god, and announce that we have discovered some previously unnoticed key theme of the play? I think not. Marsyas, in my opinion, is present in the text; but only as a momentary glimmer. Good divination stops there; it recognizes a necessary constraint. Bad divination drives out good, which is why Richard Levin's amusing book *New Readings versus Old Plays*,[7] which concerns itself mostly with unconstrained divinations, has an excuse for being so wrong about the art of interpretation. It is true that people are always looking for new thematic keys to very well known plays, and that they often behave foolishly; but it doesn't follow that they are wrong to look. What calls for discussion (not here, not now) is the nature of the constraints. Meanwhile it is enough to say that this tiny part of *Coriolanus* seems to have no extensive relationship with the whole, and testifies simply to the extraordinary intellectual vivacity and freedom of association—the peripheral vision, as it were—that make the late verse of Shakespeare so inexhaustible a source of surprise.

We are now no longer talking about divination as a branch of emendation; so it is important to emphasize not only that there continue to be constraints, just as there are in emendation, but that the existence of constraints should not be misunderstood as a virtual ban on new interpretations of old texts.

> **"What a strange memory it would have been for one. Those deserted grounds, that empty hall, that impersonal, voluble voice, and—nobody, nothing, not a soul."**
>
> **The memory would have been unique and harmless. But she was not a girl to run away from an intimidating impression of solitude and mystery. "No, I did not run away," she said. "I stayed where I was—and I did see a soul. Such a strange soul."**

I shall try to illustrate this point from the last of the extracts. It is quite long because I had to get the two expressions "not a soul" and "I did see a soul." The source is Conrad's *Under Western Eyes*; Natalia Haldin is telling the narrator what happened when she visited Peter Ivanovitch, the great anarchist revolutionary, in his villa at Geneva. She stood around in a dusty hall, listening to the great man's voice in another room; and she might have left without seeing anyone, without seeing a soul. However, the *dame de compagnie,* the oppressed Tekla, turned up, so she did see a soul. It would be possible to say that Conrad's control of English idiom was never perfect (there are undoubtedly unidiomatic expressions in this as in the other novels), and that he wrongly supposed that if you could say in English "I didn't see a soul" you can also say "I saw a soul." This would be a way, in effect, of writing the awkward expression out of the text. But to my mind that is an illicit act; it is conceivable that a native English speaker would have intuitively avoided this locution, but it is fortunate for us that Conrad did not feel himself disqualified from writing in English because he was Polish. Nor do we resent the other forms of alien-ness his misfortune of birth enabled him to import into our fiction.

The word *soul* (with a great many variants such as "specter," "phantom," "spirit," "ghoul") occurs many dozens of times in Conrad's novel, very often with an unidiomatic quality which serves to draw attention to it. It is, in fact, a characteristic of many long passages of the book, especially in dialogue (we must remember that it is mostly Russians who are doing the talking, Eastern behavior under Western eyes), that it takes a considerable effort of specialized attention on the part of the reader not to see and hear the language employed as extremely odd. Conrad, who wanted to sell his books, was always willing to cater to the kind of reader who has been brainwashed into the right kind of narrowed attentiveness, but he wanted to do other things as well, and a good reader will certainly divine, particularly at such moments as the one I am discussing, that several apparently incompatible things are going on at once: that the word *soul* is here overdetermined, belonging not merely to a colloquial dialogue but also to a "string" or plot of soul references that only very occasionally appears relevant to the simple action of the piece, and in fact constitutes an occult plot of its own. In cases like this the best emblem of the diviner is the third ear of the psychoanalyst; if Conrad is committing a parapraxis when he says "I did see a soul," then that slip is of high analytical importance. And it is worth adding that given the kind of book one is reading, a book in which some measure of divinatory activity on the part of the reader is actively solicited (a *good* book, in our normal view of the matter), all occult relevances count; the question of intention does not arise.

I am now talking about divination on a rather larger scale. There are constraints upon it, certainly; but one must not be deterred by the skepticism, sometimes the ignorant contempt, of one's peers. On the other hand, there is a difference, which the diviner himself must judge, between Shakespeare's Marsyas and Conrad's "soul." In simpler cases one may depend more on a professional consensus. And I must here add, since there must certainly be in my audience a number of future scholars and also diviners, that there is great satisfaction to be had from solving the sort of problem most unprejudiced people can see to be a problem, and to offer a solution that can command assent straightforwardly, as a matter of evidence. If I may be autobiographical for a second, I got as much pleasure out of explaining the presence of the chickens in *The House of Seven Gables* as from any more high-flown divinatory attempt;[8] the explanation had the merit of being falsifiable; it involves a leap of some kind, but a leap anybody can take, then check whether he lands in the same place. Of course he had better not do it in ignorance, but then, as I have argued, no divinatory leap can really be taken in ignorance, however inspired, any more than it can be taken by somebody who has devoted all his study to the theory of leaping.

Intuition, that is, needs support from knowledge, whether we are editing a text or simply reading a novel. We need it even when we are reading undemanding books. We are required to do something, our share, even if that share is deliberately kept to a minimum. Coding operations are called for, even as they are in ordinary conversation. More difficult books reduce their audience by calling for a degree of competence higher than that. Some books we are inclined to think of as great very often make enormous demands, and may also contain fewer indications as to how they are to be read. Such books call forth interpretations which go beyond the consensus; they will probably *include* that consensus and then vary according to the predispositions and perspectives of the individual interpreter, who will nevertheless hope to have them accepted, though there is a high risk that they will be dismissed as counter-intuitive. When we are reading these great books with a proper regard for their complexity, with a sense that we, like their authors, are exploring labyrinths of interpretative possibility, we are diviners (good and bad) just as certainly as Bentley or Housman. Housman once remarked that if a manuscript read just *o* he would have no hesitation in reading *Constantinopolitanus* if he divined that to be the true reading;[9] I think we ought to take similar risks, though remembering that Housman really did know a great deal, and so must we.

We may well believe, then, that there is some continuity between the skills of the old *divinatio* and those of modern reading. Schleiermacher was quite right to borrow the expression for a different sort of interpretation. If you look once more at the second extract, you will have once more a sense of interpretative chastening. No two people could come up with the same answer, or if they did, they would both be wrong. There are, it is conceivable, texts which similarly defy the reader of longer discourses: they would be what Roland Barthes calls *scriptible* texts, quite *illisible,* a sort of a-consensual utopia. In other cases an editor makes a reasoned choice, and we can do that also, appealing to the institutional consensus of comparably qualified persons. In still others, one may make a sensible conjecture (which might get us back from *vanished spirits* to *varnished sprits*). In others we need to be peculiarly attentive before we see that divination is called for anyway, as in the first Forster piece, and this is commonly our position when reading novels, which have a traditional duty to be clear and explicit. For all the operations I have touched upon in the editorial activity are paralleled on a grosser scale in the reading of long texts. Interpretation in that large sense still calls for the kind of skill and courage we associate with a Housman.

For, finally, there is something all we diviners ought to remember. Long after Hermes began the affair, long after Schleiermacher, there was a revolution in the analysis of long texts and in the interpretation of narrative; we correctly associate with it the name of Freud. Since his day we have learned to attend (to screw ourselves up into the posture of attending) not only to what is explicitly stated and conveniently coded, but to the condensations and displacements, the puns and parapraxes, to Shakespeare's Marsyas and Conrad's "soul." In fact it seems we are taking our time about learning the lesson; we are rather slow to pursue occulted senses, evidences of what is not immediately accessible. It is the mark of what I call a classic text that it will provide such evidence; if it were not so, the action of time and the accumulation of interpretations would exhaust it or make it redundant. When we admit that something more remains to be interpreted we are in fact calling for divination. It may be very refined, it may be very silly, and in either case it will probably be rejected by other interested parties. But it has to continue. In a sense the whole future depends upon it.

That, in short, is our justification. Our kind of divination, like the older kind, contributes to the sense and the value of the inheritance. The great scholars, sure of their inspiration and often full of vanity, liked to say the gift was innate; whether it is or not, nobody will claim that it can be effective without learning, without competence, without a knowledge of books and methods that can be acquired by labor. Without the science there can be no divination; without the divination the science is tedious. So here is my last word to this audience: as to divination, see first that you are born with it. Then, by disciplined labor (whether it is described as philological or hermeneutic, or whether it is simply the acquisition of a perfect knowledge of a text or a corpus of texts) make yourself able to use the gift.

(1979)

NOTES

1. The *Printing and Proof-reading of the Shakespeare First Folio*, 2 vols. (Oxford, 1963).

2. "The Uncommon Reader," *Bennington Review,* no. 3, Dec. 1978.

3. (Oxford, 1968; 2nd. ed. 1974), p. 212.

4 James Thorpe, *Principles of Textual Criticism* (Huntington Library, 1972), 30, 27.

5. *Dunciad* III. 27-28; see Aubrey L. Williams, *Pope's Dunciad* (London, 1955), pp. 82-83.

6. In the Arden Shakespeare (6th ed., 1958).

7. Chicago, 1979.

8. *The Classic* (New York, 1975), chapter 3.

9. Reynolds and Wilson, *Scribes and Scholars,* p. 211. Incidentally, a compositor setting Massinger's play *The Emperor of the East* changed the word *Courte* into *Constantinople*; a copy survives in which the author corrected it. (See John Crow, "Editing and Emending," in Sheldon P. Zitner, ed., *The Practice of Modern Literary Scholarship* (New York, n.d.), pp. 161–75.)

To the Tally of My Soul: Whitman's Image of Voice

Harold Bloom

WHERE DOES THE INDIVIDUAL ACCENT of an American poetry begin? How, then and now, do we recognize the distinctive voice that we associate with an American Muse? Bryant, addressing some admonitory lines, in 1830, "To Cole, The Painter, Departing for Europe," has no doubts as to what marks the American difference:

> Fair scenes shall greet thee where thou goest—fair,
> But different—everywhere the trace of men,
> To where life shrinks from the fierce Alpine air.
> Gaze on them, till the tears shall dim thy sight,
> But keep that earlier, wilder image bright.

Only the Sublime, from which life shrinks, constitutes a European escape from the trace of men. Cole will be moved by that Sublime, yet he is to keep vivid the image of priority, an American image of freedom, for which Emerson and Thoreau, like Bryant before them, will prefer the trope of "wildness." The wildness triumphs throughout Bryant, a superb poet, always and still undervalued, and one of Hart Crane's and Wallace Stevens's legitimate ancestors. The voice of an American poetry goes back before Bryant, and can be heard in Bradstreet and Freneau (not so much, I think, in Edward Taylor, who was a good English poet who happened to be living in America). Perhaps, as with all origins, the American poetic voice cannot be traced, and so I move from my first to my second opening question: how to recognize the Muse of America. Here is Bryant, in the strong opening of his poem, "The Prairies," in 1833:

> These are the gardens of the Desert, these
> The unshorn fields, boundless and beautiful,
> For which the speech of England has no name—
> The Prairies. I behold them for the first
> And my heart swells, while the dilated sight
> Takes in the encircling vastness. . . .

Bryant's ecstatic beholding has little to do with what he sees. His speech swells most fully as he intones: "the Prairies," following on the prideful reflection that no English poet could name these grasslands. The reflection itself is a touch awkward, since the word after all is French, and not Amerindian, as Bryant knew. No matter; the beholding is still there, and truly the name is little more important than the sight. What *is* vital is the dilation of the sight, an encircling vastness more comprehensive even than the immensity being taken in, for it is only a New England hop, skip, and a jump from this dilation to the most American passage that will ever be written, more American even than Huck Finn telling Aunt Polly that he lies just to keep in practice, or Ahab proclaiming that he would strike the sun if it insulted him. Reverently I march back to where I and the rest of us have been before and always must be again, crossing a bare common, in snow puddles, at twilight, under a clouded sky, in the company of our benign father, the Sage of Concord, teacher of that perfect exhilaration in which, with him, we are glad to the brink of fear:

> . . . Standing on the bare ground,—my head bathed by the blithe
> air and uplifted into infinite space,—all mean egotism vanishes. I
> become a transparent eyeball; I am nothing; I see all; the currents
> of the Universal Being circulate through me; I am part or parcel
> of God. . . .

Why is this ecstasy followed directly by the assertion: "The name of the nearest friend sounds then foreign and accidental . . ."? Why does the dilation of vision to the outrageous point of becoming a transparent eyeball provoke a denaturing of even the nearest name? I hasten to enforce the obvious, which nevertheless is crucial: the name is not forgotten, but loses the sound of immediacy; it becomes foreign or out-of-doors, rather than domestic; and acci-dental, rather than essential. A step beyond this into the American Sublime, and you do not even forget the name; you never hear it at all:

> And now at last the highest truth on this subject remains unsaid; probably cannot be said; for all that we say is the far-off remember-ing of the intuition. That thought by what I can now nearest approach to say it, is this. When good is near you, when you have life in yourself, it is not by any known or accustomed way; you shall not discern the footprints of any other; you shall not see the face of man; you shall not hear any name;—the way, the thought, the good, shall be wholly strange and new. . . .

"This subject" is self-reliance, and the highest truth on it would appear to be voiceless, except that Emerson's voice does speak out to tell us the influx of the Newness, in which no footprints or faces are to be seen, and no name is to be heard. Unnaming always has been a major mode in poetry, far more than naming; perhaps there cannot be a poetic naming that is not founded upon an unnaming. I want to leap from these prose unnamings in Emerson, so prob-lematic in their possibilities, to the poem in which, more than any other, I would seek to hear Emerson's proper voice for once in verse, a voice present triumphantly in some many hundreds of pas-sages throughout his prose:

> Pour, Bacchus! the remembering wine;
> Retrieve the loss of me and mine!
> Vine for vine be antidote,
> And the grape requite the lote!
> Haste to cure the old despair,—
> Reason in Nature's lotus drenched,
> The memory of ages quenched;
> Give them again to shine;
> Let wine repair what this undid;
> And where the infection slid,
> A dazzling memory revive;
> Refresh the faded tints,
> Recut the aged prints,

> And write my old adventures with the pen
> Which on the first day drew,
> Upon the tablets blue,
> The dancing Pleiads and eternal men.

But why is Bacchus named here, if you shall not hear any name? My question would be wholly hilarious if we were to literalize Emerson's splendid chant. Visualize the Sage of Concord, gaunt and spare, uncorking a bottle in Dionysiac abandon, before emulating the Pleiads by breaking into a Nietzschean dance. No, the Bacchus of Ralph Waldo is rather clearly another unnaming. As for voice, it is palpably absent from this grand passage, its place taken up not even by writing, but by rewriting, by that revisionary pen which has priority, and which drew before the tablets darkened and grew small.

I am going to suggest shortly that rewriting is an invariable trope for voicing—that direct transcription of the rhythm and force of speech so highly prized by modernism—within a poem, while voicing and reseeing are much the same poetic process, a process reliant upon unnaming, which rhetorically means the undoing of a prior metonymy. But first I am going to leap ahead again, from Emerson to Stevens, which is to pass over the great impasse of Whitman, with whom I have identified always Hart Crane's great trope: "Oval encyclicals in canyons heaping / The impasse high with choir." Soon enough this discourse will center upon Whitman, since quite simply he *is* the American Sublime, he *is* voice in our poetry, he is our answer to the Continent now, precisely as he was a century ago. Yet I am sneaking up on him, always the best way for any critic to skulk near the Sublime Walt. His revisionism, of self, as of others, is very subtle; his unnamings and his voices come out of the Great Deep. Stevens's are more transparent:

> Throw away the lights, the definitions,
> And say of what you see in the dark
>
> That it is this or that it is that,
> But do not use the rotted names.

* * *

Phoebus is dead, ephebe. But Phoebus was
A name for something that never could be named.
There was a project for the sun and is.

There is a project for the sun. The sun
Must bear no name, gold flourisher, but be
In the difficulty of what it is to be.
* * *

This is nothing until in a single man contained,
Nothing until this named thing nameless is
And is destroyed. He opens the door of his house

On flames. The scholar of one candle sees
An Arctic effulgence flaring on the frame
Of everything he is. And he feels afraid.

What have these three unnaming passages most in common?
Well, what are we doing when we give pet names to those we
love, or give no names to anyone at all, as when we go apart in
order to go deep into ourselves? Stevens's peculiar horror of the
commonplace in names emerges in his litany of bizarre, fabulistic
persons and places, but though that inventiveness works to break
casual continuities, it has little in common with the true break with
continuity in poets like Lewis Carroll and Edward Lear. Stevens,
pace Hugh Kenner, is hardly the culmination of the poetics of
Edward Lear. He may *not* be the culmination of Whitman's poetics
either, since that begins to seem the peculiar distinction of John
Ashbery. But like Whitman, Stevens does have a link to the
Lucretian Sublime, as Pater the Epicurean did, and such a Sublime
demands a deeper break with commonplace continuities than is
required by the evasions of nonsense and fantasy. The most
authentic of literary Sublimes has the Epicurean purpose of rendering us discontented with easier pleasures in order to prepare us for
the ordeal of more difficult pleasures. When Stevens unnames he
follows, however unknowingly, the trinity of negative wisdom
represented by Emerson, Pater, and Nietzsche. Stevens himself
acknowledged only Nietzsche, but the unfashionable Emerson and

Pater were even stronger in him, with Emerson (and Whitman) repressedly the strongest of strains. Why not, after all, use the rotted names? If the names were things that never could be named, is not one name as bad anyway as another? Stevens's masterpiece is not named *The Somethings of Autumn,* and not only because the heroic desperation of the Emersonian scholar of one candle is not enough. Whether you call the auroras flames or an Arctic effulgence or call them by the trope now stuck into dictionaries, the auroras, you are giving your momentary consent to one arbitrary substitution or another. Hence Emerson's more drastic and Bacchic ambition; write your *old* adventures, not just your new, with the Gnostic pen of our forefather and foremother, the Abyss. I circle again the problematic American desire to merge voicing and revisionism into a single entity, and turn to Whitman for a central text, which will be the supposed elegy for Lincoln, *When Lilacs Last in the Dooryard Bloom'd. So* drastic is the amalgam of voicing, unnaming, and revisionism here that I take as prelude first Whitman's little motto poem, *As Adam Early in the Morning,* so as to set some of the ways for approaching what is most problematic in the great elegy, its images of voice and of voicing.

What can we mean when we speak of the *voice* of the poet, or the voice of the critic? Is there a pragmatic sense of voice, in discussing poetry and criticism, that does not not depend upon the illusions of metaphysics? When poetry and criticism speak of "images of voice," what is being imaged? I think I can answer these questions usefully in the context of my critical enterprise from *The Anxiety of Influence* on, but my answers rely upon a post-philosophical pragmatism which grounds itself upon what has worked to make up an American tradition. Voice in American poetry always necessarily must include Whitman's oratory, and here I quote from it where it is most economical and persuasive, a five-line poem that centers the canon of our American verse:

As Adam early in the morning,
Walking forth from the bower refresh'd with sleep,
Behold me where I pass, hear my voice, approach,

Touch me, touch the palm of your hand to my body as I pass,
Be not afraid of my body.

What shall we call this striding stance of the perpetually passing
Walt, prophetic of Stevens's singing girl at Key West, and of
Stevens's own Whitman walking along a ruddy shore, singing of
death and day? Rhetorically the stance is wholly transumptive,
introjecting earliness, but this is very unlike the Miltonic transum-
ing of tradition. Walt is indeed Emerson's new Adam, American
and Nietzschean, who can live as if it were morning, but though
he is *as* the Biblical and Miltonic Adam, that "as" is one of
Stevens's "intricate evasions of as." The old Adam was not a savior,
except in certain Gnostic traditions of Primal Man; the new,
Whitmanian Adam indeed is Whitman himself, more like Christ
than like Adam, and more like the Whitmanian Christ of
Lawrence's *The Man Who Died* than like the Jesus of the Gospels.

Reading Whitman's little poem is necessarily an exercise both
in a kind of repression and in a kind of introjection. To read the
poem strongly, to voice its stance, is to transgress the supposed
boundary between reading or criticism, and writing or poetry.
"As" governs the three words of origins "Adam," "early," and
"morning"—and also the outgoing movement of Whitman, walking forth refreshed from a bower (that may be also a tomb), emerging from a sleep that may have been a kind of good death.
Whitman placed this poem at the close of the *Children of Adam*
division of *Leaves of Grass,* thus positioning it between the defeated
American pathos of *Facing West from California's Shores* and the
poignant *In Paths Untrodden* that begins the homoerotic *Calamus*
section. There is a hint, in this contextualization, that the astonished reader needs to cross a threshold also. Behold Whitman as
Adam; do not merely regard him when he is striding past. The
injunctions build from that "behold" through "hear" and
"approach" to "touch," a touch then particularized to the palm, as
the resurrected Walt passes, no phantom, but a risen body. "Hear
my voice" is the center. As Biblical trope, it invokes Jehovah walking in Eden in the cool of the day, but in Whitman's American

context it acquires a local meaning also. Hear my voice, and not just my words; *hear me as voice.* Hear me, as in my elegy for President Lincoln, I hear the hermit thrush.

Though the great elegy finds its overt emblems in the lilac-bush and the evening star, its more crucial tropes substitute for those emblems. These figures are the sprig of lilac that Whitman places on the hearse, and the song of the thrush that floods the western night. Ultimately these are one trope, one image of voice, which we can follow Whitman by calling the "tally," playing also on a secondary meaning of "tally," as double or agreement. "Tally" may be Whitman's most crucial trope or ultimate image of voice. As a word, it goes back to the Latin *talea* for twig or cutting, which appears in this poem as the sprig of lilac. The word meant originally a cutting or stick upon which notches are made so as to keep count or score, but first in the English and then in the American vernacular it inevitably took on the meaning of a sexual score. The slang word "tallywoman," meaning a lady in an illicit relationship, and "tallywhack" or "tallywogs," for the male genitalia, are still in circulation. "Tally" had a peculiar, composite meaning for Whitman in his poetry, which has not been noted by his critics. In the odd, rather luridly impressive death-poem, *Chanting the Square Deific,* an amazing blend of Emerson and an Americanized Hegel, Whitman identifies himself with Christ, Hermes, and Hercules and then writes: "All sorrow, labor, suffering, I, tallying it, absorb it in myself." My comment would be: "Precisely *how* does he tally it?," and the answer to that question, grotesque as initially it must seem, would be: "Why, first by masturbating, and then by writing poems." I am being merely accurate, rather than outrageous, and so I turn to *Song of Myself,* section 25, as first proof-text.

Dazzling and tremendous how quick the sun-rise would kill me,
If I could not now and always send sun-rise out of me.

We also ascend dazzling and tremendous as the sun,
We found our own O my soul in the calm and cool of the daybreak.

My voice goes after what my eyes cannot reach,
With the twirl of my tongue I encompass worlds and volumes of
    worlds.

Speech is the twin of my vision, it is unequal to measure itself,
It provokes me forever, it says sarcastically,
Walt you contain enough, why don't you let it out then?

Come now I will not be tantalized, you conceive too much of
    articulation,
 Do you not know O speech how the buds beneath you are folded?
Waiting in gloom, protected by frost,
The dirt receding before my prophetical screams,
I underlying causes to balance them at last,
My knowledge my live parts, it keeping tally with the meaning of
    all things,
Happiness, (which whoever hears me let him or her set out in
    search of this day.)
My final merit I refuse you, I refuse putting from me what I
    really am,
Encompass worlds, but never try to encompass me,
I crowd your sleekest and best by simply looking toward you.

Writing and talk do not prove me,
I carry the plenum of proof and every thing else in my face,
With the hush of my lips I wholly confound the skeptic.

At this, almost the mid-point of his greatest poem, Whitman is
sliding knowingly near crisis, which will come upon him in the
crossing between sections 27 and 28. But here he is too strong,
really too strong, and soon will pay the price of that over-strength,
according to the Emersonian iron Law of Compensation, that
nothing is got for nothing. Against the sun's mocking taunt: "See
then whether you shall be master!" Whitman sends forth his own
sun-rise, which is a better, a more Emersonian answer than
Melville's Ahab threatens when he cries out, with surpassing
Promethean eloquence: "I'd strike the sun if it insulted me!" As an
alternative dawn, Whitman crucially identifies himself as a voice, a
voice overflowing with presence, a presence that is a sexual self-

knowledge: "My knowledge my live parts, it keeping tally with the meaning of all things." His knowledge and sexuality are one, and we need to ask: how does that sexual self-knowing keep tally with the meaning of all things? The answer comes in the crisis sequence of sections 26–30, where Whitman starts with listening and then regresses to touch, until he achieves both orgasm and poetic release through a Sublime yet quite literal masturbation. The sequence begins conventionally enough with bird song and human voice, passes to music, and suddenly becomes very extraordinary, in a passage critics have admired greatly but have been unable to expound:

> The orchestra whirls me wider than Uranus flies,
> It wrenches such ardors from me I did not know I possess'd
>   them,
> It sails me, I dab with bare feet, they are lick'd by the
>   indolent waves,
> I am cut by bitter and angry hail, I lose my breath,
> Steep's amid honey'd morphine, my windpipe throttled in
>   fakes of death,
> At length let up again to feel the puzzle of puzzles,
> And that we call Being.

This Sublime antithetical flight (or repression) not only takes Whitman out of nature, but makes him a new kind of god, ever-dying and ever-living, a god whose touchstone is of course voice. The ardors wrenched from him are operatic, and the cosmos become stage machinery, a context in which the whirling bard first loses his breath to the envious hail, then sleeps a drugged illusory death in uncharacteristic silence, and at last is let up again to sustain the enigma of Being. For this hero of voice, we expect now a triumphant ordeal by voice, but surprisingly we get an equivocal ordeal by sexual self-touching. Yet the substitution is only rhetorical, and establishes the model for the tally in the Lincoln elegy, since the sprig of lilac will represent Whitman's live parts, and the voice of the bird will represent those ardors so intense, so wrenched from Whitman, that he did not know he possessed them.

After praising his own sensitivity of touch, Whitman concludes section 27 with the highly equivocal line: "To touch my person to some one else's is about as much as I can stand." The crisis section proper, 28, centers upon demonstrating that to touch his own person is also about as much as Whitman can stand. By the time he cries out: "I myself went first to the headland, my own hands carried me there," we can understand how the whole 1855 *Song of Myself* may have grown out of an early notebook jotting on the image of the headland, a threshold stage between self-excitation and orgasm. Section 28 ends with frankly portrayed release:

> You villain touch! what are you doing? my breath is tight
>   in its throat,
> Unclench your floodgates, you are too much for me.

The return of the image of breath and throat, of voice, is no surprise; nor will the attentive reader be startled when the lines starting section 29 take a rather more affectionate view of touch, now that the quondam villain has performed his labor:

> Blind loving wrestling touch, sheath'd hooded sharp-tooth'd
>   touch!
> Did it make you ache so, leaving me?

Since Whitman's "rich showering rain" fructifies into a golden, masculine landscape, we can call this sequence of *Song of Myself* the most productive masturbation since the ancient Egyptian myth of a god who masturbates the world into being. I suggest now (and no Whitman scholar will welcome it) that a failed masturbation is the concealed reference in section 2 of the *Lilacs* elegy:

> O powerful western fallen star!
> O shades of night— moody, tearful night!!
> O great star disappear'd—O the black murk that hides the star!
> O cruel hands that hold me powerless— helpless soul of me!
> O harsh surrounding cloud that will not free my soul.

The cruel hands are Whitman's own, as he vainly seeks relief from his repressed guilt, since the death of Father Abraham has rekindled the death, a decade before, of the drunken Quaker carpenter-father, Walter Whitman, Senior. Freud remarks, in *Mourning and Melancholia,* that:

> . . . there is more in the content of melancholia than in that of normal grief. In melancholia the relation to the object is no simple one; it is complicated by the conflict of ambivalence. This latter is either constitutional, i.e. it is an element of every love-relation formed by this particular ego, or else it proceeds from precisely those experiences that involved a threat of losing the object. . . . Constitutional ambivalence belongs by nature to what is repressed, while traumatic experiences with the object may have stirred to activity something else that has been repressed. Thus everything to do with these conflicts of ambivalence remains excluded from consciousness, until the outcome characteristic of melancholia sets in. This, as we know, consists in the libidinal cathexis that is being menaced at last abandoning the object, only, however, to resume its occupation of that place in the ego whence it came. So by taking flight into the ego love escapes annihilation. . . .

Both conflicts of ambivalence are Whitman's in the *Lilacs* elegy, and we will see love fleeing into Whitman's image of voice, the bird's tallying chant, which is the last stance of his ego. Freud's ultimate vision of primal ambivalence emphasized its origin as being the dialectical fusion/defusion of the two drives, love and death. Whitman seems to me profounder even than Freud as a student of the interlocking of these antithetical drives that darkly combine into one Eros and its shadow of ruin, to appropriate a phrase from Shelley. Whitman mourns Lincoln, yes, but pragmatically he mourns even more intensely for the tally, the image of voice he cannot as yet rekindle into being, concealed as it is by a "harsh surrounding cloud" of impotence. The miraculous juxtaposition of the two images of the tally, sprig of lilac and song of the hermit thrush, in sections 3 and 4 following, points the possible path out of Whitman's death-in-life:

3

In the dooryard fronting an old farm-house near the
white-wash'd palings,

Stands the lilac-bush tall-growing with heart-shaped leaves
      of rich green,
With many a pointed blossom rising delicate, with the
      perfume strong I love,
With every leaf a miracle—and from this bush in the dooryard,
With delicate-color'd blossoms and heart-shaped leaves of
      rich green,
A sprig with its flower I break.

4

In the swamp in secluded recesses,
A shy and hidden bird is warbling a song.
Solitary the thrush,
The hermit withdrawn to himself, avoiding the settlements,
Sings by himself a song.

Song of the bleeding throat,
Death's outlet song of life, (for well dear brother I know,
If thou wast not granted to sing thou would'st surely die).

Whitman breaks the *talea,* in a context that initially suggests a
ritual of castration, but the image offers more than a voluntary surrender of manhood. The broken lilac sprig is exactly analogous to
the "song of the bleeding throat," and indeed the analogy explains
the otherwise baffling "bleeding." For what has torn the thrush's
throat? The solitary Song itself, image of wounded voice, is the
other *talea,* and has been broken so that the soul can take count of
itself. Yet why must these images of voice be broken? Whitman's
answer, a little further on in the poem, evades the "why" much as
he evades the child's "What is the grass?" in *Song of Myself* 6, for
the *why* like the *what is* unknowable in the context of the
Epicurean Lucretian metaphysics that Whitman accepted.
Whitman's answer comes in the hyperbolic, daemonic, repressive
force of his copious overbreaking of the tallies:

Here, coffin that slowly passes,
I give you my sprig of lilac.

(Nor for you, for you alone,

Blossoms and branches green to coffins all I bring,
For fresh as the morning, thus would I chant a song for you
   O sane and sacred death.

All over bouquets of roses,
O death, I cover you over with roses and early lilies,
But mostly and now the lilac that blooms the first,
Copious I break, I break the sprigs from the bushes,
With loaded arms I come, pouring for you,
For you and the coffins all of you O death.)

Why should we be moved that Whitman intones: "O sane and sacred death," rather than: "O insane and obscene death," which might seem to be more humanly accurate? "Death" here is a trope for the sane and sacred Father Abraham, rather than for the actual father. Whitman's profuse breaking of the tallies attempts to extend this trope, so as to make of death itself an ultimate image of voice or tally of the soul. It is the tally and not literal death, our death, that is sane and sacred. But that returns us to the figuration of the tally, which first appears in the poem as a verb, just before the carol of death:

And the charm of the carol rapt me,
As I held as if by their hands my comrades in the night,
And the voice of my spirit tallied the song of the bird.

"My knowledge my live parts, it keeping tally with the meaning of all things" now transfers its knowledge from the vital order to the death drive. I am reminded that I first became aware of Whitman's crucial trope by pondering its remarkable use by Hart Crane, when he invokes Whitman directly in the "Cape Hatteras" section of *The Bridge*:

O Walt!—Ascensions of thee hover in me now
As thou at junctions elegiac, there, of speed,
With vast eternity, dost wield the rebound seed!
The competent loam, the probable grass,—travail
Of tides awash the pedestal of Everest, fail
Not less than thou in pure impulse inbred
To answer deepest soundings! O, upward from the dead

Thou bringest tally, and a pact, new bound
Of living brotherhood!

   Crane's allusion is certainly to the *Lilacs* elegy, but his interpretation of what it means to bring tally "upward from the dead" may idealize rather too generously. That Walt's characteristic movement is ascension cannot be doubted, but the operative word in this elegy is "passing." The coffin of the martyred leader passes first, but in the sixteenth and final section it is the bard who passes, still tallying both the song of the bird and his own soul. That the tally is crucial, Crane was more than justified in emphasizing, but then Crane was a great reader as well as a great writer of poetry. Flanking the famous carol of death are two lines of the tally: "And the voice of my spirit tallied the song of the bird" preceding, and: "To the tally of my soul" following. To tally the hermit thrush's carol of death *is* to tally the soul, for what is measured is the degree of sublimity, the agonistic answer to the triple question: more? less? equal? And the Sublime answer in death's carol is surely "more":

Come lovely and soothing death,
Undulate round the world, serenely arriving, arriving,
In the day, in the night, to all, to each,
Sooner or later delicate death.

Prais'd be the fathomless universe,
For life and joy, and for objects and knowledge curious,
And for love, sweet love—but praise! praise! praise!
For the sure-enwinding arms of cool-enfolding death.

Dark mother always gliding near with soft feet,
Have none chanted for thee a chant of fullest welcome?
Then I chant it for thee, I glorify thee above all,
I bring thee a song that when thou must indeed come,
    come unfalteringly.

Approach strong deliveress,
When it is so, when thou hast taken them I joyously sing the dead,
Lost in the loving floating ocean of thee,
Laved in the flood of thy bliss O death.

If this grand carol, as magnificent as the Song of Songs which is Solomon's, constitutes the tally or image of voice of the soul, then we ought now to be able to describe that image. To tally, in Whitman's sense, is at once to measure the soul's actual and potential sublimity, to overcome object-loss and grief, to gratify one's self sexually by one's self, to compose the thousand songs at random of *Leaves of Grass,* but above all, as Crane said, to bring a new covenant of brotherhood, and here that pact is new bound with the voice of the hermit thrush. The bird's carol, which invokes the oceanic mother of Whitman's *Sea-Drift* cosmos, is clearly not its tally but Whitman's own, the transgressive verbal climax of his own family romance. When, in the elegy's final section, Whitman chants himself as: "Passing the song of the hermit bird and the tallying song of my soul," then he prepares himself and us for his abandonment of the image of the lilac. And, in doing so, he prepares us also for his overwhelming refusal or inability to yield up similarly the darker image of the tally:

> Yet each to keep and all, retrievements out of the night,
> The song, the wondrous chant of the gray-brown bird,
> And the tallying chant, the echo arous'd in my soul . . .

The tally is an echo, as an image of voice must be, yet truly it does not echo the carol of the hermit thrush. Rather, it echoes the earlier Whitman, of *Out of the Cradle Endlessly Rocking,* and his literary father, the Emerson of the great *Essays.* But here I require an *excursus* into poetic theory in order to explain image of voice, and its relation to echo and allusion, and rather than turn to as recondite a theorist as myself, I rely instead on a great explainer, John Hollander, who seems to me our outstanding authority upon all matters of lyrical form. Here is Hollander upon images of voice, and their relation to the figurative interplay I have called "transumption," since that is what I take "tally" to be, Whitman's greatest transumption or introjection or Crossing of Identification, his magnificent overcoming both of his own earlier images of poetic origins and of Emerson's story of how poetry comes into being, particularly American poetry. First Hollander, from his book, *The Figure of Echo and Allusion*:

> . . . we deal with diachronic trope all the time, and yet we have no name for it as a class. . . . The echoing itself makes a figure, and the interpretive or revisionary power which raises the echo even louder than the original voice is that of a trope of diachrony. . . .
>
> I propose that we apply the name of the classical rhetoricians' trope *of transumption* (or *metalepsis* in its Greek form) to these diachronic, allusive figures. . . .
>
> Proper reading of a metaphor demands a simultaneous appreciation of the beauty of a vehicle and the importance of its freight. . . . But the interpretation of a metalepsis entails the recovery of the transumed material. A transumptive style is to be distinguished radically from the kind of conceited one which we usually associate with baroque poetic, and with English seventeenth-century verse in particular. It involves an ellipsis, rather than a relentless pursuit, of further figuration. . . .

Hollander then names transumption as the proper figure for interpretive allusion, to which I would add only the description that I gave before in A *Map of Misreading*: this is the trope-undoing trope, which seeks to reverse imagistic priorities. Milton crowds all his poetic precursors together into the space that intervenes between *himself and the truth*. Whitman also crowds poetic anteriority, Emerson, and the Whitman of 1855–1860 into a little space between the carol of death and the echo aroused in the soul of the elegist of *Lilacs*. Emerson had excluded the questions of sex and death from his own images of voice, whether in a verse chant like *Beaches* or a prose rhapsody like *The Poet*. The earlier Whitman had made of the deathly ocean at night his maternal image of voice, and we have heard the hermit thrush in its culmination of that erotic cry. Whitman's tally transumes the ocean's image of voice, by means of what Hollander calls an ellipsis of further figuration. The tally notches a restored Narcissism and the return to the mode of erotic self-sufficiency. The cost is high as it always is in transumption. What vanishes here in Whitman is the presence of others and of otherness, as object–libido is converted into ego–libido again. Father Abraham, the ocean as dark mother, the love of comrades, and even the daemonic *alter ego* of the hermit thrush all fade away together. But what is left is the authentic American image of voice, as the bard brings tally, alone there in the night among the fragrant pines except for his remaining comrades, the knowledge of death and the thought of death.

In 1934 Wallace Stevens, celebrating his emergence from a decade's poetic silence, boldly attempted a very different transumption of the Whitmanian images of voice:

> It was her voice that made
> The sky acutest at its vanishing.
> She measured to the hour its solitude.
> She was the single artificer of the world
> In which she sang. . . .

The tally, in *The Idea of Order at Key West*, becomes the "ghostlier demarcations, keener sounds" ending the poem. A year later, Stevens granted himself a vision of Whitman as sunset in our evening land:

> In the far South the sun of autumn is passing
> Like Walt Whitman walking along a ruddy shore.
> He is singing and chanting the things that are part of him,
> The worlds that were and will be, death and day.
> Nothing is final, he chants. No man shall see the end.
> His beard is of fire and his staff is a leaping flame.

It is certainly the passing bard of the end of *Lilacs*, but did he chant that nothing is final? Still, this is Walt as Moses and as Aaron, leading the poetic children of Emerson through the American wilderness, and surely Whitman was always proudly provisional. Yet, the tally of his soul had to present itself as a finality, as an image of voice that had achieved a fresh priority and a perpetually ongoing strength. Was that an American Sublime, or only another American irony? Later in 1935, Stevens wrote a grim little poem called *The American Sublime* that seems to qualify severely his intense images of voice, of the singing girl and of Whitman:

> But how does one feel?
> One grows used to the weather,
> The landscape and that;
> And the sublime comes down
> To the spirit itself,
> The spirit and space,
> The empty spirit
> In vacant space.
> What wine does one drink?
> What bread does one eat?

The questions return us full circle to Emerson's *Bacchus,* nearly a century before:

> We buy ashes for bread;
> We buy diluted wine;

This is not transumptive allusion, but a repetition of figurations, the American baroque defeat. But that is a secondary strain in Stevens, as it was in Emerson and in Whitman. I leap ahead, past Frost and Pound, Eliot and Williams, past even Hart Crane, to conclude with a contemporary image of voice that is another strong tally, however ruefully the strength regards itself. Here is John Ashbery's *The Other Tradition,* the second poem in his 1977 volume, *Houseboat Days:*

> They all came, some wore sentiments
> Emblazoned on T-shirts, proclaiming the lateness
> Of the hour, and indeed the sun slanted its rays
> Through branches of Norfolk Island pine as though
> Politely clearing its throat, and all ideas settled
> In a fuzz of dust under trees when it's drizzling:
> The endless games of Scrabble, the boosters,
> The celebrated omelette au Cantal, and through it
> The roar of time plunging unchecked through the sluices
> Of the days, dragging every sexual moment of it
> Past the lenses: the end of something.

Only then did you glance up from your book,
Unable to comprehend what had been taking place, or
Say what you had been reading. More chairs
Were brought, and lamps were lit, but it tells
Nothing of how all this proceeded to materialize
Before you and the people waiting outside and in the next
Street, repeating its name over and over, until silence
Moved halfway up the darkened trunks,
And the meeting was called to order.

                                     I still remember
How they found you, after a dream, in your thimble hat,
Studious as a butterfly in a parking lot.
The road home was nicer then. Dispersing, each of the
Troubadors had something to say about how charity
Had run its race and won, leaving you the ex-president
Of the event, and how, though many of these present
Had wished something to come of it, if only a distant
Wisp of smoke, yet none was so deceived as to hanker
After that cool non-being of just a few minutes before,
Now that the idea of a forest had clamped itself
Over the minutiae of the scene. You found this
Charming, but turned your face fully toward night,
Speaking into it like a megaphone, not hearing
Or caring, although these still live and are generous
And all ways contained, allowed to come and go
Indefinitely in and out of the stockade
They have so much trouble remembering, when your forgetting
Rescues them at last, as a star absorbs the night.

I am aware that this charming poem urbanely confronts, absorbs, and in some sense seeks to overthrow a critical theory, almost a critical climate, that has accorded it a canonical status. Stevens's Whitman proclaims that nothing is final and that no man shall see the end. Ashbery, a Whitman somehow more studiously casual even than Whitman, regards the prophets of belatedness and cheerfully insists that his forgetting or repression will rescue us at last, even as the Whitmanian or Stevensian evening star absorbs the night. But the price paid for this metaleptic reversal of American

belatedness into a fresh earliness is the yielding up of Ashbery's tally
or image of voice to a deliberate grotesquerie. Sexuality is made
totally subservient to time, which is indeed "the end of something," and poetic tradition becomes an ill-organized social meeting
of troubadours, leaving the canonical Ashbery as "ex-president / Of
the event." As for the image of voice proper, the Whitmanian confrontation of the night now declines into: "You found this /
Charming, but turned your face fully toward night, / Speaking into
it like a megaphone, not hearing / Or caring. . . ." Such a megaphone is an apt image for Paul de Man's deconstructionist view of
poetic tradition, which undoes tradition by suggesting that every
poem is as much a random and gratuitous event as any human
death is.

Ashbery's implicit interpretation of what he wants to call *The
Other Tradition* mediates between this vision of poems as being totally cut off from one another, and the antithetical darkness in which
poems carry over-determined relationships and progress toward a
final entropy. Voice in our poetry now tallies what Ashbery in his
Syringa, a major Orphic elegy in *Houseboat Days,* calls "a record of
pebbles along the way." Let us grant that the American Sublime is
always also an American irony, and then turn back to Emerson and
hear the voice that is great within us somehow breaking through
again. This is Emerson in his journal for August, 1859, on the eve
of being burned out, with all his true achievement well behind him,
but he gives us the true tally of his soul:

> *Beatitudes of Intellect.*—Am I not, one of these days, to write con-
> secutively of the beatitude of intellect? It is too great for feeble
> souls, and they are over-excited. The wine-glass shakes, and the
> wine is spilled. What then? The joy which will not let me sit in my
> chair, which brings me bolt upright to my feet, and sends me strid-
> ing around my room, like a tiger in his cage, and I cannot have
> composure and concentration enough even to set down in English
> words the thought which thrills me—is not that joy a certificate of
> the elevation? What if I never write a book or a line? for a
> moment, the eyes of my eyes were opened, the affirmative experi-
> ence remains, and consoles through all suffering.

WHEN LILACS LAST IN THE DOORYARD BLOOM'D
BY *WALT WHITMAN*

1

WHEN lilacs last in the dooryard bloom'd,
And the great star early droop'd in the western sky in the night,
I mourn'd, and yet shall mourn with ever-returning spring.

Ever-returning spring, trinity sure to me you bring,
Lilac blooming perennial and drooping star in the west,
And thought of him I love.

2

O powerful western fallen star!
O shades of night—O moody, tearful night!
O great star disappear'd—O the black murk that hides the star!
O cruel hands that hold me powerless—O helpless soul of me!
O harsh surrounding cloud that will not free my soul.

3

In the dooryard fronting an old farm-house near the whitewash'd
    palings,
Stands the lilac-bush tall-growing with heart-shaped leaves of rich
    green,
With many a pointed blossom rising delicate, with the perfume
    strong I love,
With every leaf a miracle—and from this bush in the dooryard,
With delicate-color'd blossoms and heart-shaped leaves of rich
    green,
A sprig with its flower I break.

4

In the swamp in secluded recesses,
A shy and hidden bird is warbling a song.
Solitary the thrush,

The hermit withdrawn to himself, avoiding the settlements,
Sings by himself a song.

Song of the bleeding throat,
Death's outlet song of life, (for well dear brother I know,
If thou wast not granted to sing thou would'st surely die.)

5

Over the breast of the spring, the land, amid cities,
Amid lanes and through old woods, where lately the violets peep'd
    from the ground, spotting the gray debris,
Amid the grass in the fields each side of the lanes, passing the
    endless grass,
Passing the yellow-spear'd wheat, every grain from its shroud in
    the dark-brown fields uprisen,
Passing the apple-tree blows of white and pink in the orchards,
Carrying a corpse to where it shall rest in the grave,
Night and day journeys a coffin.

6

Coffin that passes through lanes and streets,
Through day and night with the great cloud darkening the land,
With the pomp of the inloop'd flags with the cities draped in black,
With the show of the States themselves as of crape-veil'd women
    standing,
With processions long and winding and the flambeaus of the night,
With the countless torches lit, with the silent sea of faces and the
    unbared heads.
With the waiting depot, the arriving coffin, and the sombre faces,
With dirges through the night, with the thousand voices rising
    strong and solemn.
With all the mournful voices of the dirges pour'd around the
    coffin,
The dim-lit churches and the shuddering organs—where amid
    these you journey.
With the tolling tolling bells' perpetual clang,

Here, coffin that slowly passes,
I give you my sprig of lilac.

7

(Nor for you, for one alone,
Blossoms and branches green to coffins all I bring,
For fresh as the morning, thus would I chant a song for you
    O sane and sacred death.

All over bouquets of roses,
O death, I cover you over with roses and early lilies,
But mostly and now the lilac that blooms the first.
Copious I break, I break the sprigs from the bushes,
With loaded arms I come, pouring for you.
For you and the coffins all of you O death.)

8

O western orb sailing the heaven.
Now I know what you must have meant as a month since I
    walk'd,
As I walk'd in silence the transparent shadowy night,
As I saw you had something to tell as you bent to me night after
    night,
As you droop'd from the sky low down as if to my side, (while
    the other stars all look'd on.)
As we wander'd together the solemn night, (for something I know
    not what kept me from sleep,)
As the night advanced, and I saw on the rim of the west how full
    you were of woe,
As I stood on the rising ground in the breeze in the cool
    transparent night,
As I watch'd where you pass'd and was lost in the netherward
    black of the night,
As my soul in its trouble dissatisfied sank, as where you sad orb,
Concluded, dropt in the night, and was gone.

9

Sing on there in the swamp,
O singer bashful and tender, I hear your notes, I hear your call,
I hear, I come presently, I understand you,
But a moment I linger, for the lustrous star has detain'd me,
The star my departing comrade holds and detains me.

10

O how shall I warble myself for the dead one there I loved?
And how shall I deck my song for the large sweet soul that has gone?
And what shall my perfume be for the grave of him I love?

Sea-winds blown from east and west,
Blown from the Eastern sea and blown from the Western sea, till
    there on the prairies meeting,
These and with these and the breath of my chant,
I'll perfume the grave of him I love.

11

O what shall I hang on the chamber walls?
And what shall the pictures be that I hang on the walls,
To adorn the burial-house of him I love?

Pictures of growing spring and farms and homes,
With the Fourth-month eve at sundown, and the gray smoke lucid
    and bright,
With floods of the yellow gold of the gorgeous, indolent, sinking
    sun, burning, expanding the air,
With the fresh sweet herbage under foot, and the pale green leaves
    of the trees prolific,
In the distance the flowing glaze, the breast of the river, with a
    wind-dapple here and there,
With ranging hills on the banks, with many a line against the sky,
    and shadows,
And the city at hand, with dwellings so dense, and stacks of chimneys,

And all the scenes of life and the workshops, and the workmen
    homeward returning.

12

Lo, body and soul—this land,
My own Manhattan with spires, and the sparkling and hurrying
    tides, and the ships,
The varied and ample land, the South and the North in the light,
    Ohio's shores and flashing Missouri,
And ever the far-spreading prairies cover'd with grass and corn.

Lo, the most excellent sun so calm and haughty,
The violet and purple morn with just-felt breezes,
The gentle soft-born measureless light,
The miracle spreading bathing all, the fulfill'd noon,
The coming eve delicious, the welcome night and the stars,
Over my cities shining all, enveloping man and land.

13

Sing on, sing on you gray-brown bird,
Sing from the swamps, the recesses, pour your chant from the bushes,
Limitless out of the dusk, out of the cedars and pines.

Sing on dearest brother, warble your reedy song,
Loud human song, with voice of uttermost woe.

O liquid and free and tender!
O wild and loose to my soul—O wondrous singer!
You only I hear—yet the star holds me, (but will soon depart,)
Yet the lilac with mastering odor holds me.

14

Now while I sat in the day and look'd forth,
In the close of the day with its light and the fields of spring, and the
    farmers preparing their crops,
In the large unconscious scenery of my land with its lakes and
    forests,

In the heavenly aerial beauty, (after the perturb'd winds and the
　　storms,)
Under the arching heavens of the afternoon swift passing, and the
　　voices of children and women,
The many-moving sea-tides, and I saw the ships how they sail'd,
And the summer approaching with richness, and the fields all busy
　　with labor,
And the infinite separate houses, how they all went on, each with
　　its meals and minutia of daily usages,
And the streets how their throbbings throbb'd, and the cities
　　pent—lo, then and there,
Falling upon them all and among them all, enveloping me with the
　　rest,
Appear'd the cloud, appear'd the long black trail,
And I knew death, its thought, and the sacred knowledge of death.
Then with the knowledge of death as walking one side of me,
And the thought of death close-walking the other side of me,
And I in the middle as with companions, and as holding the hands
　　of companions,
I fled forth to the hiding receiving night that talks not,
Down to the shores of the water, the path by the swamp in the
　　dimness.
To the solemn shadowy cedars and ghostly pines so still.

And the singer so shy to the rest receiv'd me,
The gray-brown bird I know receiv'd us comrades three,
And he sang the carol of death, and a verse for him I love.

From deep secluded recesses,
From the fragrant cedars and the ghostly pines so still,
Came the carol of the bird.

And the charm of the carol rapt me
As I held as if by their hands my comrades in the night,
And the voice of my spirit tallied the song of the bird.

Come lovely and soothing death,

Undulate round the world, serenely arriving, arriving,
In the day, in the night, to all, to each,
Sooner or later delicate death.

Prais'd be the fathomless universe,
For life and joy, and for objects and knowledge curious,
And for love, sweet love—but praise! praise! praise!
For the sure-enwinding arms of cool-enfolding death.

Dark mother always gliding near with soft feet,
Have none chanted for thee a chant of fullest welcome?
Then I chant it for thee, I glorify thee above all,
I bring thee a song that when thou must indeed come, come unfalteringly,
Approach strong deliveress,
When it is so, when thou hast taken them I joyously sing the dead,
Lost in the loving floating ocean of thee,
Laved in the flood of thy bliss O death.

From me to thee glad serenades,
Dances for thee I propose saluting thee, adornments and feastings for thee,
And the sights of the open landscape and the high-spread sky are fitting,
And life and the fields, and the huge and thoughtful night.

The night in silence under many a star,
The ocean shore and the husky whispering wave whose voice I know,
And the soul turning to thee O vast and well-veil'd death,
And the body gratefully nestling close to thee.

Over the tree-tops I float thee a song,
Over the rising and sinking waves, over the myriad fields and the prairies
  wide,
Over the dense-pack'd cities all and the teeming wharves and ways,
I float this carol with joy, with joy to thee O death.

15

To the tally of my soul,
Loud and strong kept up the gray-brown bird,
With pure deliberate notes spreading filling the night.

Loud in the pines and cedars dim,
Clear in the freshness moist and the swamp perfume,
And I with my comrades there in the night.

While my sight that was bound in my eyes unclosed,
As to long panoramas of visions.
And I saw askant the armies,
I saw as in noiseless dreams hundreds of battle-flags,
Borne through the smoke of the battles and pierc'd with missiles I
    saw them,
And carried hither and yon through the smoke, and torn and
    bloody,
And at last but a few shreds left on the staffs, (and all in silence,)
And the staffs all splinter'd and broken.

I saw battle-corpses, myriads of them,
And the white skeletons of young men, I saw them,
I saw the debris and debris of all the slain soldiers of the war,
But I saw they were not as was thought,
They themselves were fully at rest, they suffer'd not,
The living remain'd and suffer'd, the mother suffer'd,
And the wife and the child and the musing comrade suffer'd,
And the armies that remain'd suffer'd.

16

Passing the visions, passing the night,
Passing, unloosing the hold of my comrades' hands,
Passing the song of the hermit bird and the tallying song of my
    soul,
Victorious song, death's outlet song, yet varying everaltering song,
As low and wailing, yet clear the notes, rising and falling, flooding
    the night,
Sadly sinking and fainting, as warning and warning, and yet again
    bursting with joy,
Covering the earth and filling the spread of the heaven,
As that powerful psalm in the night I heard from recesses,

Passing, I leave thee lilac with heart-shaped leaves,
I leave thee there in the dooryard, blooming, returning with
    spring.

I cease from my song for thee,
From my gaze on thee in the west, fronting the west, communing
    with thee,
O comrade lustrous with silver face in the night.

Yet each to keep and all, retrievements out of the night,
The song, the wondrous chant of the gray-brown bird,
And the tallying chant, the echo arous'd in my soul,
With the lustrous and drooping star with the countenance full of
    woe,
With the holders holding my hand nearing the call of the bird,
Comrades mine and I in the midst, and their memory ever to
    keep, for the dead I loved so well,
For the sweetest, wisest soul of all my days and lands—and this for
    his dear sake,
Lilac and star and bird twined with the chant of my soul,
There in the fragrant pines and the cedars dusk and dim.

(1980)

THE POLITICS
OF MODERN CRITICISM

DENIS DONOGHUE

THERE IS A FAMOUS PASSAGE in Trotsky's *Literature and Revolution*, the fifth chapter, where a quiet rebuke delivered to the Futurists becomes an attack on the Formalists. Trotsky insists that art is a function of social man, and that it plays a subsidiary rather than a primary role in the social process. Formalism, he maintains, is merely a version of Idealism. It ignores the social and historical factors which constrain what an artist may do; it discounts the psychological unity of social man. Formalists are engaged in "the superstition of the word." Followers of St. John, they believe that "in the beginning was the Word." But we believe, Trotsky says, that "in the beginning was the deed: the word followed, as its phonetic shadow."

These alternatives, word or deed, were made available to Trotsky in a passage from the first part of Goethe's *Faust*, where Faust is engaged in an experimental translation of the sentence from St. John. He starts by taking it at its apparent word: "in the beginning was the Word." But it strikes Faust as implausible; he cannot bring himself to give "the Word" the prize. He tries again: "in the beginning was the Mind." But that, too, seems doubtful. Is Mind, he asks, the creative source? Recoiling from that commitment, he tries again: "in the beginning there was Force." But something, presumably the source of his own inspiration, warns him not to accept that version. "The Spirit helps me," he reports, as if to say, "Now I have it right." So he concludes: "In the beginning was the deed."

Trotsky does not rehearse these several possibilities; he goes in a leap from word to deed. He does not say what a deed is, or what it means to give priority to the deed rather than to the word. John refers, evidently, to an inaugural word, and in the nature of the case the word is divine, since it has not proceeded from anything but itself. The word in John has regularly been associated with spoken truth, the original truth that makes possible every subsequent act or statement of truth. Those who think of it most devoutly construe it as the sign of God's presence, understood by analogy with a human voice saying something to somebody. It is "in the beginning" because no other conceivable beginning answers so fully the desires to which it is addressed. The origin it posits is divine, but not alien, since the analogy of personal presence, as in a voice that speaks to us, makes it radically answerable to our desires.

Trotsky does not say what a deed is. He does not even refer to *vita activa*, which Hannah Arendt has defined as "human life insofar as it is actively engaged in doing something." The reason is that the supreme form of a deed is already before Trotsky's eyes, the revolution of 1917 which he personifies as October. October is the revolution, understood as fulfilling the type of action in a public world, where men make their history by such deeds. They make their history, subject to finite constraints: human life is therefore a series of mediations between factors voluntary and involuntary. A philosophy of action is likely to regard the deed as separable from the word, and to value the word only when it fortifies the deed it serves. The word is the rhetoric in the cause of the deed. Trotsky speaks as a philosopher of action for whom such a philosopher has already been authenticated as October.

Two years later, in 1926, Boris Eichenbaum replied to Trotsky without mentioning him: he was as silent toward Trotsky as Trotsky was toward Goethe. Eichenbaum's essay on the theory of the "Formal Method" argues that Formalism is an aesthetic concern; it studies the character of literary works in the hope of discovering what literature is, and what distinguishes it from other things. Eichenbaum took care to distinguish Formalism from Symbolism. Symbolism, he said, was indeed idealistic, rotten with subjectivity. Formalism was based upon "scientific positivism"; it was determined to work toward a science of literature, a functional poetics. It was not concerned with causes, but with functions. The study of literary genetics clarifies only the origin of a device: the function of the device in the poem can be explained only by poetics. Eichenbaum deals with the problem of form and content by setting it aside: form is in its own right everything it needs to be, concrete, dynamic, self-contained.

Eichenbaum's defense of Formalism consists mainly in his saying that it has particular work to do and that it believes in the wisdom of minding its own business: its business is with literariness, the fact that a work of literature is indeed literary or poetic rather than practical. He does not point to the strong tradition of Formalism in Russian fiction, a tradition that does not start with Bely's *Petersburg* or end with Nabokov's *Pale Fire*. But he refers to Roman Jakobson and Viktor Shklovsky and to the critical interests they share. Jakobson is severe upon historical or psychological critics; he compares them to policemen who, bewildered in trying to arrest one man, take the desperate course of arresting everyone in sight. Critics who wander into psychology, the history of ideas, and so forth are helpless, he says; they forget that the price of such wandering is that they use literary masterpieces "only as defective, secondary documents." Presumably Jakobson means that a poem or novel which is used to illustrate some situation in history or psychology is denied its true life in favor of the half-life of being an illustration.

Eichenbaum uses Shklovsky to expound the idea of estrangement, an idea which modern criticism has found congenial. The idea means to say that in ordinary life we deal with nearly everything by recognizing it and passing on, as we deal with the wallpaper in our rooms. The function of art is corrective. It causes us to look at things as if for the first time; we see them as if they were strange to us rather than familiar. Perception, as distinct from casual recognition, is an aesthetic act: it should be prolonged in that character. The purpose of a poetic image is not to present to our minds the approximate meaning of an object, or to replace an object by its meaning, but to induce in us a special perception of the object, the creation of its vision rather than the mere recognition of its use. Shklovsky means that when we merely recognize something we see not the object but its local usefulness. But when we perceive it, we grasp it in its true character, which is far richer than its utility. Such a perception is a pleasure to the perceiver, and the character of the pleasure is aesthetic rather than moral or social. Estrangement is therefore at the furthest remove from the punctual sense of an object, the sense by which we deal with it as it is passing or has already passed into familiarity. Eichenbaum's addition to Shklovsky is to say that when we perceive an object in a full aesthetic sense, we perceive it as form. The form is not a mere envelope containing the substance or content: we see the object as if it were form, which it becomes, under that attention.

Eichenbaum does not take up Trotsky's challenge about the priority of word or deed, but it is clear that Formalism has no interest in a philosophy of action which demands that a deed be considered apart from its word or prior to it. What Nabokov calls "aesthetic bliss" is to be felt among the words, and never apart from them; it is a property of the experience of being among words. As a linguistic or poetic theory, Formalism is bound to say that a word is logically prior to the speaker who speaks it or the writer who writes it; more strenuously, that it is also temporally prior in the sense that we are born into a world already to some extent mediated by language—if not by language as such, then by the particular mother tongue we soon begin to learn. The theory of Formalism does not require anyone to believe that man is a mere function of the linguistic codes he learns to negotiate. His context includes other factors, starting with body and its faculties. Kenneth Burke has emphasized that the bodily senses give us certain animal reports about the world into which we are thrown: these reports can be taken as immediate, if not absolutely then relatively by comparison with the personal acts of mediation which we perform as ideas and concepts. But it would take only a slight push in the Formalist direction to reach the point of arguing that the bodily senses, too, are already coded. The ear can only hear; it can only report audible events, beginning with the message that the events are of this nature. Finer adjustments, distinguishing between the character of one event and other events which have to be assigned to the same category, are made later. But the first reports from the bodily senses are rough, if useful, and they are given in prescribed forms.

I have gone into the argument between Trotsky and Eichenbaum because it identifies, in a context now safely historical, what is still the main ideological argument in literary criticism. We can see the issue more clearly by seeing it at a certain historical remove. The current debate in literary theory is sometimes regarded as politically neutral: it is often assumed that there is no necessary connection between literary theories and moral or political principles. But if you scratch a theory you find a principle, and if you find a principle closely attended by a rhetoric in its favor, you find theory, principle, and rhetoric adding up to an ideology. I maintain that the question of the priority of word over deed, or of deed over word, is still the main question of criticism, the question that divides one critic from another to a degree that makes further debate virtually impossible. The matter is not resolved by distinguishing between priority temporal, narrative, and logical. Temporal priority simply means that one event took place before another. Narrative priority means that the events are already joined in a formal relation. "John died, and later Mary died" indicates temporal priority, leaving otherwise moot the question of the relation between John and Mary. "John died, and then Mary died of grief" indicates priority both temporal and narrative. Logical priority means that one term depends upon a more fundamental term as the ground of its meaning.

If you say that in the beginning was the deed, you are bound to regard language and literature as secondary matters, however important in their ways, and you are likely to have a pretty rudimentary theory to account for both. Your central interests are likely to turn upon history and politics. When literature comes into the question, you are likely to argue that the character of language as such, or even of a particular language, is not crucial. A theory of language which presents it as an instrument in the service of action and communication will probably answer your requirements. The fact that a novel may be translated from one language to another, with only as much loss as the common reader takes in his stride, is bound to gratify you. Literature can then be construed not as what is lost in translation but as what survives translation. But if you maintain that in the beginning was the word, and that the very notion of a deed is a function of language, you are likely to find your choice commitments in semiotics and linguistics, with the support of whatever metaphysical or anti-metaphysical tradition you find most persuasive. But it would be naïve to think that the Formalist argument is ideologically neutral.

I have maintained that the argument between Trotsky and Eichenbaum has remained central to the understanding of criticism. But the context of the dispute has changed. Trotsky and Eichenbaum argued in the context of October. It was assumed by both parties that the proletarian revolution was a success in principle and, as for the fact, a success which would soon be completed. October had come. Trotsky assumed that bourgeois domination was a thing of the corrupt past; the future was to be a new thing in the hands of the workers. Literature would have to acknowledge and endorse it: the poetic imagination would give itself to the new vision, and set aside its flirtation with decadence. What Eichenbaum felt on this issue, I have no idea; but it is reasonable to assume that he felt misgivings about the secondary status of literature, and hoped to make a case for its independence.

It is a commonplace that the literature of the past two centuries, so far as it has been a literature of high spiritual ambition, has been an effort to escape from the middle class, or at least to provide the sentiment of escaping from that class. Modern poets and novelists have fostered the assumption in their readers that the true essence of our lives does not coincide with our bourgeois existence, that our real lives are lived not here but elsewhere. F. W. Bateson once interpreted Romanticism as the shortest way out of Manchester. Modern literature has sought the shortest way out of the suburbs; or it has permitted its readers to stay in the suburbs, on condition of staying there in bad faith. The social form of this attitude was seen most clearly in the counterculture of the years after 1968, a counterculture predicated upon a pastoral vision of landscape and fellowship, free from the official culture of cities and bureaucracy. But modern literature was already a counterculture. Georg Simmel pointed out, in *The Philosophy of Money* (1900), that the aesthetic experience in modern literature corresponds to an attitude of carefully maintained reserve, of distance from the commodity relations imposed by a culture based on money. It is easy to see Eliot's early poems as attempts to make a quiet space for a self deemed acutely vulnerable to the forces surrounding it. In that respect, high art in our century has always proposed a counterculture, if we take the dominant culture as a bourgeois power.

The attack upon bourgeois values has come in our time from Left and Right: it is still an open question which of these forces has delivered the more damaging considerations. I shall say a little about each.

From the Left, Lévi-Strauss's work has emphasized the imperial motive in modern forms of communication and exchange, the imposition of writing, as in printed documents, upon native populations, so that they may be controlled by law. Since ignorance of the law is held to be no excuse, there is a moral requirement that the citizen should be able to read the laws he has to obey. Lévi-Strauss has also made much of the Western ideology by which we spread the assumption that the laws of our society are authenticated by laws of nature which, to be accepted, have only to be known. Roland Barthes's entire work was an attempt to show how far an ironic relation to bourgeois values, which he derided as "the bourgeois myth," could go. He regarded modern forms of communication as a conspiracy between writer and reader on the analogy of that between producer and consumer. The bourgeois novelist writes a novel which is read, generally, in the passive sense of being consumed by the reader. Bestsellers normally put the reader into such a state of passivity. Barthes's answer was to try to break the conspiracy by proposing forms of reading in which the reader produces the text, reads it in his own way, at his own speed and in fulfillment of his own desire, to thwart the rhetorical force the writer is exerting upon him. The best reading, according to Barthes, is the most outlandish, the most excessive. The reader tries to overcome not the writer but the bourgeois myth with which he has conspired. Instead of taking dictation from the writer, the reader should engage in the play of codes, knowing them to the point of discounting their design upon him. The aim is not the consumption of an official meaning but the play of pleasure, as diverse as possible. So the conspiracy between the novelist and the society which rewards him for producing yet another consumer object is, at least marginally, broken.

It is not clear how a reader is supposed to acquire the ironic force to defeat the bourgeois myth, since he is a product of it. The theory would say, I assume, that at some pitch of revulsion an intelligent reader would recoil from subservience to his society, and would turn against the statutory objects it offered and elude their force by recourse to his own. Barthes encourages the reader in this direction because he resents the bourgeois program of transforming the reality of the world into a coded image of the world: a bourgeois society is ingenious in persuading its citizens that history is nature, or rather, that history is the temporal form of nature. People are persuaded to prefer signs that don't look like signs. As a class, according to Barthes, the bourgeoisie does not want to be named, it wants to give the impression that it, too, has issued directly from nature, that its power is not a mere historical event like any other but rather a state of being, guaranteed by laws of nature. Barthes wants to show his readers how to discredit the signs they receive, first by knowing that they are signs, and then by detecting the ideology that has produced them. If all else fails, Barthes encourages the reader to detach himself from society and cultivate his private garden of pleasures.

Michel Foucault's work is concerned with the ways in which power is exercised in bourgeois society, particularly in such matters as the treatment of mental illness, crime, and sexuality. He proposes to dislodge bourgeois man from the vanity of assuming that he is immortal or that the universe was made in his favor. Much of Foucault's rhetoric is designed to make people feel tired of themselves, disgusted with their shallowness in having conspired with bourgeois society to create a justifying mythology. His readers cannot suppose themselves strong enough to defeat bourgeois power, but they can put themselves somewhat beyond its reach by anticipating the otherwise constraining forms it will take. Foucault's project, then, is to remove from bourgeois power its mystery if not its venom. But it has been argued, notably by Frank Lentriccia, that Foucault gives a misleading impression: his account of the exercise of power is finally innocuous because it presents that exercise as "multiple, automatic and anonymous." Within its own terms, bourgeois society is a success story, a best seller, because it has established a machine of power-relations that works throughout society, everywhere, from top to bottom. Power is everywhere, by being nowhere in particular. But if this is the case, Foucault cannot find a point of entry at which resistance or attack would be effective. In the end, or indeed at any stage in the transaction, there is nothing to be done, except to contemplate the fact that we are like so many common soldiers deployed in strategic movements of which they are ignorant. Foucault's reader is not impelled to change anything, since to make any difference it would be necessary to change everything at once. Working apparently in political terms, Foucault lets his reader conclude that political action is pointless. Reading Foucault is in that respect like reading Beckett: it does not incite you to do anything.

On the face of it, Jacques Derrida's rhetoric seems more challenging. He returns to what we have taken to be the source, the first word of presence and discourse, and he denies that it is the source; it is merely the focus of our nostalgia, our homelessness, it is what we yearn for when we feel the need of authority, some guarantee that our presence in the world is the proper consequence of Being itself, our founding uttering Father. Derrida would accustom us to live with mobility, to do without a stable center, to forgo an origin. But he does not allow us to cultivate the insignia of orphanage; we are not orphans, because we have never had a parent. He allows us to retain the notion of a center, but only as a function, not a subject; as one function among many, entirely without privilege, it is merely a vehicle of play, like any other.

Derrida's admonition is so complete that it is useless to take refuge in one social rhetoric rather than another; they are all compromised equally. But his descriptions of nostalgia have especially in view the petit-bourgeois satisfactions which he regards as vulgar consolation prizes. But the defect of his project is that it breaks every practical connection, so far as it is credited, between thought and action; its skepticism leaves the reader free to conclude that since, as in Foucault, there is nothing to be done, he may as well proceed as if his actions were just as feasible as he had fancied them to be. Derrida's skepticism is so thoroughgoing that it is impossible to live and act in its light; very soon we have to start again upon our lives even if our motives remain much the same as they were before the question of skepticism was raised.

I have spoken of these attacks as coming from the Left, but they do not issue from any Left that exists in formal political terms. The objection to bourgeois values is not completed by proposing a practical alternative in any party of the Left, and certainly not in the French Communist Party, the object of nearly universal contempt. The arguments, after 1945, among Sartre, Camus, and Merleau-Ponty have at least established the fact that a neo-Marxist apocalyptic vision cannot be fulfilled by any political party or movement that exists. Barthes wrote of the Left with notable sympathy, but he did not suggest that a vote for Socialism or Communism would solve any problem of bourgeois domination. The Left I have invoked is a hypothetical position which is accorded every merit except existence in the world. It is not necessary that it should exist; it is enough that it live in the critic's mind, sustained by an antithetical relation to everything he fears and detests in the bourgeois culture at hand. It is hardly necessary to say that an ironic or subversive relation to bourgeois values depends to an embarrassing degree upon the values it derides.

The real problem is that an attack upon bourgeois values, if it comes from the Left, has only two possibilities: it can deconstruct bourgeois rhetoric, disclosing interests of class which present themselves as laws of nature; or it can establish itself in some relation to Marx or Marxism, doing whatever it can to keep itself free from the taint of Stalinism. The first possibility has been developed most fully by Barthes; the second has been attempted, despite the experience of French intellectuals since the War, by critics as diverse in other respects as Lukács, Marcuse, Althusser, Foucault, Raymond Williams, Irving Howe, and Frederic Jameson. In some cases the Marxism is fairly close to its official source; in other cases, it is transposed and transformed through the interpretations of such post-Marxist thinkers as Adorno, Benjamin, and Gramsci. But the critic's problem is to retain a dynamic relation to Marxism while disengaging himself from the proletarian vision which in Marx as in Gramsci seems increasingly specious. There is no sign that a victorious proletariat would remain a proletariat in any sense that matters; matters, I mean, in the sense of remaining true to the spirit of its Marxist origin. The workers would join the middle class and hire other people, the latest immigrants, Algerians, West Indians, the Irish in London, Puerto Ricans in New York, Italians and Turks in Germany, to do the menial chores. In England, the workers are already in the middle class: the culture for which D. H. Lawrence felt so warmly no longer exists. There is no point in talking about hegemony and the evils of reification so long as the facts of the case are these and not other. There is no longer a social class to which critics on the Left can appeal, as Trotsky appealed to the October people. This would not matter much if the history of the Left were not presented as a visionary apocalypse, in which the proletariat is featured as subsuming history itself. There is no

October, except in the graduate seminar where the production of
an edifying vision is mistaken for a victory in the streets.

Critics on the Left, in default of a proletarian constituency,
have two main procedures. They can attack bourgeois culture and
blame it for the plight of "the wretched of the earth," amounting
to millions if you include the poor in the Third World, starving
people in India, Uganda, Biafra, Latin America, repressed groups in
Eastern Europe, and if you add, nearer home, blacks, homosexuals,
criminals, outcasts, and women. The same bourgeois culture can
also be blamed, as in Jameson's commentaries on Freud and psy-
choanalysis, for the repression which brought out, as an answer to
it, the politics of desire and transgression which he recalls, nostalgi-
cally, from 1968.

The second procedure is to let middle-class readers remain in
that class in every comfortable sense, but to stay there in bad faith,
holding as a secular version of spirituality the essentialist notion that
their true life is elsewhere. I have mentioned this procedure
already, but a further remark is permissible: the procedure is congenial to the intelligentsia, who show no sign of giving up bourgeois
comfort but resent the society that provides it. Critics recognize
that in the past forty years or so, bourgeois society has learned that
a politics of confrontation is unnecessary. Radical ideas are no
longer dangerous: they lost their power to hurt when bourgeois
societies discovered that such ideas could be accommodated, and at
last domesticated, by a sufficiently clammy embrace. What critics
on the Left most bitterly resent is not that a bourgeois society pun-
ishes them but that it patronizes them.

The attack upon bourgeois values from the Right is a familiar
story, so I can be brief. It has usually been represented as a revolt
against the spirit of the age, so far as that spirit presents itself as liberal and democratic. The vice of democracy is that it fosters mediocrity. Writers as different in other respects as Eliot, Pound, Yeats,
Lawrence, and Wyndham Lewis attacked bourgeois liberalism on
the grounds that it was content with the least a society might hope

to achieve by way of intelligence and order; that it reduced people to the same dreary level of faceless anonymity. These writers appealed, beyond the conventions of daily life, to the idea of an operative intelligence, or to the form a superior mind would take in the world. Eliot appealed to the idea of Tradition, which in his later work he construed as Orthodoxy or the continuity of Christianity. Pound appealed to the lucidity of intelligence, and to certain moments in the past when the values of intelligence, lucidity, and form were embodied in a specific relation to political power. By these comparisons, it seemed to him that democratic life amounted to "a mess of mush." Yeats thought, at least in his early years, that bourgeois culture, the conventions of towns, might still be defeated by the combined force of peasant and aristocrat, linked in their relation to land and to the continuities of race and custom. In his last years he put more trust than hindsight would approve in the exercise of power by great men, supposedly enlightened in the manner he ascribed to certain Renaissance princes. He was not, in fact, a Fascist, but Fascism had a better chance of gaining his approval than Nazism, because its most spectacular version was enacted on his beloved Italian soil and he could not help believing that somewhere beneath those marching feet he could hear the sweet sounds of Urbino, "the wise Duchess," and Lady Elilia adorning the theme. Wyndham Lewis's allegiance was German rather than Italian. For some years he found Hitler, rather than Mussolini, the exemplar of superiority, the type of Exceptional Man. Hitler was the political form of genius, imposing his will upon people who would otherwise have sunk into nothingness and anonymity. Intelligence, according to Lewis, was a force to be directed against the pieties of bourgeois liberalism.

It is as true of the Right as of the Left that there is no social class in which the approved values are embodied. Wyndham Lewis knew enough of English aristocratic life to know that exceptional intelligence was not one of its attributes. But the difference between Right and Left in this matter is that the Right never had such a class, or at least not since the Renaissance. There has been nothing to correspond, in the rhetoric of the Right, to Trotsky's October. The Right has always appealed to a critical few, already culturally privileged, and it has encouraged them to believe that their privilege is justified by the values of order and intelligence they have espoused. As for the faceless masses, the Right has regarded them as the monstrous form of force, of energy beyond the reach of mind; to be transformed, if possible, by education and authority, else civilization is ruined. The values endorsed by the Right do not exist in any social class, but they are found in art and literature. The criteria upon which the rhetoric of the Right is based are aesthetic rather than moral: a politics is to be derived from an aesthetic. A society is to be judged as a place fit or unfit for artists to live in; its qualities are to be those found in the structure of a work of art. No wonder Lawrence left England and kept moving around the world, hoping to find a space available for his choice metaphors.

There has also been an attack upon bourgeois values from within the bourgeois family, from people who feel no visionary zeal for any other class and think the best hope is in persuading the middle class to rise above its ordinary state. From Matthew Arnold to Wallace Stevens, John Crowe Ransom, Lionel Trilling, and Jacques Barzun, liberal humanists have been urged to earn the right to exist.

In *Culture and Anarchy* Arnold represented the three major social classes in England by a severe characterization of each; they were Barbarians, Philistines, and Populace. He conceded that a few in each class were free of the limitations of their class, but in the end he appealed to the middle class, not as it was but as it might still become. Arnold distinguished between one's ordinary self and one's best self: one's ordinary self entertains without question the values of one's class, such as they are; one's best self rises, if not beyond class, then at least to a degree of lucidity and consideration rarely found in individuals and never as a characteristic of a class. In *Culture and Anarchy* he identifies one's best self with right reason.

"It is not easy," he says, "with our style of proceeding, to get beyond the notion of an ordinary self at all, or to get the paramount authority of a commanding best self, or right reason, recognized." Presumably one's best self is to be achieved by establishing a critical relation to the values of one's class; taking up a stance of "creative dissatisfaction," to use Karl Mannheim's phrase. In Arnold's terms, it is to be achieved by taking thought, by choosing not to be supine, by living among fresh and true ideas, the best that has been thought and said in the world, and by striving toward the clarity in moral judgment which Arnold praised as Hellenic rather than Hebraic. While it is true that anyone could act upon Arnold's prescription, it is clear that he placed his hope, short of placing his confidence, in the "best self" of the middle class, the class he saw coming into power after the Reform Acts. The middle class was already coming into power, but it had not shown any sign of having earned it. Arnold did not celebrate the bourgeois victory, but he encouraged his readers to hope that the middle class, assured of its power, would take enough care, if constantly admonished, to strive toward its best self.

Stevens's sense of the relation between poetry and politics was intermittent: goaded into it, he felt sensitive enough on the subject to defend himself. He did not yearn for

> A time in which the poets' politics
> Will rule in a poets' world . . .

partly because he saw no reason to trust poets in their political judgments, and partly because he believed that the poet should never be entirely of the world in which he lives: he should remain a little aside from its orthodoxy. Political sentiments came readily to Arnold, but Stevens had to remind himself of them. On those occasions, his recommendations were compatible with the idea of a comfortable bourgeois life, purged of its vulgarity. In *The Necessary Angel* he refers to the statue of Jackson in Washington. Jackson, Stevens says, is raising his hat in a gay gesture, saluting the ladies of his generation. "One looks at this work of Clark Mills," he continues, "and thinks of the remark of Bertrand Russell that to acquire immunity to eloquence is of the utmost importance to the citizens of a democracy." Stevens's remark is interesting, subject to the qualification that only in a democracy would immunity to eloquence even arise. Stevens's poetry is consistent with the politics of minding one's own business and doing one's work, but it rests, too comfortably, upon the assumption that a good life requires a certain amount of money, some leisure in the evening, enough aesthetic interest to buy books and a few paintings, and the patrician flair which enables one to live a little aside from ordinary life.

Ransom's program is often described as aristocratic, but it has nothing to do with any organization of society for which aristocrats have been responsible: he does not yearn for Urbino. The values he espoused depend upon the idea of a gentleman, but they do not require blue blood. The image of the Southern plantation-owner, reading the *Aeneid* in the intervals of supervising the conduct of his estate, charmed Ransom a little, but not as much as it charmed Allen Tate and Donald Davidson. Ransom's aesthetic creed was not based upon that image. He argued in *The World's Body* that it is the function of a proper society to transform appetitive or instinctual values into aesthetic values. He favored a way of life notable for reserve and courtliness, but still compatible with the idea of a gentleman, which I take to be the middle-class citizen in his best self. I do not recall that Ransom wrote, as Barzun did, of the "hatred of high bourgeois culture" issuing from "nearly every novel, play, painting, or artist's biography" that finds a place on the popular part of the curriculum in our universities, but he would have found Barzun's attitude congenial.

But the most sustained admonition from within the bourgeois family has come from Lionel Trilling. In "Reality in America" he reflected upon the modern American evaluation of Dreiser and James, and especially upon the indulgence liberal readers have given to Dreiser and withheld, on the same issues, from James. Trilling related this discrepancy to "the political fear of the intellect" in American liberal culture. "In the American metaphysic," he argued, "reality is always material reality, hard, resistant, unformed, impenetrable, and unpleasant: and that mind is alone felt to be trustworthy which most resembles this reality by most nearly reproducing the sensations it affords." The essays in *The Liberal Imagination* are attempts to persuade the American middle-class reader, the man or woman of vaguely liberal inclination, to rise beyond the easy assumptions of that class, to question them, and to achieve by such interrogation his or her best self. When Trilling appealed to "the educated class," he meant the middle class on its most thoughtful occasions. If his later books are lugubrious by comparison with *The Liberal Imagination*, the reason is that Trilling felt, especially after 1968, that the bourgeois liberal had allowed himself to be undermined, shamed out of his virtues while adhering to his vices. He had put up no resistance to "Modernism in the streets."

The liberal tradition from Arnold to Trilling has acknowledged that there is a split between the bourgeois liberal's ordinary self and his best self. For his ordinary self there is, apparently, nothing to be said. But the situation has changed in the years since Trilling's death. Till recently, the ordinary self of the bourgeois liberal was recognizable as decent, humane, tolerant, even if his relation to these virtues was lazy or complacent. But in the past few years there has emerged, not for the first time, a form of Social Darwinism. The bourgeois liberal feels himself under a sustained siege: the attack has been proceeding for so long, and from sources of such loudly claimed moral superiority, that the bourgeois liberal feels himself intimidated, if not humiliated.

It is time to say that the bourgeois liberal has a strong case, if he would make it. I am thinking of the values Arnold thought sufficiently worthwhile to identify with the best self as the personification of an ideal State; the values which Trilling, espousing the idea of Society rather than that of the State, recognized as providing the setting for whatever an individual might achieve, the context in which his freedom consorts with his constraint. I am also thinking of R. P. Blackmur, a critic who cannot be accused of letting bourgeois culture off lightly. It was Blackmur who said that "the true business of literature, as of all intellect, critical or creative, is to remind the powers that be, simple and corrupt as they are, of the turbulence they have to control. There is a disorder vital to the individual which is fatal to society. And the other way round is also true." It was Blackmur, too, who defined bourgeois humanism as "the treasure of residual reason in live relation to the madness of the senses" and went on to say that "bourgeois humanism is the only conscious art of the mind designed to deal with our mega-lopolitan mass society: it alone knows what to *do with* momentum in its new guise; and it alone knows it must be more than itself without losing itself in order to succeed." I read these sentences as Blackmur's version of the bourgeois liberal according to his best self. It is evident that Blackmur, from the considered possibilities in front of him and all around his mind, could not think of any other power that stood a chance of maintaining in live relation the devil of pure behavior and the order which exists only as an aspiration and never as something achieved once and for all. As things stand, the bourgeois humanist is in danger of losing himself before he has any further chance of being more than himself. He loses himself when he gives in to the intimidation, from whatever source, which tells him that he has no right to live.

Much of this intimidation takes the form of undermining the common assumptions of freedom which go into notions of the self. The self, it is insisted, does not exist: what exists is a site marking our penury. Or the self is merely a function of many codes in their diverse relations. In *Allegories of Reading,* commenting on Rilke's tropes, Paul De Man says that "neither love nor the imagining power of the deepest nostalgias can overcome the essential barren-ness of the self and of the world." It is hard to believe that this sen-tence is a disinterested response to Rilke's poems; it seems clear that it comes with a largely personal urgency. If so, we have to ask: by comparison with what, precisely, is the self barren; and by com-parison with what other world is our own world barren? It is easy to imagine selves and worlds richer than our own, but only because we have seen some tokens of them around us. Criticism, De Man says, is "the deconstruction of literature, the reduction to the rigors of grammar of rhetorical mystifications." The mystifications to which he is most alert are those which suppose "the autonomous power to will of the self." I have never come upon such a supposition. I can't think of any literature in which the self claims to act with such a degree of autonomy. The relation between autonomy and constraint may be posited in one spirit or another, but only a wild angelist would present the self in free-floating independence of its conditions.

The modern version of Trotsky's "in the beginning was the deed" usually takes a political form. A critic working along that line would say: we take thought so that we may the better take action, and we resort to words so that, in taking action, we may the better identify our purpose. I find this motive in Edward Said's recent essays, especially those in which he scolds critics on the American Left for thinking that their rhetoric of the graduate seminar strikes a real blow for freedom. But the sense that "in the beginning was the deed" does not necessarily take a political form. Harold Bloom's criticism, for instance, is founded upon a belief in the will, a consciousness that knows the movement of its desire and acts upon that knowledge. Bloom is a humanist in his assumption that will and imagination are two names for the one thing, the one energy. We call it will when we think of its context chiefly as predicament and its action as defensive to begin with. We call it imagination when we think of its context as problematic and its action as creative or productive. To Bloom, as to Kenneth Burke, the mind is genuinely known as agent; it acts, of course, subject to conditions and limitations. The reaction Bloom posits between a strong poet and his precursor is an act of will, and the "crossings" he finds in poems are crises in a drama of the will and what opposes it. Bloom is so completely a critic of will, action, deed, and imagination that he regards Deconstruction as mere idolatry of words, a fetishization of Language.

But Deconstruction does not say: "in the beginning was the Word." It retains the form of John's sentence only to insist upon a skeptical sense of it, as if to say: "there was no beginning; nor was a word spoken." Or, in a more prosaic version: at any moment there is Language, a deceptive and mystifying set of relations, impersonal and arbitrary, its delusory power capable indeed of being known but not of being defeated, even by the doomed irony which alone knows enough to undermine its rhetoric. It follows that the language posited by Deconstruction is not any particular language but Language as such, abstracted from all the concrete experiences in which it is found. Figurativeness corresponds not to any inventive possibilities which people have found, with pleasure, in the presence of the imagination among the words it engages, but rather to the mystification inscribed, apparently, upon life itself.

Is it possible to make peace between adepts of word and adepts of deed? There may be, at the moment, no clear desire for peace: peace would produce a drop in the liveliness of the critical situation. My own sense of the matter is that we may find peace by giving up talking about language and talking, instead, about discourse. Discourse is close enough to language to satisfy nearly everybody, but it acknowledges the active and intentional character of speech. A similar possibility is provided by Ben Belt's *The Double Witness*. Mr. Belt uses an epigraph from Machado's *Juan de Marina* as a provoking context for his poem "Boiling the Egg." "Poetry is the word in its time," Juan says, "and students of poetry must maximize the temporality of their verse. . . . All our class exercises have been devoted to this end. . . . I especially remember a poem called Boiling the Egg." Now if we think of poetry as the word in its time, we cannot be tempted to identify it with Language as such, which is distinctly not the word in its time but the abstract principle of which words are at best the particles. The word in its time is addressed to its listeners and readers, and it is timely if the word is what is wanted, all the better if the want has only been known vaguely till the words for it have been found. But the word in its time is also what it has become with its histor-

ical memories, associations, and resonance's, the wealth of which
is what F. R. Leavis had in view when, thinking of Shakespeare
and Blake, he emphasized the dependence of their achievements
upon what made them possible, the English language, "a rich,
supple, and exquisitely vital language," with the values which such
a language couldn't but possess.

(1981)

THE MAKING OF A CRITIC

IRVING HOWE

SOMETIMES BY SPEAKING TRUTH, sometimes by shows of brilliance, sometimes by sheer nerve, *Partisan Review* had clawed its way to cultural strength. The magazine could now hoist reputations, push a young writer into prominence, and deal out punishment to philistines, middlebrows, and fellow travelers. Because it stood for something, *Partisan Review* gained influence. It evoked fear among opponents, rage among academics. William Dean Howells had once joked that anyone can make an enemy, the problem is to keep him. This skill *Partisan Review* had mastered.

At the thought of "those characters out there"—that is, beyond the Hudson—cursing and fearing him, Philip Rahv, the dominant editor of the magazine, used to chortle with pleasure. (My image of chortling is of his large body heaving up and down, in appreciation of the discomforts of others.) Rahv ran the magazine as if he were a party leader or parliamentary whip, spinning threads of maneuver so complex they sometimes sped past their intended victims. Whenever I met him, he would propose that I write something to "smash them." Always there was a "them," from Stalinists to New Critics. Rahv cultivated a Marxist style without its political context, and among our "opponents" only Allen Tate responded satisfactorily, for in his splendid Southern manner he was always ready to charge into battle. No wonder Rahv and Tate became friends: nothing but ideas stood between them.

Most of the New York writers were still young. "Veterans" like Sidney Hook and Philip Rahv, William Phillips and Meyer Schapiro, Harold Rosenberg and Clement Greenberg were in their forties. Younger people, very talented, kept appearing: Randall Jarrell, Elizabeth Hardwick, Saul Bellow, Robert Warshow. Not all of these sympathized with *Partisan* politics, but most felt at home with its homelessness. The magazine had a heady cosmopolitan air in those days, with contributions from Eliot and Orwell, Gide and Sartre. Anti-Stalinist leftism created a fragile bond across borders: one kept a kinship with writers like Orwell, Silone, and Camus without having ever met them. There was a visible pride in the capabilities of mind. There was an impatience with that American tradition which regards writing as an outpouring of untainted intuition. There was a spirit of arrogance which kept out lesser souls, smaller talents.

Now that Hitlerism was destroyed, intellectuals felt they had to reach out for new ideas, new modes of sensibility fitting the postwar world. Dissatisfied or bored with Marxism, many *Partisan* writers started to shake off the very idea of system. In spring 1946 the magazine put out a remarkable issue, "New French Writing," that included Sartre's powerful essay on anti-Semitism, Camus's reflections on the myth of Sisyphus, and the work of other French writers, all testifying to the upheaval caused by war, captivity, and resistance.

What now began to absorb the New York writers was a search for some principle by which to order the world after Hitler, culture after the Holocaust. The idea of centrality replaced the ideology of Marxism, though the idea can be seen as a stepchild of the ideology. To be central meant to engage with questions that gave our time its peculiarly terrible character. T. S. Eliot in his poetry had been central; Trotsky had for a time been central; and in the postwar years Kafka seemed central, if only in the purity of his desolation. The idea of the central was slippery: that was what made it attractive.

In the late forties Lionel Abel wrote a piece challenging the older assumption of the centrality of modernist culture and radical politics; that was no longer true, he said, though what had replaced them he did not know. No, said Harold Rosenberg. *He* believed the historical crisis which had spawned modernism was so persistent, so unrelenting, "there is no place for art to go but forward." Why so? Hadn't we been saying the same thing about politics, and didn't political life somehow not go "forward?" Still, if Abel was right, as I now believe, the question remained, what might come after modernist culture and radical politics? No one quite foresaw the benefits of several decades of relative affluence and reconsolidated democracy in Western society. No one foresaw that until the Marxist lenses, or blinkers, were lowered. So a race broke out, some of the *Partisan* sprinters heading straight for the castle of centrality while others were distracted by sideshows of novelty.

A year or two after the war one began to hear about existentialism, associating it mainly with the names of Sartre and Camus and thinking of it not as a formal philosophy but as a testimony springing from the ordeal of Europe. It seemed more attractive in voice than in doctrine. It swept aside the rigidities of deterministic systems, the Left's traditional reliance on "historical forces." It sought to implant a new strength in the *sentiment* of freedom, not by claiming for it transcendent validation or even historical grounding, but by placing it at the heart of our need, perhaps our desperation. "We have arrived," wrote Nicola Chiaromonte, "at humanity's zero hour and history was senseless; the only thing that made sense was that part of man which remained outside of history, alien and impervious to the whirlwind of events. *If,* indeed, such a part existed." That "if" was transformed by desire into an "as if," becoming the burden of Camus's rebel.

In America existentialism led to no literary groups or schools, but it forced writers back to an apprehension of some essential, naked man: a mere idea of man, if you wish, but an idea rich in salvage. In some unsystematic way the writings of Sartre and Camus left a strong mark. Of the two Sartre had the more powerful mind, but politically and "personally" (though I never met him) I felt closer to Camus. Sartre seemed an unresting machine for the manufacture of theories, while Camus, in his veiled bewilderments and unveiled vanities, struck one as more humane. You might learn from Sartre, but you could talk with Camus. And in Camus there were two saving presences: the individual person, a stranger stammering with doubt, and the physical world, shore, ocean, sun.

There was also, it must be admitted, a disturbing softness in Camus, a weakness for noble rhetoric. Still, I thought of him as a comrade, as I could not think of Sartre. For it was Camus who said: "The great event of the twentieth century was the forsaking of the values of freedom by the revolutionary movements. . . . Since that moment a certain hope had disappeared from the world and a solitude has begun for each and every man." That was how I felt in those years, though I would not have put it quite so grandly, with quite so much assurance about the "solitude" of "each and every man." But then, I told myself, Camus was French.

Ideology crumbled, personality bloomed. Perhaps there was a relation between the two? The New York writers, unmoored and glad to be, began to take pleasure in constructing elaborate public selves. The *Partisan* group had done its best work during the late thirties and early forties; now its scattered members, tasting the sweets of individuality, were beginning to do their best individual work. In the search for centrality, they yearned to embrace (even crush) the spirit of the age.

Do I delude myself in thinking there was something peculiarly Jewish in this need to wrestle with the hovering *Zeitgeist*? With appropriate flair and chaos, here were a number of them, cut off from traditional attachments either Jewish or American, casting themselves as agents of the problematic, straining for high thought and career.

The first New York writer with whom I became friendly was a recent arrival from Chicago. *Wunderkind* grown into tubby sage, Isaac Rosenfeld radiated a generosity that melted the crustiest New York hearts. It was easy to imagine him, as his childhood friend Saul Bellow recalled, getting up to a debating club in school, still in short pants, and reading an essay on Schopenhauer; it was not hard to imagine him in a Vilna yeshiva, elucidating points of Talmud. Owlish and jovial but with sudden lilts of dignity, loving jokes even more than arguments, he had a mind strong at unsystematic reflection, though he never quite found the medium, either in fiction or essay, to release his gift. He was also a delicious mimic.

Visiting Isaac I would beg him to do his Yiddish version of Prufrock (*ikh ver alt, ikh ver alt, un mayn pupik vert mir kalt*, I grow old, I grow old and my belly-button grows cold). Isaac was our golden boy, for there was an air of yeshiva purity about him that made one hope wildly for his future. Profligate with his being, his time, his thought, he lacked only that cunning economy which enables writers to sustain lengthy careers.

I learned from Isaac the possibility of a life unflinching in restlessness. He became a wanderer, physically and intellectually, out of step even with his own dybbuk. He played minor parts for a time in a third-rate Yiddish theatrical troupe: he closed himself into a Reichian orgone box to grasp superior energies. Jewish to his bones, he sought a way of leaping beyond those constraints which in our time signify Jewishness—and all that stood in his way was his body, his country, his time. At 38 he died, in lonely sloth.

When I knew him, in his few happy years after the war, Isaac made me feel the world was spacious. There was room for him and room for me. Our friendship didn't last long: he must have smiled at my opinions, while I fretted at the splashing away of his gifts. All we had in common was being young, Jewish, in love with English words, and a rationalism no one can escape whose childhood had been soaked with Yiddish. Isaac chose to move beyond that rationalism, as I could not, but even while fearing the price he must pay, I envied his staggering freedom.

Little remains of this flawed, noble spirit: a minor first novel, some fine critical miniatures, and a legend of charm and waste, a comic intelligence spent upon itself. I visited Isaac as friend but attended Harold Rosenberg as audience. Never have I known anyone who could talk with such unflagging manic brilliance, pouring out a Niagara of epigrams. In the late forties Harold was not yet a famous art critic, and the consciousness of public power that shadowed him was not yet a barrier. Whatever fears may have assailed him, he surely could not have known the fear of running dry that haunts so many writers. Harold was Harold as granite is granite. He lived by a consciousness of historical crisis, making himself theoretician, prophet, advance man, and inner critic of aesthetic modernism. The sectarianism of the radical vanguard he re-enacted through the hermeticism of the artistic vanguard.

As Harold rasped along in his high-pitched voice, did he ever so much as notice who stood before him? I used to think when visiting his studio: suppose I were suddenly to drop dead, would he stop talking? All the while he was the most ingenuous of democrats, one ear being as good as another. I would leave his studio gasping from overstimulation. If only I could "bottle" all I had heard, there'd be enough to work with for a year. But his ideas could not be "bottled"; they had a curious way of evaporating into the upper air. It was as if they came alive only through his voice.

What I learned from Harold Rosenberg was not a particular idea, since he had so many, but the wonders of abundance and still more, the satisfaction of going one's own way. In those years Harold was somewhat isolated, having remained closer to his apolitical Marxism than most other New York writers to their political ideas. If this isolation bothered him, he never showed it. A man who could fill a room with his lunging, arrowed body and rivet attention through his stammer of phases: why should he feel unhappy about his isolation?

Years later his old friend Lionel Abel would sum up the essence of the man: "That which is prior to, more fundamental than radicalism in art, radicalism in action, is the homelessness of spirit that gave rise to both. . . . Harold addressed himself to making clear that no alternative to, or ideological therapy for, our condition of homelessness has yet been found, and until something of that order is discovered, our only valid works of art, our only valid actions, must continue to express a certain distance from things, from others, and even from ourselves." Thirty years ago I could not have made so lucid a claim for this spirit of modernism, but some glimmer of it I had, and that may be why I found myself so dizzied by the hammerings of Rosenberg's mind.

Even when brief, such friendships brought lasting rewards, but there were also missed occasions, the result of shyness and vanity.

Long before I thought of becoming a literary critic I read with admiration essays William Troy was printing in *Partisan Review*. He was not part of its inner circle and had no apparent interest in politics; but each time he wrote—on Lawrence or Fitzgerald or Virginia Woolf—I admired his lucidity. Troy was a "pure" critic, and he helped unsettle my provincial notions about what criticism had to be. There was an austerity to his work, a hard, undeviating concentration on the text, which set him apart from other contributors to the magazine: he never bothered to be merely brilliant, he never rattled his emotions in one's ear. Several times in the late forties I started writing him notes of admiration but always destroyed them, suspecting I might be trying to cozy up to a famous man. A few years after Troy's death I met his widow, the poet Leonie Adams, and when I told her of my repeated failure to write him about my feelings, she let out a kind of moan. In the fifties he had been a troubled man, uncertain of himself and his work, and the admiration of a young stranger, she said, might have given him pleasure. She wheeled on me: "Why did you worry so much about your motives? Suppose they weren't pure? Don't you see that what matters is what we *do*?" Her words shaming me as few stronger rebukes ever have, I turned away in silence, to carry with me through the years a dislike of that vanity which drapes itself as a scruple.

I used to think of the rise of the New York intellectuals as an historical sport, caused by an overflow of energies from the children of Jewish immigrants. So it was. But now I also see this "singular event" as imbedded in the deeper rhythms of American culture, rhythms of shock, break, and intrusion by alien roughnecks.

Suppose we agree to look upon the history of American culture as a grudging retreat from visions of cultural autarchy. The appearance of the New York writers should then be seen not just as a rude, alien intrusion but also as a step in the "Europeanizing" of American culture. Among *Partisan* writers there was a conscious intent, not without touches of grandiosity, to capture the idea of

Europe for America. That meant the idea of *another* culture, an older culture, one richer in moral possibilities, steeped in bloodier experiences, and closer to the tragic than ours could be. Other American writers had reached out toward Europe, from Henry James to T. S. Eliot. The New York writers were coming at the end of a line, but even at the end, the idea of Europe gave them a renewed energy. Themes of cultural return figure strongly in their work: in the dissemination of Russian modes and sensibilities, in the championing of the great modernists, in the popularizing of Marxist ideas, in the insistence that, to be serious, literature must now be international.

Their international perspective came from a provincial experience. Most of the New York writers stemmed from the world of immigrant Jews, having come to articulateness at a moment when there was a strong drive both to break out of the ghetto and to leave the bonds of Jewishness entirely. By the late thirties Jewishness as sentiment and cultural source played only a modest part in their conscious experience. What excited them was the idea of breaking away, willing a new life. They meant to declare themselves citizens of the world and, that succeeding, might then become writers of this country.

The Jewish immigrant milieu had branded on its children marks of separatism while inciting fantasies of universalism. It taught them to conquer the gentile world in order finally to yield to it. Strategic maneuvers of the vanguard had first been mapped out on gray immigrant streets.

With that immigrant culture our relations were far more tormented than we could possibly know. Denial and suppression, embarrassment and shame: these words would not be too harsh. Take so simple a matter as the pen name chosen by *Partisan*'s chief editor: I knew of course what "rahv" meant yet years passed before it dawned on me that Philip wanted to present himself as the chief *rabbi* of our disbelieving world, choosing, in a paradox typically Jewish, to blur his Jewish identity by adopting an aggressively Jewish name.

We wanted to shake off the fears and constraints of the world in which we had been born, but when up against the walls of gentile politeness we would aggressively proclaim our "difference," as if to raise Jewishness to a higher cosmopolitan power. This was probably the first time in the course of American cultural history that a self-confident group of intellectuals did not acknowledge the authority of Christian tradition. A whole range of non-Christian references was now reaching at least some American literary people, terms like Hasidism, place names like Chelm, proper names like Sholom Aleichem. *Partisan Review* was just starting to confront its anomalous position as the voice of emancipated Jews who refused to deny their Jewishness. Surprising assertions broke through. I recall my shock, rather a pleasant shock, when reading in the late forties Clement Greenberg's attack on Arthur Koestler for accepting the "majority gentile view" of the east European Jews. "It is possible," wrote Greenberg, "to adopt standards of evaluation other than those of Western Europe. It is possible that by 'world-historical' standards the European Jews represent a higher type of human being than any yet achieved in history. I do not say that this is so, but I say it IS possible and that there is much to argue for its possibility." *Partisan* writers may have felt a twinge of embarrassment before these words, but I suspect Greenberg was also expressing some of their deeper feelings.

Little wonder that portions of the native intellectual elite, or ragtail poseurs trying to shimmy their way to elite status, found the modest fame of the New York writers insufferable. Soon they were mumbling that American purities of speech and spirit were being contaminated in the streets of New York. (When I first met John Crowe Ransom and heard that lovely man speak of "toid" avenue, I was stunned: had his speech also been contaminated in the streets of New York? It turned out that some Tennessee speech sounded, at least to my dull ear, like that of Brooklyn. But Ransom said "toid" without worrying about the goyim.)

Anti-Semitism had become publicly disreputable in the years after the Holocaust, a thin coating of shame having settled on civilized consciousness; but that hardly meant that some native writers would lack a vocabulary for private use about those New York usurpers, those Bronx-and-Brooklyn wise guys who proposed to reshape American literary life. When Truman Capote later attacked the Jewish writers on television he had the dissolute courage to say what more careful gentlemen said quietly among themselves.

A sprig of genteel anti-Semitism was also entwined with the ivy of our more notable departments of English. When I tell my students that only forty years ago so distinguished a literary man as Lionel Trilling had trouble finding a job in the academy because he was Jewish and therefore judged by his "peers" to be deaf to the "Anglo-Saxon spirit" of English literature, those students stare at me in disbelief. Their disbelief was made possible by an earlier generation's discomforts.

The New York writers introduced a new voice in American literary life: a roughening of tone, a burst of demotic speech. Here perhaps they did have some kinship with earlier writers like Whitman and Melville, who had also brought a plebeian strain into American writing. The gentility against which writers like Theodore Dreiser had rebelled was quite beyond the reach of the New York writers clawing their way out of immigrant quarters. Gentility seemed comic. It was a device for making us squirm, reminding us of our uncouthness; and we repaid with contempt, as well as a rather ungenerous suspicion toward those of our own, like Trilling, who had mastered the art of manners (not after all, when you come down to it, so forbidding or impossible).

These New York writers constituted the first intelligentsia in American history—which is a shade different from a group of intellectuals. An intelligentsia as defined by Renato Poggioli is "an intellectual order *from the lower ranks* . . . an intellectual order whose function was not so much cultural as political. . . ." Poggioli had in mind the Russian writers of the late nineteenth century, but one can find points of similarity with the New York writers. We too came mostly from "the lower ranks" (later composing rhapsodies about the immigrant parents from whom we insistently fled). We too wrote with polemical ferocity. We too stressed "critical thinking" and opposition to established power. We too flaunted claims to alienation.

A footnote about this "Russianness" of the New York milieu came from Lionel Abel in the forties. Invoking "the tradition of the *Partisan*," Abel wrote: "For good or ill, modern politics is a *school of rudeness.* . . . The exquisite aristocratic tact which subtly specified the circumstances under which things could be called by their right names is today something we know about largely from books, not from anybody's public behavior."

Insurgent groups hoping to rouse anger against established authority will always be tempted to violate rules of decorum. In its early years *Partisan Review* was often rude, sometimes for no reason whatever, as if to demonstrate its sheer prickliness. But there were serious reasons, too. Rudeness was not only the weapon of cultural underdogs, but also a sign that intellectual Jews had become sufficiently self-assured to stop playing by gentile rules.

The story of the New York writers has curious similarities to the story of the Southern writers. Allen Tate once remarked that "the distinctive Southern consciousness was quite temporary. It has made possible the curious burst of intelligence that we get at the crossing of the ways. . . ." Can we not say something fairly similar about the New York writers? Both groups were about equally cut off from the mainstream of American culture, about equally assertive in affirming their minority splendor, about equally ideological in styles of thought (though in New York it was called, oddly, "scientific," and in Nashville, quaintly, "poetic"). The Southerners, too, were on the lookout for centrality. Their relation to literary modernism was somewhat less inhibited than that of the New York writers; their politics almost as ill-at-ease with American liberalism. No wonder conflict melted into a gingerly friendship, plight calling to plight, ambition to ambition.

The "crossing of the ways" about which Tate spoke must always prove to be temporary, yet it is this sense of historical tremor which can give point and urgency to literary work. One thinks back to Delmore Schwartz's stories, to the early fiction of Bellow and Malamud, to Rahv's literary criticism, to Hook's social criticism, to the London Letters of Orwell, to Robert Motherwell on modern art, to the learned incisiveness of Meyer Schapiro, to the drama criticism of Mary McCarthy and Eleanor Clark, to Dwight Macdonald's social journalism. Writers of alien opinion also began to find a place in *Partisan Review*: Eliot, Tate, Gide. Nothing in my lifetime has quite equaled this.

There were limitations, too. The *Partisan* group had its orthodoxies: it would have been astonishing to hear a good word for Trollope or Thackeray, a modest recognition of Arnold Bennett or E. A. Robinson. Taste had its narrow boundaries, and one took pride in the narrowness. *Partisan Review* cut enormous segments of the literary past out of its scrutiny—a parochialism of the present, as if the modern were the whole of literature.

Connections with the American cultural past were shaky. Rahv played a leading role in the Henry James revival, but not many *Partisan* critics were sufficiently grounded in the native cultural tradition. They didn't know enough about Puritanism and enriched views of it provided by recent scholarship; they accepted too uncritically Henry James's notion of "a paucity of experience" as explanation for the peculiarities of nineteenth-century American writing; they failed to consider that the tradition of New England Puritanism could yield significant weights of experience.

Not that the "paucity of literature" idea—that nineteenth century American literature, locked into the Puritan heritage, feared to engage with social power and sexuality—was entirely mistaken. But it was inadequate to the richness of the native past, and patronizing as well. Why were the New York critics indifferent to Perry Miller's version of American-literary history? Perhaps because they felt uneasy with Miller's probings into religious thought. Perhaps because they were suspicious of anything coming out of the Harvard English department, which they regarded as a nest of WASP gentility and literary fellow-traveling. Perhaps because they saw no need to trouble themselves with "mere" academic scholarship.

Between ourselves and the native tradition there were real barriers of taste and value. What could we make of all the talk, both from and about Emerson, which elevated individualism to a credo of life? Nothing in our tradition prepared us for this. The whole complex of Emersonianism seemed pale, disabling, genteel, an individualism of vaporous spirituality. Now I know better, or think I do. And perhaps we did not want to recognize what might be genuinely revolutionary in that strand of Emerson's thought which placed a central value on a shared vision of personal autonomy. In any case, I found the classical Americans, especialy Emerson and Thoreau, deficient in those historical entanglements that seemed essential to literature because inescapable in life. I surely would have agreed with Henry James's judgment that Emerson leaves "a singular impression of paleness" and lacks "personal avidity." Born, as we liked to flatter ourselves, with the bruises of history livid on our souls, the New York writers wanted a literature in which experience overflowed, engulfed, drenched. So, with the exception of Alfred Kazin, we abandoned Emerson even before encountering him, and in later years some of us would never draw closer than to establish amiable diplomatic relations.

But this was a position that could not long be sustained. Anyone who approaches American literature even casually must recognize that, except for Edith Wharton, every major American writer bears the stamp of Emerson. To evade Emerson is to evade America. Yet this very "alienation" from the native mainstream did contribute something valuable to *Partisan* writings on American fiction and poetry. It contributed the voice of the outsider. It contributed a skeptical European sensibility that refused to take at face value claims for the moral sublimity of our nineteenth-century literature and insisted upon the most rigorous standards—comparison with the great Russians and modernist French—in judging that literature.

My own responses were as impassioned as they were confused. At the forefront limped wily club-footed Ambivalence, god of

Modernism, and behind straggled such lesser spirits as Eager Ambition and Self-Protective Withdrawal. More important, however, was a persuasion that the New York intellectual world really did function as a free market of ideas and talents, closer to the norms of *laissez-faire* than any capitalist society I had ever heard of. In our little world competition was fierce, not much mercy shown to losers, and the clamor of self incessant. Yet no entrenched monopoly was tolerated or traditional caste privileges honored simply because they were traditional. Anyone with talent or a fresh idea could elbow into the market and set up a stall. The competitors might even help a little. There was equal opportunity to soar or tumble. There was also envy and nastiness: when Philip Rahv or Delmore Schwartz finished tearing apart a friend, little remained but a stack of bones. Still, gifts mattered, ideas mattered. Of manners there was perhaps little, of passion an abundance.

Coming into this world, I had the good sense to listen. I listened to Delmore Schwartz entangle himself in his own wit, as he declared T. S. Eliot a culture hero yet ripped apart his "Christian" snobbism. I listened to Lionel Trilling slide through categories— "the will," "the moral imagination"— the exact meaning of which remained elusive. I listened to Philip Rahv chart American literary relations through lurid diagrams of power. The greatest listening was still two or three years away, the listening to Meyer Schapiro. But in my impatient scrappy way, pocketing a phrase here and a thought there, I listened hard.

And imitated. How else does one learn? Becoming a literary critic seemed fairly easy: it was something one might pick up in a few months. Becoming a writer seemed very hard: it would take several decades. My notion about criticism was a piece of foolishness, half-jokingly indulged, but my idea about writing was serious.

All you needed to be called a literary critic, it seemed, was a determination to read with charged attention and a pencil in the clutch of your fingers. Marking passages up and writing things down, you quickly discovered that reading had become spoiled with purpose. Then you tried to chart the articulated patterns of a novel or poem, its narrative line or theme, its interplay of event and character, quite as a specialist might study x-rays. You might also pick up a few semi-technical terms like "structure," "vision," and "sensibility" without inquiring too closely into their meaning. Finally you tried to locate whatever in a text seemed distinctive, some nuance of perception or tone of voice—but here the whole fantasy about the easiness of writing criticism came tumbling down and then you had to stare at the blinding hardness, perhaps the sheer helplessness of the whole enterprise, before which only fools and pedants thought "method" a protective shield. I remember how hard it was for me when I had to review a book by a new and gifted writer—say, Malamud's first collection of stories—and "*all*" I wanted to do was describe whatever seemed distinctive in his style.

Not once did I ever hear anyone in New York talk about "critical method": it would have been regarded as bad form. Most New York writers didn't think of themselves as critics primarily; they thought of themselves as writers who did criticism, and the difference seemed important.

Decidedly more interesting than theories of criticism was the act of writing. I knew that my prose had a certain vigor, but was deficient in nuance, ease, modulations of tone and pace. So I decided to imitate, not the style of one or another critic, which would have been disastrous, but the common style of the *Partisan* essay. And by imitating a common style I might develop a personal style. I studied the way these writers negotiated rapid thrusts, extreme condensations, the rhetoric of anti-rhetoric. I played with mixtures of high seriousness and street colloquialism, a style John Hollander has called "New York Baroque." I sought that vibration of intensity which seemed the mark of our moment. I learned that this charged, burning style would not work for anything longer than an essay.

Wondering if I could ever match the fluent wit of Elizabeth Hardwick or the rhetorical plenitude of Alfred Kazin, I narrowed my homework to simple effects. How do you begin a literary piece so as to hold attention? George Orwell was masterful at this, probably because he had none of the American literary snobbism about doing "mere journalism." Take the opening of his Dickens essay: "Dickens is one of those writers who are well worth stealing." Who but a brute or hopeless academic would not keep reading after a sentence like that? Edmund Wilson, by contrast, did not strive for striking leads, perhaps assuming that the majesty of his presence would be enough to hold his readers. Philip Rahv came on like a slow thunder of manifestoes. Trilling would begin with a simulated hesitation but soon plant a hint that just ahead lay some revelation about the ways in which "we"—"the educated class-es"—were misconstruing "the cultural situation."

Such attentiveness made me aware of the essay as a form, the most natural for literary criticism. What might one make of it? Only a master like D. H. Lawrence could profit from giving way to personality or idiosyncracy; only a semi-master like Van Wyck Brooks could manage "poetic" evocations of a text. Usually the essay required a margin of impersonality, or a showing forth of per-sonality through indirection. You also had to learn how and when to quote—sparingly, like a pause in the flow of your voice: Tate was skilled at this, Wilson too. Most critics, I decided, had never learned how to do a plot summary without breaking the rhythm of their argument. Hardest of all was to find fresh ways of describing a writer's style, the usual repertoire of descriptives having long ago lost its freshness.

There were two main verbal resources, I concluded somewhat naïvely, that critical writers might call upon, and these were imagery and syntax. V. S. Pritchett was blessed with imagery. But those of us not so blessed had to keep a strict eye on syntax, learn-ing to shape and stretch, as a physiotherapist works with muscles. Among critics Newton Arvin was a master of the supple elaborate sentence; Edmund Wilson was also skilled with complex sentences, but less for imagistic vividness than for hammering together a group of propositions. Aware that the heavenly dispenser had denied me a gift of imagery and suspecting it would be a long time, if ever, before I could approach Arvin and Wilson in their syntacti-

cal virtuosity, I looked about for other models. The idea was to
imitate writers much better than oneself yet not hopelessly out of
range. (One evening I tried to write a critical piece in the manner
of D. H. Lawrence; the next morning I stealthily dropped it in the
wastebasket.) So I decided to work hard in order to write like
Orwell—not, heaven knows, that I succeeded, but still, it made
sense to try, since whatever strength of style I had lay in a certain
incisiveness.

As for being a literary critic, why, come to think of it, should I
want to be one? That it was enjoyable to read and write about
books did not then seem a sufficient reason: now I think it is. That
literary criticism apparently required no special preparation seemed
at first encouraging, until the appalling thought struck me that a
craft requiring no special preparation might require just about
every kind of preparation. I came to see that the critics I most
admired were men for whom criticism mattered because it could
serve as open-ended humanist discourse. Precisely what made it
tempting also made it treacherous: the endlessness of possibility.
The best critics of all schools took for granted that a literary text
merited respect for its integrity, but saw no reason to stop there.
Obeying the command of limit, they realized that it also signified
there were stretches of perception beyond that limit, which one
might yet bring to bear upon the literary work.

I was stumbling upon an idea that could be traced back to
Matthew Arnold and soon would be picked up by Randall Jarrell:
that in a secular age literary criticism carries a heavy burden of
intention, becoming a surrogate mode of speech for people
blocked in public life. Unable to fulfill directly their visions of politics, morality, and religion, critics transfer these to the seemingly
narrower channels of literary criticism. Precisely this spilling over of
thought and passion has made criticism so interesting in our time—
so perilous too. The dominant formal claim of modern criticism
has been an insistence upon treating literature as autonomous; the
main actual circumstance, a pressure for extra-literary connections.
The most valuable critics have often doubled as cultural spokes-

men, moral prophets, political insurgents. Especially in the years after the war, when so many hopes had turned to dust, literary criticism appealed to segments of the intellectual classes as a discipline in which it was still possible for the mind to move dispassionately and freely. A terrifying freedom: to make criticism into a reflection upon our most serious concerns or to reduce it to undisciplined reverie, grandiose and wanton.

Unsure as I was about the place of literary criticism, I was still less sure about my own small beginnings as a critic. How seriously should I take this venture? Not too much, I told myself, solemnly on guard against solemnity. Spending one's life writing about the writings of other people seemed a fairly inglorious prospect. I used to say to friends—with a defensiveness surely transparent—that criticism was "an amiable way to pass the time." Until, that is, history would beckon me to greater callings. . . .

As I came to know the New York critics and, a bit later, the New Critics, I saw that the most gifted among both groups were inclined toward a mildly ironic depreciation of the whole enterprise. All took criticism to be a secondary discipline, dependent on primary creation; and if critics forgot this they would soon be puffing themselves up with ridiculous affectations. People like Tate and Wilson, Trilling and Arvin took their work seriously enough, but all of them spoke with humor, or irritation, about the tendency of modern criticism to make itself a major subject for study.

For a moment it seemed in New York as if the life of the mind could be regarded as a "permanent revolution" of consciousness, a ceaseless dynamic of motion and change. Neither rest nor retreat: that was the way. Influenced by figures as diverse as Eliot and Trotsky, the New York writers proposed to link a defense of modernist culture with a politics of anti-Stalinist radicalism. It was an attractive idea; it lacked durability.

In Europe this union of the *advanced* had flourished only briefly, perhaps in Paris during the late nineteenth century, perhaps in Berlin during the twenties. Such an alliance could not be stable.

The European Left was often middlebrow in cultural style, seldom inclined to sympathize with rebellious experiments. The European avant garde was apolitical when not reactionary. A scrutiny of European culture between, say, 1875 and 1930 would have shown that the literary avant garde and the political Left could really not form a comfortable partnership. But here in America there was this important difference: no one in the *Partisan* circle was proposing actually to bring together *people* from the Left and from the literary and artistic worlds; all that was envisaged was a yoking of two sensibilities within an isolated circle. If this represented a misunderstanding, it was, not for the first time, a productive one.

Partisan Review sanctioned the idea—perhaps the most powerful cultural idea of the century—that there existed an all-but-incomparable generation of modern masters who represented for our time the highest reaches of the imagination. The magazine also helped win respect for a generation of European writers—Silone, Koestler, Malraux, Orwell, Serge—not in the first rank of novelists but who served as moral spokesmen for the homeless independent Left.

The union of the *advanced*, much as it entranced and enabled, was an idea that could not long endure. Avant gardes march forward, but not necessarily to the same tune or in the same direction. By the time the *Partisan* writers came along, both the literary and political avant gardes were living off remembered glories and lacked the vitality needed for a shared upsurge. Modernism was not moving along a necessary line of purpose or progress. At least politically, many of its heroes were quite prepared for a backward spiral, some dreaming of recreated aristocratic decorums, and still others—a distressing number—yielding to authoritarianisms of right and left. It became fashionable in the earlier decades of this century for advanced writers—Joyce stands out as a wonderful exception!—to dismiss liberal democracy as a breeding ground of the mediocre masses and thereby an enemy of high culture. No; the union between cultural modernism and independent radicalism was neither a proper marriage nor a secure liaison; it was a meeting between parties hurrying in opposite directions, brief, hectic, messy.

The prolonged historical crisis that had provided the impetus to modernism might persist into the end of the twentieth century, but that did not ensure that modernism would still be able to flourish. Modernism, as George Lukács observed, despairs of human history; it abandons ideas of a linear development or progress; it even falls back, in extreme instances, upon notions of a universal *condition humaine*, a rhythm of eternal recurrence, or even a blockage of the entire human enterprise. Yet within the literary realm modernism signifies ceaseless change, turmoil, reaction. The more history comes to be seen as mired in endless crisis, the more must art take on a relentless dynamism; as if Hegel's "cunning of reason" had been driven out of its high place as motive force of history and exiled to culture.

How long can this stand-off continue, with history grinding its wheels in the ruts of insoluble crisis and culture ceaselessly inventing new modes of experiment? Must not a breakdown occur sooner or later, wearying of nerves, a pull toward entropy?

It would have been hard to ask, even to think of, such questions several decades ago, for precisely an acute sense of history blocked the vision of less dramatic historical options. The New York writers also discovered that their relation to literary modernism was less authoritative and more ambiguous than they liked to suppose. The battles for Joyce and Eliot had been fought in earlier decades and by now were mostly won. The New York writers came toward the end of the modernist experience, just as they came at what may yet be judged the end of the radical experience, and as they certainly came at the end of the immigrant Jewish experience. One shorthand way of describing this situation, a cause of both their fevered brilliance and their fevered instability, is to say that *they came late.*

The earlier radicalism of the New York Intellectuals had been thin, anxious, problematic. They had no choice: the crisis of socialism was world-wide, with no end in sight, and felt most keenly in countries that lacked mass movements of the Left. No version of orthodox Marxism could now retain a hold on intellectuals who had suffered the trauma of abandoning the Leninist *Weltanschauung* and had come to realize the extent to which the politics of this century, most of all the rise of totalitarianism, called into question Marxist categories.

Yet if the radicalism of the New York intellectuals lacked firm political foundations, it played a major role in their own history. The thirties, however much they might scorn that decade or pretend to forget it, represented their time of fervor. The radicalism of the thirties gave them their distinctive style: a flair for polemic, a taste for the grand generalization, an impatience with what they regarded (often parochially) as parochial scholarship, and internationalist perspective.

Their essayistic style was a style of nervousness, strewn with knotty and flashy phrases, impatient with transitions and other concessions to dullness. It willfully called attention to itself as a token of bravura, a mixture of mandarin elegance and street outcry. I think I know a few of its sources: the early Van Wyck Brooks, a superb essayist in *America's Coming of Age*; Edmund Wilson; and some Continental writers too, Valèry and Eliot. But finally the *Partisan* writers *made it up*, out of their visions of what a cosmopolitan style might be. In most of these essays there was an aura of *tornament*, the writer as gymnast with one eye on other rings, or the writer as skilled infighter juggling knives. It was a style that easily evoked strong distaste, even fear. "Ordinary readers" were often left with the fretful sense that they were not "in," the beauties of polemic racing past their eyes. Oldline academics declared the New York writers to be "unsound."

The New York writers developed a style of brilliance, and a style of brilliance is often hard to bear. At its best this style represented a certain view of the intellectual life: freelance dash, peacock strut, knockout synthesis. It celebrated the idea of the intellectual as antispecialist. It celebrated the writer as roamer among theories, as dilettante connoisseur, as *Luftmensh* of the mind. It could be wonderful, it could turn rancid. Our partial assimilation—roots loosed in Jewish soil but still not torn out, roots lowered into American soil but still not fixed—gave us a seemingly endless range of possibilities. These were not really endless, of course, but it was good that for a time they should seem so. Well or poorly, we tried to live by that vision of Ishmaelite pride and independence that Melville had called the way of the loose-fish. It was a vision that could not last very long, since need and caution, realism and loss of nerve, erosion and complication would finally do it in. Decades later I still ask myself, what better than to be a loose-fish?

(1982)

THE USES OF DECADENCE: WILDE, YEATS, JOYCE

RICHARD ELLMANN

VICTORIAN MELANCHOLY disclosed its uneasiness in the concept of decadence. The word began to be used in England about 1850, as if the distentions of empire necessarily entailed spiritual decline and fall. Decadent was not a word that Ruskin or Arnold found congenial: Ruskin preferred "corruption" and Arnold "philistinism" and "barbarism." But decadence, with implications of the fading day, season, and century, had an unfamiliar ring and gradually came to seem the right word. As if to confirm its rightness, the principal guardians of the Victorian age in statecraft and in literature ailed and then died symbolically as well as literally. Most were gone by the time the 'nineties started. "The woods decay, the woods decay and fall."

What distinguished decadence from corruption or philistinism was that it could be discussed with relish as well as with concern. Gautier, whose writings were in vogue in England as well as in France, declared in his preface to Baudelaire's *Les Fleurs du Mal* in 1868 that the decadent spirit was in harmony with the contemporary crisis. He interpreted decadence as the extreme point of maturity of a civilization. Paul Verlaine could accordingly announce in 1883 with *Schadenfreude* rather than discomfiture, *"Je suis l'Empire à la fin de la Décadence."* Dying cultures make the best cultures. A few months after Verlaine's poem came Huysmans' novel *A Rebours* to give decadence the force of a program. His decadent nobleman (decadents are always male and preferably noble; female decadents are called by other names) has no normal tastes. A determined quester for unheard-of pleasures, he collapses at last in neurasthenia, but of the most glamorous kind. This powerful work outlasted all other decadent prose because it established a new type—the sampler, who keeps changing his drink, who moves from one inordinate and esoteric fancy to another. *A Rebours* became at once a favorite book of Whistler, Wilde, George Moore, Arthur Symons. Wilde and Moore wrote books that in part derived from it, and something of the book's effect rubbed off on Wilde's life as well. The cult of the green carnation, for instance, probably stemmed from Des Esseintes' peculiar notion that, while artificial flowers were to be preferred to natural ones, best of all would be natural flowers that looked like artificial ones. (A florist in the Burlington Arcade painted white carnations green every day.) What was also valuable about *A Rebours* was that it criticized decadence even while touting it. The intricate schemes of Des Esseintes to amuse himself with new sensations are checked as much by Huysmans' sardonic irony as by their inherent futility, and Huysmans, while never indifferent to his hero, avoids identification with him.

A Rebours was read with more solemnity than it was written with, and remained for a time the Bible of decadence. Devotees of that movement were as determined in their advocacy as its bourgeois adversaries in their rejection. They flourished, however, for only a few years in Paris, during the 'eighties. By the time English writers took an interest in decadence it had already lost its lustre, or what they labeled (in a mistranslation of Baudelaire) "its phosphorescence of putrescence." In England nobody called himself a decadent, though it was a fine epithet to ascribe to someone else. Ten years after Verlaine's poem Arthur Symons published his article in *Harper's* on "The Decadent Movement in Literature." Symons expressed wry fondness for decadence as "a new and interesting and beautiful disease," but within a few years he acknowledged that the decadent movement had been "an interlude, a half-mock interlude." He was persuaded later to call the movement symbolist rather than decadent, a change of title which had already taken place in Paris ten years earlier. The element of mockery was overt in Oscar Wilde's references to decadence in the late 1880s. He spoke of a new club called "The Tired Hedonists" who he said "wore faded roses in their buttonholes" and "had a sort of cult for Domitian." The essay in which he evoked this fantasy movement was "The Decay of Lying," the title itself a mockery of decadence.

The fact that in England decadence never gained the status of a literary movement did not keep people from taking sides about it. It was a subject of debate, it affected the course of literature, it did everything but exist. What opponents of decadence meant by the word was principally its parent movement, aestheticism. The battle lines had been drawn early in the century in two books. One was Gautier's *Mademoiselle de Maupin* (1837); the other, Kierkegaard's *Either/Or* (1843). Gautier provided a heroine with bisexual tastes; in his preface he scorned morality, social utility, and nature as points of reference for art. Art was amoral, useless, and unnatural. Kierkegaard took up aesthetic man, as opposed to ethical man, and anatomized the way in which aesthetic man sought to be absorbed in a mood, a mood which must necessarily be only a fragment of himself. For fear of losing the mood, he cannot afford to reflect; nor can he attempt to be more than what he for that mood-moment is. He moves from sensation to sensation, much in the manner that Pater was later to extol; Kierkegaard seems to be refuting Pater before Pater wrote.

During the century both aestheticism and anti-aestheticism gathered force. In Joyce's *Stephen Hero* the president of the college warns Stephen, "Estheticism often begins well but ends in the vilest abominations. . . ." The term could still be used without reproach, however. In 1868 Pater described the Pre-Raphaelites under the honorific title of the "aesthetic movement." But the counter movement had its weapons of ridicule. In 1881 Gilbert's *Patience* presented an aesthete—Bunthorne—as effeminate and narcissistic. Up to now no memorable type of decadent aestheticism had been evolved in English literature to match Huysmans' character Des Esseintes, but Pater tried to establish one with his *Marius the Epicurean*, published two years after *A Rebours*. Marius is also a sampler, attracted to a series of cults like a series of sensations; one of them is a new Cyrenaicism, which as Pater explains "from time to time breaks beyond the limits of the actual moral order, perhaps not without some pleasurable excitement in so bold a venture." As his double negative indicates, Pater was a cautious man. His Marius is cautious too, and cannot be said to succumb to Cyrenaicism or to Christianity either; he seeks the impassioned realization of experience, but in so sobersided a way as to deprive aestheticism of its unwholesomeness. (For true decadent aestheticism a gamey whiff of the Borgias is required.) Pater situated his story in imperial Rome during the reign of Marcus Aurelius, and so left it open for someone else to provide a more modern and English instance. This was exactly what Wilde tried to furnish in *The Picture of Dorian Gray*, first published four years after *Marius* and part of the same cycle of novels.

The familiar ways of attacking decadent aestheticism were to quarrel with its supposed morbidity and pretentiousness, its narcissism, its excesses in technique and language, its concern with mere sensation, its artificiality and abnormality. Most of these criticisms could easily be turned against those who made them. Wilde said that if one looked for examples of decay, one would find them among the sincere, the honest, the earnest. In *Ecce Homo* Nietzsche declares, "Agreed that I am a decadent, I am also the reverse." By his lights "morality itself" was "a symptom of decadence." It was a revenge upon life, an attempt to "unself man" (*Ecce Homo*). In *Stephen Hero* Joyce acknowledged that at moments Stephen showed signs of decadence, then added, "But we cannot but see a process to life through corruption." One man's decadence was another man's renaissance. Mallarmé saw in the dying century "the fluttering of the veil of the temple," as if some infinite revelation were in store ("*Crise des vers*"). So Yeats wrote an essay under the title of "The Autumn of the Flesh" in 1896, and said in 'ninetyish rhythm, "I see, indeed, in the arts of every country those faint lights and faint colours and faint outlines and faint energies which many call 'the decadence' and which I, because I believe that the arts lie dreaming of things to come, prefer to call the autumn of the flesh." The best season is autumn, and the best time of day is of course the Celtic twilight, which also heralded a victory of moonlit spirit over sunlit matter. Wilde, less mystically, offered the heraldic figure of the new man, the *do-nothing*, a creature who emerges only after five in the afternoon, what used to be called "the lounge lizard." In a period when Victorians were infernally busy in misdoing everything, what really needed to be recognized was what he called "the importance of doing absolutely nothing." Under cover of indolence, which others were free to call decadence if they liked, Wilde proposed to transform society.

The debate about decadence achieved such resonance that any account of the 'nineties must take notice of it. C. E. M. Bowra reports in his *Memoirs* that Yeats wrote to him, "The 'nineties was in reality a period of very great vigour, thought and passion were breaking free from tradition." The allegation that they were decaying prompted writers to disprove the charge. In so doing, they had to rethink problems of art, language, nature, life, religion, myth. Wilde is the supreme example. He had adopted aestheticism while still at Trinity College, Dublin, and in the early 1880s he went to America to present the doctrine under the title of the English renaissance. At the time he was between two versions of aestheticism. One, deriving from Gautier, and supported by Whistler, extolled art for its absolute uselessness and its elitism, and denied that it had any but a perfunctory connection with life and nature. The other held that art could remake the world. In America Wilde spent most of his time extolling beauty, but he also urged that artistic principles might beautify houses and dress as well as life generally. This meant that it was not useless, nor necessarily elitist.

Wilde preached renaissance for a whole year to the Americans, then returned and went to Paris. He found himself there *en pleine décadence*. Parisian decadence made his inveterate proselytizing for undefined beauty seem somewhat out of date. Soon after returning to England, Wilde made clear in a review that he did not at all accept that art was for art's sake. That slogan referred only to what the artist feels when he is composing, and had nothing to do with the general motive of art. Toward the end of the 'eighties Wilde propounded such a general motive of art in "The Decay of Lying." In this he turned Aristotle on his head by saying that art does not imitate nature, nature imitates art. It was a paradox that no one had been able to state so succinctly before, though it had certainly been implied by the romantics. The effect was not to divorce art from life, as Whistler and Gautier would do, but to bring the two together again, though with the priorities changed. The difference between Wilde and the romantics was not in estimating the value of art, but in putting so much emphasis as Wilde did on artifice. When he said, "A sunset is no doubt a beautiful thing, but perhaps its chief use is to illustrate quotations from the poets," he was suggesting that artists were not only the Shelleyan unacknowledged legislators, but the quickeners of perception. Nature as we know it is built up out of imaginative fictions. Strip as we will, we will never be naked.

People fall in love because poets have talked up that sentiment. They limp because Byron limped; they dress up because Beau Brummel did; Wilde's point here being that people are affected not only by the works of art that are written down, but by the works of art that are lived. This view of art was not at all elitist; it was democratic and inescapable. Wilde set himself against the contempt that Whistler expressed for art critics, which derived from Gautier's comment, "There was no art criticism under Julius II." Wilde's contrary view was, "The Greeks were a nation of art critics," and he would have said the same of the Italians of the Renaissance. For criticism was one way in which expression could recognize its cultural antecedents. In his other great essay, "The Critic as Artist," he explained that if it were not for criticism art would merely repeat itself. But since all fine imaginative work is self-conscious and deliberate, the role of criticism is to subvert what has just been done, by confronting it with what was done before and elsewhere. The critical faculty brings to bear "the concentrated experience of the race" as opposed to momentary consolidations arrived at by individual artists. Art is a great subverter, but always in danger of forgetting to subvert. Criticism prevents art from forgetting, prevents it from sinking into conformity. The image of subversion leads Wilde to see the artist and the critic within the artist as in some sense criminal. He disrupts, he destroys as he creates. In pursuing ever ampler and as yet unaccepted versions of the world, the artist is always breaking bonds.

The effect is to challenge all effigies, all that is established, such as the established virtues. Chastity is a virtue that, as Renan says, nature cares little for, and art, according to Wilde, correspondingly little. Charity creates a false sense of obligation, since the rich have no right to their wealth any more than the poor to their poverty. As for self-sacrifice, Wilde says that only a thoroughly secular age like our own deifies it, for self-sacrifice is a survival of the self-mutilation of the savage and part of the old worship of pain. (This was not his final word on the subject.) It involves exactly that contraction of impulse, that narrowing in, which art sets itself to overcome. Wilde examines, or rather cross-examines, all the accepted virtues. So he takes up the virtue of presence of mind. He had a story to illustrate this. Once, in a crowded theater, the audience saw smoke rising from the wings. They panicked and ran for the exits. But a leading actor, a man with presence of mind, went to the proscenium and called out, "Ladies and Gentlemen, there is nothing to worry about. This tiny disturbance is of no consequence. The real danger to you is your own panic. The best thing for you to do is to go back to your seats." They all turned and went back to their seats, and . . . were burned to a crisp.

The virtues are all to be tested afresh, then, and in fact all things require testing. The artist, equipped with a critical eye that constantly enforces a larger context—as for example, of Greece and Rome as well as Christianity, has this task to perform. We speak of the artistic imagination, but what we mean is this eye for "the concentrated experience of the race" which keeps the new from solidifying. Writ large, this shift in perception brings a new dispensation—Wilde speaks of it as the "new Hellenism," as in youth he had spoken of it as the Renaissance. Does it matter whether we call it decadent or resurgent? He thinks not, and simply says, "When that day dawns, or sunset reddens," as if either phrase would do so long as we recognize that the world will be changed.

Without having read Nietzsche, Wilde had arrived at something of the same view of things. In their different ways, both were constructing a new man, what Wallace Stevens called a "major man." Wilde did not share Nietzsche's elaborate view of the genealogy of morals, by which Christianity overturned the pagan virtues and put a morality of slavery in their places; but he did see hypocrisy all about him, masquerading as seriousness. His conception of the major man was of the artist who dared to "harrow the house of the dead." Nietzsche would have agreed.

In making the artist an advance man rather than a camp follower of his society, Wilde implied that the artist is by necessity as well as by choice a deviant. His sense of his own sexual deviation helped him to find justification for this view. (Later writers such as D. H. Lawrence also made an alliance between their sexual and their artistic needs.) In Wilde's time the word homosexual was not in use, but there was no less need to find warrant for what it signified. Wilde became the first writer in English since Christopher Marlowe to make a case for it in public. One of his ways of doing so is to attack homosexuality's enemies the puritans. He does so in his plays in the 'nineties as he demonstrates, in one play after another, that moral questions are too complex to be solved by puritan mottoes. He never defended homosexuality overtly, except once at his trial, and the present generation, happily uncloseted, are sometimes indignant with him for not having made himself more convincingly and openly the victim of society, the first "Homintern martyr" (in Auden's phrase). I think Wilde felt he could be more effective by opening a window here and there than by seeking martyrdom through taking off the roof, and given the age in which he lived, that monstrous age, who can say that he was wrong? He saw himself as a rebel, not as a missionary. Homosexuality was not a cause, it was a way of affronting complacency. In three works, between 1889 and 1892, Wilde therefore outraged heterosexual smugness.

The first was *The Portrait of Mr. W.H.*, which played with the idea that Shakespeare was a homosexual, and that he wrote the sonnets to his "dearmylove," Mr. W.H. He does not actually endorse the view, but he disseminates it. Wilde had begun his perilous campaign to bring this forbidden theme into literature by reconstructing the image of Shakespeare himself. He continued this campaign in *The Picture of Dorian Gray*. Dorian not only espouses decadence, he decays in every way except physically, the physical decay being consigned till the book's end to his portrait. He is driven to ruin men and women alike, as if his love in either mode were genuine only to the extent that it is tainted. As in *A Rebours* or for that matter in *The Waste Land*, a later decadence, both forms of love are introduced as equally corrupt. Wilde did not celebrate homosexuality, but then, neither did Proust. In both writers, this deviation is described in terms of unhappiness. But to mention it at all in a society which pretended it did not exist was courageous, and for Wilde, as events proved, foolhardy. The book is also a criticism of the aesthete-type, who samples sins and regrets it. Dorian lacks the motive of art, has only its artificializing mechanism. He enslaves instead of emancipating himself. We almost forgive him because he is so beautiful. In *Salomé* the pageboy loves the Syrian soldier, but this is only one of the erotic relationships suggested. For the Syrian, like Herod, loves Salomé, Salomé loves John the Baptist, John the Baptist loves Jesus. All love appears as deviation, and no deviation is superior to any other. All bring their tragic consequences. Wilde improves upon the Bible also by making Iokanaan as hysterical in hatred as Salomé is hysterical in love, so that the reader feels about the same concern for his being decapitated and for her being smothered. Originally Wilde intended to have both of them decapitated as if to confirm their parity. Wilde said elsewhere that renunciation, like excess, brings its own punishment, chastity being just as tendentious as debauchery. Mario Praz finds that the play exhibits the *femme fatale* in all her cruelty, but it seems to exhibit rather the uncontrollability of passion. Though Praz claims it is all plagiarized, and is baffled by its surviving better than other versions, the reason is simple—only Wilde's *Salomé* reconstitutes the entire legend, St. John as well as Salomé, and in terms of a strong and original attitude.

With these writings Wilde stretched the domain of literature: he suggested that art might deal critically with moral taboos as part of an effort to remake the world. As Herbert Marcuse says, art shatters everyday experiences and anticipates a different reality principle. Wilde did for English literature almost single handedly what a score of writers in France had been attempting for a dozen years. The result was soon apparent. A. E. Housman was empowered to write, in the year of Wilde's trial, *A Shropshire Lad,* with its thinly veiled interest in boys; he sent it to Wilde as he was being released from prison. The next year Rhoda Broughton, who did not like Wilde but was quick to sense the way the wind was blowing, wrote her novel *Faustina,* which is the first Lesbian novel in English. Even Henry James wrote a series of works which took advantage of the freedom that Wilde had won for art even while losing his own freedom. Among them perhaps the most important for my purpose is *The Turn of the Screw* (1897) in which James indicates that boy and valet, and girl and governess, pair off for long hours together, and that the boy is expelled from school for some unnameable act of corruption of his schoolmates, which is described as being "against nature." Of course his offense is never specified. By presenting, even if with deliberate vagueness, homosexuality in terms of the corruption of children by adults, James follows Wilde's lead in broaching the subject, and he too associates it with bad conduct, though he too was inclined that way. It is in large part thanks to Wilde, then, both to his books and to his trial testimony, that the taboo against writing about homosexual behavior or other forms of sexuality begins to be lifted in England. Opening our eyes has been the principal labor of modern literature.

In only one of his works did Wilde attempt to say what the

renaissance would be like. That is *The Soul of Man under Socialism*. It would be a time when art would be triumphant, when people would develop freely, when there would be a new Hellenism devoid of the slavery that marked the old Hellenism, when nobody would have to be concerned about the poor, because there would be no poor, nobody would fight for property, because there would be none, nobody would marry because marriage, being merely an extension of property, would also be abolished. In his letter to Douglas, *De Profundis*, Wilde imagined in muted terms that Christ, whom he now accepted at last, but as the supreme aesthete, would bring about a renaissance by being recognized as a model—for Christ created himself, out of his own imagination, and asserted the imagination as the basis of all spiritual and material life. There are no laws, only exceptions. Sin and suffering were for him modes of perfection. So Wilde found place for suffering, at last, as leading to reconstitution of the terms of existence.

Yeats was in many ways a disciple of Wilde. When he was eighteen he heard Wilde give a lecture in Dublin, and when he was twenty-two he met Wilde at the home of William Ernest Henley. This was the famous occasion when Wilde praised Pater's book on the Renaissance—"It is my golden book. I never travel anywhere without it, but it is the very flower of decadence; the last trumpet should have sounded the moment it was written." "But," someone interjected, "would you not have given us time to read it?" "Oh, no," said Wilde, "there would have been plenty of time afterwards, in either world." Wilde was praising Pater for his deca- dence, and also suggesting that Pater's readers might as likely go to hell as to heaven. He recognized the ambiguity of Pater's morality. But the decisive moment in the early relationship of Wilde and Yeats came after the Christmas dinner at Wilde's to which Yeats was invited in 1888, when he was twenty-three. At 16 Tite Street he saw the extraordinary decor—drawing room and dining room done in white, not only walls but furniture and rugs too, the only exception being the red lampshade suspended from the ceiling. This cowled a terra cotta statue which stood on a diamond-shaped cloth in the middle of a white table. After dinner Wilde brought out the proofs of his essay, "The Decay of Lying," and read it to Yeats. It had a profound effect. Yeats was quite prepared to believe that lies were better than truth, for he had already written in "The Song of the Happy Shepherd,"

> The woods of Arcady are dead
> And over is their antique joy;
> Of old the world on dreaming fed;
> Grey Truth is now her painted toy.

He would say this more vigorously in his verse dialogue, "Ego Dominus Tuus," where the first of the two speakers, Hic, pleads for sincerity and veracity so that one can be what one really is, and the second, Ille, pleads for masks and images to enable one to be more than one really is. Ille of course wins. In his edition of Blake Yeats redefined truth in the light of aestheticism: it is "the dramatic expression of the most complete man." Pater and Wilde would have approved.

Much of "The Decay of Lying" deals with the value of images in shaping our awareness of the world. Wilde insists, for example, that "the whole of Japan is a pure invention. There is no such country, there are no such people." It is a concoction of the artists, to which they have given the name *Japan*. Yeats would do something similar with Byzantium, which in his poems must be taken as a pure invention also. It bears no resemblance to the historical Constantinople, but is a city of imagination made by its artists, a magnificent "instead" conjured up by an aging Irishman seeking an antidote for his own time. In his first poem on the subject, Yeats made the city somewhat static and he wrote a second poem to give it the dynamism that he, like Wilde, regarded as essential to avoid art's repeating itself.

Although Yeats in the 'nineties scouted the idea of literary decadence, he wrote many poems about the decadence of the modern world. When he says in "The Second Coming," "Things fall apart, the center cannot hold, / Mere anarchy is loosed upon the world," he has at least the satisfaction of finding in the rough beast that "slouches towards Bethlehem to be born" an image of the mock-renaissance that decadence will bring. His poetry is full of anguish over the world's decadence in poem after poem:

> Though the great song return no more
> There's keen delight in what we have:
> The rattle of pebbles on the shore
> Under the receding wave.

When Edward VII is crowned he writes:

> I have forgot awhile
> Tara uprooted, and new commonness
> Upon the throne—and crying about the streets
> And hanging its paper flowers from post to post.

But it was not only English decadence he resented, it was Irish decadence too, as in "Romantic Ireland's dead and gone, / It's with O'Leary in the grave," or, more largely, "Many ingenious lovely things are gone." Yet he never loses hope, and a renaissance is almost always in the offing. "Easter 1916," which declares that "A terrible beauty is born," makes the claim that in tragic failure Ireland has achieved heroic rebirth. The great sacrifice is a true Easter, as the poet is the first to recognize.

Yeats identified decadence much as Wilde did, as all the things that the Victorians celebrated as evidences of health. He spoke derisively of "that decadence we call progress." The Victorian poets had allowed morality·and religion to fill their art with impurities, such as the "doctrine of sincerity." Victorian morality was particularly blameworthy. So he says in *A Vision* (1925), "A decadence will descend, by perpetual moral improvement, upon a community which may seem like some woman of New York or Paris who has renounced her rouge pot to lose her figure." He insisted even in his early work that fantasy and caprice would lose their necessary freedom if united either with good or with evil. Wilde sometimes referred distantly to a *higher ethics*, which would completely revise moral standards, and Yeats was prompted to try to redefine good and evil, in terms of an aesthetic point of view. In *A Vision* (1925) he said that for men of the coming age, good would be that "which a man can contemplate himself as doing always and no other doing at all." This definition underlies poems such as the ones in which Yeats sanctions, "the wild old wicked man," or praises Crazy Jane against the Bishop, or pleads for vital personality instead of dead character, for laughter instead of solemnity. For he too like Wilde knew the terrible unimportance—or even danger — of being earnest. Artists are in league with lovers because they too are in search of an amplified consciousness. Appropriately, however, when Yeats in "Under Ben Bulben" denounces the present,

> Scorn the sort now growing up
> All out of shape from toe to top,
> Their unremembering hearts and heads
> Base-born products of base beds,

as if all beds could not be called base—or no beds at all, he asks the Irish *poets* to overcome this decadence. It is they who must engender renaissance of the imagination, to rescue "this foul world in its decline and fall,"

> . . . gangling stocks grown great, great stocks run dry,
> Ancestral pearls all pitched into a sty,
> Heroic reverie mocked by clown and knave.
>
> ("A Bronze Head")

Like Wilde, Yeats insists on the ulterior motive of art to reshape the world in which we live. This renaissance is always in the making. Sometimes it is present in the deeds of great men, in intense love, in images of poets, or in the way the language, often clogged and impeded, suddenly begins to dance.

And here we come to recognize that each Yeats poem is likely to begin in decadence, and to end in renaissance. The decay may be physical, as in "The Tower," or "Sailing to Byzantium," or cultural, as in "Nineteen Hundred and Nineteen." There are of course many variations—sometimes the point is to show that apparent decadence is not true decadence, as in "No Second Troy," and sometimes, as in "The Cold Heaven," the decadence continues into the afterworld, where heaven proves to be hell. But in general the poems present decadence in order to overcome it. The mind contends with some decadent fact or thought or image, then puts it aside in favor of some radiant recovery, a renaissance in little. Yeats does the same thing when he takes up whole civilizations, as if they too at recurrent intervals were artistically rescued from decadence. He expresses this idea most powerfully in "The Gyres":

> Conduct and work grow coarse, and coarse the soul,
> What matter? Those that Rocky Face holds dear,
> Lovers of horses and of women, shall,
> From marble of a broken sepulchre,
> Or dark betwixt the polecat and the owl,
> Or any rich, dark nothing disinter
> The workman, noble and saint, and all things run
> On that unfashionable gyre again.

Lovers of horses and of women—Yeats could have said artists directly but he avoids the term, not wishing to be totally aesthetic. The term artist had become much less honorific than it was in Wilde's time, yet the artist's role in conjuring up the best of life out of marble or air is implicit.

In Wilde and Yeats decadence becomes the term to turn upon their antagonists. The decadents are those who accept the acquisitive, insensitive, unimaginative world, with all its morality, sincerity, and seriousness. This world exists only as a distortion of reality, as Blake would also have said. Wilde could celebrate art more directly in his time than was possible in Yeats's more ironical age, and while Yeats believed as fully as Wilde did that the mind of man can be rescued by art, he had to be wary in praising a faculty that others were quick to belittle. If Yeats is occasionally circumspect, Joyce is even more so. By his time silence, exile, and cunning are required. Yet, though he would not have said so, Joyce was in the same tradition.

He rarely discusses decadence or renaissance in general terms as
Wilde and Yeats had. The word aesthetic was used by him to
describe a philosophical theory, not adjectivally to pat art on the
back. He even called Yeats an aesthete in a derogatory way, meaning that Yeats had been too ethereal and so had drifted about. Joyce
wanted his renaissance closer to earth. He began by particularizing
the waste-land qualities of life in Ireland. He has Mr. Dedalus say at
the Christmas dinner in *A Portrait*, "A priestridden godforsaken
race." In "The Day of the Rabblement," Joyce's first published
work, he called the Irish the "most belated race in Europe." Later
Stephen Dedalus in *A Portrait* says that Ireland is "the old sow that
eats her farrow." Joyce, as a writer of fiction based on close observation, makes a more detailed attack upon hypocrisy than either
Wilde or Yeats—he shows his countrymen pretending to piety and
goodness but actually using religion and morality to curb individual
lives with cruelty and repressiveness. In *Dubliners* he presented his
initial indictment of Ireland, in terms of its inertness, repression,
and corruption. Yet *Dubliners* does not rest in the portrayal of decadence. It establishes by tacit antithesis what it is the country lacks.
Even while he portrays the fallen state of his countrymen, Joyce
introduces three elements of possible relief. The first is a sympathy
usually latent and unstated, for thwarted lives. The second is the
evident pleasure taken by the author in Dublin humor. If Joyce
were merely excoriating, the humor would be a continual irrele-
vance. But it is not irrelevant; it keeps suggesting that even squalor
can be funny, as if to enable us to withdraw a little from mere disgust or horror, and yet by prodding the muscles with which we
laugh to keep us from detachment. Through humor we tumble to
our likeness with others. The third is the reserved, fastidious diction and occasional bursts of lyricism. It is as if Joyce were proclaiming that all is chaos, but doing so in heroic couplets. When
even the most mentally impoverished situations are described so
deftly, so reservedly, so lyrically, the style itself offers the lost
rhythms, the missing emotional possibilities, the absent structure.
The age weeps, the rhythm smiles. So as hopes are dashed, enter-

prises doomed, love unrequited or warped, sympathy, humor, and lyricism keep reminding us that life need not necessarily be so incomplete. Joyce is not being inconsistent then, in the last story of *Dubliners*, "The Dead," where his hero is forced to acknowledge that there can be passion in parochialism and primitivism. The country may be decadent, yet still worth saving.

If the description of decadence is by example rather than generalization, so is the description of renaissance. Yet that Joyce hoped for a renaissance was something he did say explicitly, though in less grandiloquent language, on a few rare occasions. The first was in his semi-autobiographical narrative essay entitled "A Portrait of the Artist," not the book that came later. He ends that essay with a promise of what, thanks to the artist, is to come:

> To those multitudes, not as yet in the wombs of humanity but surely engenderable there, he would give the word: Man and woman, out of you comes the nation that is to come, the lightening of your masses in travail; the competitive order is employed against itself, the aristocracies are supplanted, and amid the general paralysis of an insane society, the confederate will issues in action.

The later novel, *A Portrait of the Artist as a Young Man*, uses a different method from *Dubliners* in that decadence is described not from various points of view, but entirely through the growing consciousness of it in the mind of the inchoate artist. The criticism of decadence is much the same but looks different because of this focus. Stephen's future depends upon his becoming an artist, but the future of Ireland depends upon it too. So he asks himself, as he thinks of his decadent countrymen,

> How could he hit their conscience or how cast his shadow over the imaginations of their daughters, before their squires begat upon them, that they might breed a race less ignoble than their own.

At the book's end, Stephen announces that he is going forth for the millionth time to "encounter the reality of experience and to forge in the smithy of my soul the uncreated conscience of my race." Joyce has stolen conscience away from the church and given it to art. He wishes to emphasize that his art will work with reality, not Zolaesque reality, which is distortion in the name of the body, and not mystical distortion, which is the name of the soul—but it is through art that he hopes to bring about this great change. As he wrote in a letter to his wife on August 22, 1912, "I am one of the writers of the generation who are perhaps creating at last a conscience in the soul of this wretched race.

Joyce had read Wilde, regarded him as a hero of literature, a victim of society; he had Buck Mulligan mock Wilde's idea of a new Hellenism, but what Mulligan mocks is what Joyce doesn't mock. Even if Joyce would not have used that slogan, *Ulysses* with its Greek title was intended to bring something like a new Hellenism about. Because *Ulysses* does so many things—Joyce worried at one point whether he was trying to do too much—this basic impulse has been lost. Yet Joyce like Stephen in *Stephen Hero* considered art to be the vital center of life. When he speaks of a conscience he means something different from the conscience then prevalent — something in tune with Wilde's higher ethics, more Hellenic than Christian. It is a conscience which is always in search of more freedom for itself, and hence for both artist and his audience. Readers of *Ulysses* have pondered endlessly whether the principal characters are reborn. They do not need to be. Their consciences have gradually defined themselves as exemplary in action and thought against the powers of the world. In *Circe* they resist final attempts to subdue them. They are the race less ignoble than their fellows for which the artist has forged a conscience. Stephen poses the negative aspect of the new era and the new conscience when he points to his head and quotes Blake against subjugation of his spirit or body, "But in here it is I must kill the priest and the king." Bloom poses the affirmative aspect when he advocates "the opposite of force, hatred, history, all that," as truly life— and when pressed says, "Love, I mean the opposite of hatred." Molly Bloom is needed to complete the picture to raise their fragmentariness to lyricism, and to show by her general approval of Bloom and Stephen that nature, to which she may be a little closer than they, responds to the values of art—sensitivity, discrimination, sympathy, understanding, and intensity of feeling. Although she is described as fleshly, she is not fleshlier than Hamlet. For her too the mind affects everything. The tenor of her thoughts is to acknowledge grudgingly that her husband, who recognizes her wit and musical talent and inner nature, is a better man than Blazes Boylan. "I saw he understood or felt what a woman is," she says. Penelope recognizes Ulysses not by his scar but by his imagination. All three characters achieve a freedom from hypocritical spirituality or empty materiality. In reading about them, the reader takes on the new conscience too. Joyce, like Wilde and Yeats, had a fifth gospel, a vision, a new bible. So reading *Ulysses*, if that book is properly understood, is a means of emancipation. One is freed by it to read about freedom.

Decadence then had its uses for Wilde, Yeats, and Joyce, as a pivot around which they could organize their work. Each in his different way summons up an opposite to decadence, the promise of an "unfashionable" age for which as artists they constitute themselves heralds. They are not decadents but counter decadents. Or we could say that they went through decadence to come out on the other side.

(1983)

LONG WORK, SHORT LIFE

BERNARD MALAMUD

I INTEND TO SAY something about my life as a writer. Since I shan't go into a formal replay of the life, this will read more like a selective short memoir.

The beginning was slow, and perhaps not quite a beginning. Some beginnings promise a start that may take years to induce a commencement. Before the first word strikes the page, or the first decent idea occurs, there is the complicated matter of breaking the silence. Some throw up before they can breathe. Not all can run to the door at the knock of announcement—granted one hears it. Not all know what it means. Simply, not always is the gift of talent given free and clear. Some who are marvelously passionate to write may have to spend half their lives learning what their proper subject matter may be.

Not even geniuses know themselves in their youth. For years Emily Dickinson was diverted from her poetry by men she felt she loved, until one day she drew the shutters in her sunlit room and sat in loneliness at her table. She had at last unearthed a way of beginning. Those who loved her appeared in her home from time to time, perhaps less to love than to cause her to write her wondrous poems of intricate feeling and intricate love.

I began to write at an early age, yet it took me years actually to begin writing. Much diverted me. As a child I told stories for praise. I went for inspiration to the movies. I remember my mother delivering me, against her will, on a wet Sunday, to a movie house to see Charlie Chaplin, whose comedy haunted my soul. After being at the pictures I recounted their plots to school friends who would listen at dreadfully long length as I retold them. The pleasure, in the beginning, was in retelling the impossible tale.

When I over-contrived or otherwise spoiled a plot, I would

substitute another of my own. I could on occasion be a good little liar who sometimes found it a burden to tell the truth. Once my father called me a "bluffer," enraging me because I had meant to tell him a simple story, not one that had elaborated itself into a lie.

In grammar school, where I lived in a state of self-enhancing discovery, I turned school assignments into stories. Once I married off Roger Williams of Rhode Island to an Indian maiden, mainly because I had worked up an early feeling for the romantic. When I was ten, I wrote a story about a ship lost in the Sargasso Sea. The vessel appeared in dreams, about to undertake a long voyage in stagnant seas. This sort of thing, to begin with, was the nature of my "gift" as a child, that I had awakened to one day, and it remained with me many years before I began to use it well. Throughout my life I struggled to define it, and to write with originality. However, once it had pointed at me and signaled the way, it kept me going even when I wasn't writing. For years it was a blessing that could bleed as a wound.

Thus began an era of long waiting.

I had hoped to start writing short stories after graduation from City College during the Depression, but they were long in coming. I had ideas and felt I was on the verge of sustained work. But at that time I had no regular means of earning a living; and as the son of a poor man, a poor grocer, I could not stand the thought of living off him, a generous and self-denying person. However, I thought the writing would take care of itself once I found steady work. I needed decent clothes; I would dream of new suits. Any work I found would make life different, I thought, and I could begin writing day or night. Yet I adamantly would not consider applying, in excess of pride, to the WPA. Years later, I judged that to have been a foolish act, or non-act.

I considered various things I might do to have time for writing, like getting up at five A.M. to work for an hour or two each morning before hitting the dreadful Sixth Avenue agencies in Manhattan to scrounge around for jobs. More often than not there were none, especially for someone with no work experience. And where there was no work there were no words.

The Second World War had begun in 1939. I was born at the beginning of the First World War, in 1914. The Second was being called "The Phony War." The French and German armies sat solemnly eying each other over the Maginot Line, yet almost not moving except for night forays. No one seemed about to launch a major attack. Neville Chamberlain, after Munich, was on his way out. He had rolled up his umbrella and was hastening away from the frightful future; Churchill came to power and was eloquently growling that Britain would never be conquered. Possibly diplomacy was in progress. Perhaps there would be no renewed conflict. Many Americans seemed to think the threat of war might expire. Many of us hoped so, though hoping was hard work; nor did it make too much sense, given the aberrations of Adolf Hitler. We worried about the inevitable world war but tried not to think of it.

Often young writers do not truly know what is happening in their lives and world. They know and they don't know. They are not sure what, in essence, is going on and are years in learning. Recently I was reading Ernst Pawel's book of the life of Kafka, and the author speaks of Kafka's "all encompassing goal in which the writer searches for his own truth." Truth or no truth, I felt the years go by without accomplishment. Occasionally I wrote a short story that no one bought. I called myself a writer though I had no true subject matter. Yet from time to time I sat at a table and wrote, although it took years for my work to impress me.

By now I had registered at Columbia University for an M.A. in English, on a government loan. The work was not demanding. I told myself what I was doing was worthwhile; for no one who spends his nights and days devoted to great works of literature will be wasting his time as a writer, if he is passionate to write.

But when did I expect to begin writing?

My answer was unchanged: when I found a job that would support my habit: the self's enduring needs. I registered for a teachers examination and afterward worked a year at $4.50 a day as a

teacher-in-training in a high school in Brooklyn. I was also applying for, and took, several civil service examinations, including those
leading to jobs of postal clerk and letter carrier. This is mad, I
thought, or I am. Yet I told myself the kind of work I might get
didn't matter so long as I was working for time to write.
Throughout these unsatisfying years, writing was still my gift and
persuasion.

It was now four years after my graduation from college, but the
four felt like fifty when I was counting. However, in the spring of
1940 I was offered work in Washington, D.C., as a clerk in the
Census Bureau. I accepted at once though I soon realized the
"work" was a laugh. All morning I conscientiously checked esti-
mates of drainage ditch statistics, as they appeared in various coun-
ties of the United States. Although the job hardly thrilled me, I
worked diligently and was promoted, at the end of three months,
to receive a salary of $1,800 per annum. That, in those times, was
"good money." What was better was that I had begun to write
seriously on company time. No one seemed to care what I was
doing so long as the record showed I had finished a full day's work;
therefore after lunch time I kept my head bent low while I was
writing short stories at my desk.

At about this time I wrote a piece for *The Washington Post,*
mourning the fall of France after the German Army had broken
through the Maginot Line and was obscenely jubilant in conquered
Paris. I felt unhappy, as though mourning the death of a civilization
I loved; yet somehow I managed to celebrate on-going life and
related acts.

Although my writing seemed less than inspiring to me, I stayed
with it and tried to breathe into it fresh life and beauty, hoping that
the gift was still in my possession, if by some magic act I could see
life whole. And though I was often lonely, I stayed in the rooming
house night after night trying to invent stories I needn't be
ashamed of.

One night, after laboring in vain for hours attempting to bring
a short story to life, I sat up in bed at an open window looking at

the stars after a rainfall. Then I experienced a wave of feeling, of heartfelt emotion bespeaking commitment to life and art, so deeply it brought tears to my eyes. For the hundredth time I promised myself that I would someday be a very good writer. This renewal, and others like it, kept me alive in art years from fulfillment. I must have been about twenty-five then, and was still waiting, in my fashion, for the true writing life to begin. I'm reminded of Kafka's remark in his mid-twenties: "God doesn't want me to write, but I must write."

There were other matters to consider. What about marriage— should I, shouldn't I? I sometimes felt that the young writers I knew were too much concerned with staying out of marriage, whereas they might have used it, among other things, to order their lives and get on with their work. I wondered whether I could make it a necessary adjunct of my writing. But marriage was not easy: wouldn't it hurt my career if I urged on myself a way of life I could hardly be sure of? One has his gift—the donnée—therefore he'd better protect it from those who seem to be without a compelling purpose in life. Many young women I met had no clear idea what they wanted to do with their lives. If such a woman became a writer's wife, would she, for instance, know what was going on in his thoughts as he worked in his sleep? Would she do her part in keeping the family going? I was often asking myself these and related questions—though not necessarily of someone who might answer them. And I was spending too much time being in love, as an uneasy way of feeling good when I wasn't writing. I needed someone to love and live with, but I wasn't going out of my way to find her.

Meanwhile, I had nailed down an evening school job in September of 1940; I then completed an M.A. thesis and began to think of writing a novel. By now I had finished about a dozen stories, a few of which began to appear in university quarterlies. One of these, "The Place is Different Now," was the forerunner of *The Assistant*. And a novel I had started while I was teaching in Erasmus Hall Evening High School, in Brooklyn, was called *The Light*

Sleeper. It was completed but not sold. Later, I burned it one night in Oregon because I felt I could do better. My son, who was about four at that time, watched me burning the book. As we looked at the sparks fly upward I was telling him about death; but he denied the concept.

Several years before that, not long after Pearl Harbor, while I was teaching at night and writing this novel, I met a warm, pretty young woman at a party. I was told she was of Italian descent and lived in a hotel with her mother and step-father, who was a musician. I observed my future wife for a while before we talked.

Soon we began to meet. Some nights she would come to Flatbush to watch me teach. We ate at Sears, or Oetgen's, and sometimes walked across the Parade Grounds to my room. We wrote each other during the week. Her letters were intense and witty, revealing an informed interest in politics and literature, in love and marriage. After the death of my own mother, I had had a step-mother and a thin family life; my wife, the child of a woman divorced young, had experienced a richer cultural life than I. And since we both wanted children we wondered how we would fare in a mixed marriage. She had been Catholic. I defined myself as Jewish.

Life in New York City was not easy or pleasant during the Second World War. Our friends Rose and James Lechay, the painter, had rented a small walk-up flat on King Street, in the Village, which we took over when they went off to live in Iowa, Jim to take Grant Wood's place as Professor of Painting at the university. After we were married we both continued working until my wife was pregnant. I taught day and evening classes, with practically no time to write. A few years later I left the evening high school and spent a year teaching in Harlem, incidentally picking up ideas for short stories like "Black Is My Favorite Color," before we decided to go west. I had now received an offer to teach at Oregon State College though I had no Ph.D. degree. In 1949, when my son was two, we moved to Corvallis, Oregon, where I taught three days a week and wrote four. In my own eyes I had become seriously a writer earning his living, though certainly not from his writing.

I think I discovered the Far West and some subject matter of my earlier fiction at almost the same time, an interesting conjunction, in imagination, of Oregon and the streets of New York. One's fantasy goes for a walk and returns with a bride.

During my first year at Oregon State I wrote *The Natural*, begun before leaving New York City. Baseball had interested me, especially its comic aspects, but I wasn't able to write about the game until I transformed game into myth, via Jessie Weston's Percival legend with an assist by T. S. Eliot's "The Waste Land" plus the lives of several ballplayers I had read, in particular Babe Ruth's and Bobby Feller's. The myth enriched the baseball lore as feats of magic transformed the game.

Soon we were making plans to go abroad. We had wanted to go earlier, but could not afford it until we experienced the fortunate coincidence of a sabbatical leave from Oregon State with a *Partisan Review*–Rockefeller Foundation grant.

We left in late August 1956, for Italy. On board the S.S. *Constitution* I spent hours studying the horizon, enjoying the sight of ocean as the beginning of more profound adventure, amid thoughts of new writing. One night we passed our sister ship, the S.S. *America*, steaming along in the mid-Atlantic, all decks alight. I felt I was on the verge of a long celebration.

Previously, my wife had been abroad twice, once at age eight, for a year in Italy, and at another time for her college junior year, in France.

I was ready for a broader kind of living with as much range in writing as I could manage. Before leaving Oregon to go abroad, I had completed *The Assistant*, and had begun to develop several of the stories that became *The Magic Barrel*, some of which I wrote in Rome.

Italy unrolled like a foreign film; what was going on before my eyes seemed close to unreality. An ancient city seemed to be alive in present time. It was larger than life, yet defined itself as our new life. I felt the need to live in a world that was more than my world to live in. I walked all over the city. I walked in the ghetto. I met Italian Jews who had been tortured by the Nazis; one man held up his hand to show his finger-shorn fist. I felt I was too much an innocent American. I wandered along Roman streets and studied Roman faces, hoping to see what they saw when they looked; I wanted to know more of what they seemed to know. On All Soul's, I walked in the Campo Verano cemetery. I visited the Ardeatine Caves where the Nazis had slaughtered Italians and Jews. Rome had its own sad way of sharing Jewish experience.

Mornings I walked my eight-year-old son to Piazza Bologna where he took his bus to the American school. At noon, after finishing my morning's work, I picked up my four-year-old daughter at her kindergarten. She would hand me her drawings as we walked home. Home was 88 Via Michelo Di Lando, not far from where Mussolini had lived with Clara Petacci, his mistress. We had made friends of our landlords. Mr. Gianolla was an old Socialist who had been forced to swallow castor oil by Mussolini's Fascist thugs. His wife, thin and energetic, talkative, courteous, was one of the rare women university graduates of her time.

I returned to Oregon to an improved situation after our year abroad. From a teacher of freshman grammar and technical report writing, I was transformed into a teacher of English literature, as though a new talent had been discovered in a surprised self. What had happened was that the two gentlemen who administered the English department had heard I was acquiring a small reputation as a serious writer of fiction, and therefore I was no longer required to teach composition only, but might be allowed, even without a doctoral degree, to teach unsuspecting sophomores a little poetry, with even a touch of Shakespeare in the night. For this relief I gave happy thanks.

Let me, at this point, say a short word about the yeas and nays of a writer teaching what is called Creative Writing. I have done it because I teach decently well, but I wouldn't recommend that anyone devote his life to teaching writing if he takes little pleasure in informing others. Elsewhere I've said about teaching creative writing that one ought to keep in mind he is not so much teaching the art of imaginative writing as he is encouraging people with talent how to work as writers. Writing courses are of limited value although in certain cases they may encourage young writers to read good fiction with the care it deserves. However, I think about a year of these courses should be enough for any serious student. Thereafter writing must become a way of life.

When my Western-born daughter appeared, my father sent us $350 for a washing machine. Once when I was twenty, he trudged up the hall stairs from his grocery store one morning. I had a summer cold and was stretched out in bed. I had been looking for a job without success. My father reached for my foot and grasped it with his hand.

"I wish it was me with that cold instead of you."

What does a writer need most? When I ask the question, I think of my father.

I had already begun to receive literary awards. It seemed to me that I did nothing to get them other than stay at the writing table, and the prizes would mysteriously appear. One day I had a phone call from New York. My publisher, Roger Straus, asked me whether I was sitting down. I said I was. He told me I had just won the National Book Award for *The Magic Barrel*.

I must know how to write, I told myself, almost surprised.

I was in a happy mood when I began to work on *A New Life*, my fourth book. Once, at Yaddo, while I was writing it, a visitor knocked at my door. I had just written something that moved me. He saw my wet eyes. I told him I was enjoying writing my book. Later the legend grew that I had wept my way through it.

During my early years at Oregon State I had gone nowhere, with the exception of our trip abroad, and a six-week visit to Montana, when Leslie Fiedler was there in the 1950s. He had sent me a copy of an article he had published in *Folio*, in Indiana. His was the first appreciation of *The Natural* that I had read by someone who knew how to read. Fiedler was always sui generis, but on the whole generous in his judgment of my work. I shan't forget that he appreciated the quality of my imaginative writing before anyone else wrote about it. That was long before Robert Redford, in his sad hat of failure, appeared on the scene, Bernard Malamud socking away at a ball that went up in the lights.

Not long after our return to Corvallis from Italy, I had a telephone call from Howard Nemerov, at Bennington College, where I was invited to teach for a year. l was glad to go. After our year abroad, stimulated by the life and art I had seen, I wasn't very patient with my experience in a small town, though my wife, after a difficult start, now enjoyed her Western life. I seized the opportunity to return to the East. She would have liked living in San Francisco, but there were no job offers. So we traveled to Vermont by way of Harvard Summer School, where I substituted for Albert Guérard. When the class filled quickly, someone at Harvard asked John Hawkes, the novelist at Brown University, to teach a second section of the course. Before long we were walking together in Cambridge streets, talking about fiction. Hawkes is a gallant man and imaginative writer. His work should be better known than it is.

In September 1961, my wife and I arrived with our kids in Bennington, Vermont. The college, an unusual place to work and learn, soon became a continuing source of education for me. My teachers were my new colleagues: Howard Nemerov, poet and faithful friend; Stanley Edgar Hyman, a unique scholar and fine critic; and Ben Belitt, a daring, original poet and excellent teacher—from all of whom I learned. My other teachers were my students, whom I taught to teach me.

Stanley Hyman reminded me of Leslie Fiedler in more ways than one. They both knew a great deal about literature, and neither found it difficult to say what. Hyman was an excellent theoretician of myth and literature. His humor kept him young and so did his appetite. Once my wife and I invited him and his wife, the writer Shirley Jackson, to a restaurant, to help us celebrate our wedding anniversary. Stanley ordered the champagne. He and Shirley lived hard, and—I think they thought—well; and almost did not regret dying young. Flannery O'Connor once described them as two large people in a small car, when they came to call on her in Milledgeville, Georgia. She showed them her peacocks.

When I think of Hyman as a critic of literature, what stands out was his honesty of self and standards. One of his favorite words was "standards," and you weren't in his league if you didn't know what he meant. He defined and explicated. He was proud of what he knew, though I remember his saying, speaking of himself, "knowledge is not wisdom." He enjoyed the fun of wit, merriment, poker, horseplay, continuous laughter. He died young.

Before I come to the end of this casual memoir, perhaps I ought to say that I served as president of American PEN (Poets, Editors, and Novelists) from 1979 to 1981. PEN had come to life in 1921 as an international organization founded in London by John Galsworthy, the British novelist and dramatist. Basically, PEN brings together writers from all over the world to meet as a fraternity, to foster literature, and to defend the written word wherever threatened.

When I was president, I began to deal more frequently with publishers after the difficult period that followed a time of consolidation in the book industry. The consolidation I refer to was not always helpful to those who wrote, and much remains to be done to improve the situation of writers, dealing in whatever way with their own publishers.

Though my publisher is a good one, I fear that too many of them are much more concerned with making money than with publishing good books that will seriously influence generations of writers in the future. Stanley Hyman had preached standards, but one tendency in publishing today is that standards are forgotten. I can't tell you how badly some books are edited these days; one excuse given is "We can't afford too much time on one book. We've got to make our profit." I'm all for profit from the work of writers, but the simple fact is that we have begun to pay more in a loss of quality in publishing than our culture can afford. Happily, many people of good will, dissatisfied with present-day publishing, are trying to find new ways to improve the industry. And some of the new presses that have begun to publish are quite good, a few even daring.

If I may, I would at this point urge young writers not to be too much concerned with the vagaries of the marketplace. Not everyone can make a first-rate living as a writer, but a writer who is serious and responsible about his work, and life, will probably find a way to earn a decent living, if he or she writes well. And there's great pleasure in writing, if one writes well. A good writer will be strengthened by his good writing at a time, let us say, of the resurgence of ignorance in our culture. I think I have been saying that the writer must never compromise with what is best in him in a world defined as free.

I have written almost all my life. My writing has drawn, out of a reluctant soul, a measure of astonishment at the nature of life. And the more I wrote well, the better I felt I had to write.

In writing I had to say what had happened to me, yet present it as though it had been magically revealed. I began to write seriously when I had taught myself the discipline necessary to achieve what I wanted. When I touched that time, my words announced themselves to me. I have given my life to writing without regret, except when I consider what in my work I might have done better. I wanted my writing to be as good as it must be, and on the whole I think it is. I would write a book, or a short story, at least three times—once to understand it, the second time to improve the prose, and a third to compel it to say what it still must say.

Somewhere I put it this way: first drafts are for learning what one's fiction wants him to say. Revision works with that knowledge to enlarge and enhance an idea, to re-form it. Revision is one of the exquisite pleasures of writing: "The men and things of today are wont to lie fairer and truer in tomorrow's meadow," Henry Thoreau said.

I don't regret the years I put into my work. Perhaps I regret the fact that I was not two men, one who could live a full life apart from writing; and one who could live in art, exploring all he had to experience and know how to make his work right; yet not regretting that he had put his life into the art of perfecting the work.

(1984)

LITERATURE AND BELIEF: THREE "SPIRITUAL EXERCISES"

BEN BELITT

READERS OF HIS *Notebooks* will not have to be reminded that I have taken the second half of my title from Gerard Manley Hopkins, who had it from St. Ignatius Loyola, who had it from the Abbot García de Cisneros. For Hopkins, the novice, preparing for the Olympiad of his induction into the Society of Jesus, the *Exercises* served the calesthenic purpose of grooming the incumbent priest for a crisis of commitment that led to the higher mysteries of his calling. For my own purposes, the choice of three devotional texts is neither worshipful nor canonical: what I would hope to do is suggest the coexistence of a sacred with a secular subtext for individual talents committed to the creation of a literature for laymen, and its imaginative encompassment in language. My concern is not with the City of God, but with a poetics for men of letters generally.

We can begin with a poor man's version of Pascal's Wager—that confidence game for pietists of little faith who prefer the fatalism of the gaming wheel to the prayer wheels and mandalas of the East. You may recall its streetsmart inelegance, its bow to the baize of the croupier's table:

> He who calls heads and he who calls
> tails are guilty of the same mistake; they
> both are wrong; the right course is not
> to wager. "Yes, but we have to wager. You
> are not a free agent; you are committed.
> Which will you have, then?" . . . "Heads:
> God exists!" If you win, you win
> everything; if you lose, you lose nothing.
> . . . *Bet He exists!*"

We can begin our little foray by putting both chips—the literature and the belief of things—on the gaming table: we can begin by assuming we believe in Bibles: *"Bet on the Bible!"* The wager, at the very least, is eschatologically advantageous. For the Laodicaeans among us, who "blow neither hot nor cold," it provides a kind of spiritual insurance which turns gambling into a species of cautionary divination. And let us, at some midpoint between idolatry and condescension, choose from the artifacts of Christian–Hebraic discourse three texts for examination without regard for the protocol of worship, in the spirit of that wager. And, as a third condition, let us be somber.

Here, whatever our stock of operative beliefs, is an avowedly devotional anthology of beliefs which has penetrated into every aspect of humane activity in the last 4000 years or more of Western European history—which is inseparable from our literature, from our ethics, from our certainties, from our anxieties, and from all the objects of our violence and tenderness equally. Bibles comprise a canon of private and public worship for believers delivered from conditional modes of assertion to absolute commitments which transcend history and touch the very plasm of reality. In applying to these texts, after all, we apply to 4000 years of our contemporaneity, as well as to the old codices of our Jewishness and our Christianity. Here are the persuaded, the assured, the convinced, the obsessed, the inspired—the saints, the heroes, the defaulters, and the "fools" (St. Paul's word) of belief; and here is the testimony of their eloquence and their dedication. I am proposing that we forfeit all definition, appeal to the textual witness of their experience, and move blindly and without baggage, into the literature of their belief.

"To ask with infinite interest," said Kierkegaard, "about a reality which is not one's own, is faith."

2

Praise ye the Lord. Praise ye the Lord from the heavens: praise Him in the heights. Praise ye Him, sun and moon: praise Him all ye stars of light. Praise Him, ye heavens of heavens, and ye waters that be above the heavens. Let them praise the name of the Lord: for He commanded, and they were created. He hath also established them forever and ever; He hath made a decree which shall not pass. Praise the Lord from the earth, ye dragons, and all deeps: fire and hail, snow and vapors, stormy wind, fulfilling His word: mountains and all hills; fruitful trees and all cedars; beasts and all cattle; creeping things and flying fowl: kings of the earth and all people; princes and all judges of the earth, both young men and maidens; old men and children: let them praise the name of the Lord. For His name alone is exalted: His glory is above the earth and heaven, He also exalteth the horn of his people, the praise of His saints; even of the children of Israel, a people near unto Him. Praise ye the Lord.

—Psalms

If the whole duty of the believer is to affirm the object of his belief, the above passage is certainly an exemplary one. Here, one feels, is the way all belief *ought* to sound—jubilant, resolute, unconditional, hyperbolical. The text is, of course, from Psalms, which in the Greek is a word deriving from *psalmos,* or a song sung to the plucking of a stringed instrument; and in the Hebrew from *tehillim,* meaning "praises." Apparently, the praiser has applied himself to his theme—the creativity of his Creator—in both senses of the word, for the passage is at once songlike and eulogistic. He begins by praising the universe in terms of its creative energies—the phenomena of light and warmth, like the sun, moon, and stars; the phenomena of order, like height, matter, and heaven; the phenomena of power, like the angels—and exhorting them in turn to praise. He celebrates all that is unknowable to him "above the heavens," and then passes on to a category of mysteries "from the earth" interpretable by him only in part: dragons and deeps, fire, hail, snow, wind, and mountains. He concludes with the theme of God's differentiated creativity—of the transformations of matter which epitomize the life-process and serve the needs of man: fruitful trees, cedars, beasts, cattle, creeping things, flying fowl, human life in its princely and rational aspects, childhood, youth, and old age, and, finally, the tribal history of Israel itself.

The data of the Psalm, however, insofar as it submits to such substantive reductions at all, are only a secondary aspect of its content. What remains primary is the *psalmos*, or the *song*, which inheres in the modality of the language itself as a kind of compositional radiance—the evangel of a productive God, which needs but a single word to sustain it: *praise*: "Praise! Praise! Praise!" It is the recurrence of this word, in all the changing urgencies of its rhythm, which gives the text its extraordinary mood of elation and certainty. The Psalm, if it is "believable" to outsiders at all today, is believable not because it recommends itself to the intelligence as a statement of demonstrable doctrine, but because it exists as an immediate datum of sensibility, as heat inheres in the tempering of a metal. The inflection is doxological, rather than logical, infectious rather than reflective. Like St. Paul, who was "determined not to know anything among you, save Jesus Christ and Him crucified," the Psalmist has concentrated all of knowledge into a single commitment: that of giving praise. He has, in other words, equated reality with jubilation. To believe rightly is to affirm joyously; and he stands ready to say *Yes!* to the mystery of creation and his own destiny because it is an article of his belief that the Creator is an aspect of his collective and individual destiny and endows it with his divine imprimatur: that Jehovah "exalteth the horn of His people . . . even the children of Israel." The rest will be regarded as "non-negotiable" by unbelievers and dismissed as a mysterium for the chosen and the privileged.

Here let us digress for a moment. Let us concede with the Psalmist that praise is an inalienable mandate of all genuinely operative religions. Let us define praise in its broadest devotional sense as the will or the wish or the need to affirm a numinous entirety of belief. Let us oppose to the idea of *praise* the idea of *appraisal*—the will or the wish or the need to *verify*, where a fundamental skepticism and self-sufficiency are implied. Let us agree that the praiser represents a mode of liturgical assent, and the appraiser, a mode of provisional corroboration: that one lies within the domain of spirit as a non-negotiable absolute, and the other, in the domain of suasion and the usable world; that one worships while the other questions, one unifies and the other atomizes, one turns to song and symbol, and the other to dialectic.

Does it follow, however, that praise must *always* exist in the believer as an irreducible intensity—that belief must always be undivided and single-hearted, like the Psalmist's, in order to be "true"? Can there be such a thing as *praiseless* belief where human worth and the viability of an ongoing cosmos are in doubt? If not, how is praise possible for the modern spirit, in a time of techniques, methodologies, and sciences which invite the skeptical manipulation of all the categories of thought and matter, and substitute cunning for awe? How can we ever hope for the joy of the Psalmist in a world that is knowable and unhaunted if his single-mindedness rests upon the haunting of a cosmos and the celebration of *mystery*? If Prospero has served us as the tutelary spirit for the *re-haunting* of a world plunging toward Renaissance omniscience, is not Hamlet the spokesman for joyless, aweless, distracted, fragmentary, postulating man?

> I have of late—but wherefore I know not—lost all my mirth, forgone all custom of exercise; and indeed, it goes so heavily with my disposition that this goodly frame, the earth, seems to me a sterile promontory, this most excellent canopy, the air, look you, this brave, o'erhanging firmament, this majestical roof fretted with golden fire, why it appears no other thing to me than a foul and pestilent congregation of vapors. What a piece of work is man! how noble in reason! how infinite in faculty! in form and moving, how express and admirable! in action, how like an angel! in apprehension how like a god! the beauty of the world! the paragon of animals! And yet, to me, what is this quintessence of dust? man delights not me: no, nor woman either, though by your smiling you seem to say so.

(II. ii)

Here, certainly, we have the obverse of the praisebearing Psalmist and the "hero of faith"; we have, instead, the divided sensibility of the appraiser, whose melancholy and mistrust alienate him from the universe at the moment of highest consent. Reversing the fable of Balaam, who was sent to curse the tents of Jacob and remained to bless them, Hamlet, it would seem, invokes the blessing as though it were a curse. Yet, for the contemporary mind, is it not also a fact that the blessing is *there*, in the only way, perhaps, that we can invoke it? And discounting the melancholia and estrangement of the speaker, are we not right in asking, after all: But isn't this a *kind* of joy? Isn't Hamlet's place with the praisers?

I think it is; and the assumption that praise implies a *joyful* vocation, or that joy, in its devotional sense, must be present in the praiser as a state of manifest sensibility, is a delusion. On the contrary, praise does not imply an *occasion* of joy, but a *premise* of joy— the belief in joy, or the creation of it out of the demand that joy *be*. For the artist, joy may even be *imagined* into existence; indeed, one of the profoundest achievements of the Romantic poets was their rediscovery of the tragic, the "strenuous," character of joy, and its affinity with despair, in their search for a principle of belief. For Keats, it was "in the very temple of delight" that "veil'd melancholy" had her "sovran shrine," and only he "whose strenuous tongue can burst Joy's grape against his palate fine" could enter. All of Michelangelo's sibyls, prophets, martyrs, warriors, diviners lean from their niches with their chins on the flat of their palms and their weight on their forearms and knucklebones, brooding on the melancholy of a scrutable universe, as though they awaited a second coming of the Sphinx, rather than Einstein's equation for energy. Out of joy, also, John Donne concludes his suite of Holy Sonnets with the cry: "Those are my best days when I shake with fear"; Kierkegaard bases his psychology of religious experience on a condition of "dread," of "fear and trembling"; Gerard Manley Hopkins declares that his heart "lo, lapped strength, stole joy" in the hours of "now done darkness" when he lay wrestling with his God. It is in the pursuit of joy that, according to Pascal, man "makes for himself an object of passion, and excites over it his desire, his anger, his fear, to obtain his imagined end, as children are frightened by the face they have blackened." And in our own time, Auden has spoken to our joy with the proposal—certainly as old as St. Paul—that "love needs death, death of the grain, our death, / Death of the old gang."

Similarly, we can account for much of the anguish and the obdurateness of Job as his sheer insistence upon joy and the will to praise, in a situation ghoulishly designed to give him no cause for either. The two themes, "Let the day perish wherein I was born!" and "I know that my Redeemer liveth!" are not two, but one, and are equally a medium of praise. Only when this is borne in mind can we account for the existence of one psalm beginning, "Make a joyful noise unto the Lord," and another beginning, "My God, my God, why hast thou forsaken me?" in a "book of praises." For further light on this paradox, we can hardly do better than appeal to the example of Job himself—the praiseless hero of faith—and to his crucial lamentation in Chapter 19.

3

Know that God hath overthrown me and hath compassed me with his net. Behold, I cry out of wrong, but I am not heard: I cry aloud but there is no judgment. He hath fenced up my way that I cannot pass and he hath set darkness in my paths. He hath stripped me of my glory and taken the crown from my head. He hath destroyed me on every side, and I am gone: and mine hope hath he broken like a tree. . . . Have pity upon me, have pity upon me, O ye my friends; for the hand of God hath touched me. . . .Oh that my words were now written! Oh that they were printed in a book! That they were graven with an iron pen and lead in the rock forever! For I know that my redeemer liveth, and that he shall stand at the latter day upon the earth: And though after my skin worms destroy this body, yet in my flesh shall I see God: whom I shall see for myself and mine eyes shall behold and not another, though my reins be consumed within me.

—Job 19

Note that the passage begins in blasphemy and ends in adoration. Job, in effect, appeals from the wisdom of God to the wisdom of man, calling the whole world to bear witness to the criminality of his Creator. God has inexplicably "overthrown" him, "compassed" him, "fenced" him, trapped him, "stripped" him, dishonored him, "destroyed" him, "broken" him. The tone is one of outraged betrayal: a loveless despot has struck at the sources of good will and an anarchy of the spirit is at hand: "I cry out of wrong, but I am not heard: I cry aloud but there is no judgment." Job implies that belief is no longer possible in a world where a cynical and destructive God has run amok—a malevolent misanthropist against whom there is neither redress nor judgment. Seemingly, the passage is moving toward a statement of man's tragic dependency upon man: henceforth, man must make his love and his belief out of his own pitiableness. Job's abandonment is all mankind's: tenderness, if it is to come at all, must be found in the circumstance of man's common vulnerability. Despair must call helplessly to despair, indignation to indignation, pity to pity: "Have pity upon me, have pity upon me, O ye my friends!" To all intents and purposes, Job is prepared to formalize his position for all time "with iron pen and lead forever" as the new humanism of the future. Yet precisely at the point when his denunciation of Jehovah has been accomplished without possibility of compromise, when hope itself has been "broken like a tree," the adoration of Job blazes out in a passage which, for entirety of belief, is unmatched in the Bible:

> I know that my redeemer liveth, and that he shall stand at the latter day upon the earth: And though after my skin worms destroy this body, yet in my flesh shall I see God: whom I shall see for myself and mine eyes shall behold and not another, though my reins be consumed within me.

Let us examine the passage more closely. Note, in the first place, that the outcry completely reverses the logic of the preceding sentences, which have emphasized only the bewilderment and demoralization of Job and implied the unknowability of God. Yet Job's word in the new context is absolute, unqualified, buoyant: "I know"—not "I pray that," or "I hope that," "I guess that," "I believe that," or any of the available synonyms which indicate a *partial* awareness *on its way* to certainty. *"Know"* carries with it the full assault of consummated belief: in the grammar of consent, it stands for a commitment graven into the tables of reality to which nothing can be added or from which nothing can be taken away. In the same way, the substitution of *redeemer* for the earlier *God* suggests that an irresistible element of doctrine has forced its way forward, "against all common sense," and transformed chaos into commitment, rebellion into adoration. Where the context would seem to invite despair—or at best, a prayer for an unknown God of redemption—God is already addressed in his role of redeemer and invested with his properties. Job's "knowledge" has already achieved the object of prayer by that "leap of faith" which renders prayer and proof equally unnecessary. God and redeemer have become interchangeable words: nothing is conceivable in the unspeakable abandonment of Job except redemption.

Similarly, the force of the word *liveth* in the new context remains to be noted. Its juxtaposition with *know* and *redeemer* is one of those triumphs of intoxicated certainty which turn belief into a species of magic; for its effect is to overturn chapters of lamentation and argument, reverse the direction of the meaning, and transform the sensibility of the speaker. Where an alternative word—*reigneth,* for example—would have produced nothing more than a pietistic formula of submission ("I know that my redeemer reigneth"), the effect of *liveth*: "I know that my redeemer liveth" is to personalize the experience of belief itself—the gross physicality of God's presence—and enact the excitement of God's nearness. For despite the chapters of complaint and inquisition, the debates and rebuttals of his "comforters," the immediate evidence of his own ill usage, the issue for Job has remained not whether his God was a *just* one, requiring the forensic mediation of experts and the skills of midrashic debate, but whether he was a *living* God, close at hand, available, and his own. The word, then is climactic, as well as poignant: for it brings to light the psychic truth which underlies the apparent, or polemical, truths of Job's endless denunciations. It is the nearness of a *living* God which renders further argument idle in the end, volatilizes all issues, and proves unanswerable. Job's wrangling and his logic and his evidence count for nothing. His comforters repeat a rubric for preachers and pedants, to no purpose. The phenomenon of life has only to insist on itself as a *fait accompli* to which the whole soul of Job bears witness, to supplant them all with a passionate image of God's manifest availability:

> Though after my skin worms destroy this body, yet in my flesh shall I see God: whom I shall see for myself and mine eyes shall behold and not another, though my reins be consumed within me.

The living God moves in the body of a malcontent. The premise of the Book of Job is essentially a *comic* one, as it was for that other agonist of self-loss, Dante Alighieri. For though the apostate "from the land of Uz" was capable of every heresy, he was incapable of disbelief.

4

> If God be for us, who can be against us? Who shall separate us from the love of Christ? shall tribulation or distress or persecution or famine or nakedness or peril or the sword? As it is written, For thy sake we are killed all day long; we are accounted as sheep for the slaughter. Nay, in all these things we are more than conquerors through him that loved us. For I am persuaded that neither death, nor life, nor angels, nor principalities, nor powers, nor things present nor things to come, nor height nor depth nor any other creature shall be able to separate us from the love of God, which is in Jesus Christ our Lord.
>
> —Romans, 8

Here, as in Job, the believer's task is a strenuous one, in that it calls for affirmation in circumstances which in themselves furnish no basis for belief: he must reconcile the apparent contradiction between a calamitous turn of events—tribulation, distress, persecution, famine, nakedness, the sword—and the absence of an intervening God. All evidence points toward the removal of God from the riotous world of His creation. The hostility of the universe extends from the very first things—life, angels, principalities, height, depth—to things present, to the very last things: martyrdom and God's love. The situation is thus an absolute test of conviction: with no help whatever from the objects of the material universe, with the circumstance of God's actual removal from events apparent to all, he must affirm the ridiculous. He must celebrate the beneficence and the actuality of his God at a time when he himself is "killed all day long" and "accounted sheep for the slaughter."

Obviously, the predicament is not a promising one for empirical demonstration: it cannot be accommodated to the processes of the laboratory or the inductive fantasies of the geometer. Even the speaker's passion is, in the long run, a disservice, since it renders him blind to the manifest absurdity of his position and denies him the tactical advantages of cunning. It is possible that, with caution and ingenuity, a case might be made for the satisfactions which are always present for the man of true faith and blameless conscience— yet the assertion that "In all these things we are more than conquerors" is a piece of inflamed bravado for which there is no evidence whatèver. In the same way, the image of "sheep for the slaughter" is almost cynical in its insensitivity: it leaves no room for heroic elaboration and equates his martyrdom with the mindless butchery of the slaughterhouse.

How, then are we to account for the thrilling plausibility of the passage and the optimism of a speaker who must make his certainty out of nothing at all: out of nonsense, paradox, and impossibility? For despite all the arguments which good sense can furnish to discredit the strategy of the speaker, the fact remains that he has established exciting contact with his hearers: he has "made his point" even if his thinking has been preposterous. Not only does his certitude strike with the immediacy of a physical sensation—as an impulse to action rather than an idea to hold in reserve—but it pursues its initiative boldly to the very end, in a masterstroke of hyperbolical absurdity:

I am persuaded that neither death, nor life, nor angels, nor principalities, nor powers, nor things present nor things to come, nor height nor depth nor any other creature shall be able to separate us from the love of God, which is in Jesus Christ our Lord.

The crucial word here, of course, is "persuaded"; but surely it is absurd in a context which has heaped persuasion in the opposite pan of the scales and stressed only the persecution of the believer. Persuaded by whom and by what? We are compelled to answer that the "persuasion" relates to none of these things: it refers to nothing whatever in the outside world, but is entirely a persuasion from within. Unlike the suasion of logic, it is not a process or an exercise in Platonic *elenchus,* but an entirety—a state of awareness, of inwardness, which cannot be altered from lesser to greater by a more or less fortunate realignment of circumstances. It can merely exist—or it can not exist: but, if it does exist, it is the factor under-lying all others—the enabling premise out of which consciousness itself creates its first cause.

Given such a state of awareness in the believer, even his *incredulity* is put to creative use and made to serve belief instead of discrediting it. Instead of freeing the skeptical process to deploy and combine and eliminate inductively, it looks *away* from the event and puts the question a second time at a higher level of intensity: "Who shall separate us from the love of Christ?" By this time, however, the question has lost its interrogative character entirely— it is no longer a call to speculation, but a mounting crescendo of conviction: "Shall tribulation or distress or persecution or famine or nakedness or peril or the sword?" The speaker has discovered that his question is literally inconceivable to thought: to put the question is to impel the certainty; and gazing directly into his cer-tainty, he turns knowledge into ecstasy: "I am persuaded that nei-ther death nor life etc., etc."

5

What can we learn about belief in its devotional sense from this triad of believers? In the first place, that belief is not an appendage, or an accessory, or an apparatus, like a Diesel engine, which exists to ensure the satisfactory operation of a second effect outside of itself. Though it is famous for moving mountains, it was not devised with this in mind. Indeed, belief is often not *devised* at all. It is not the product, in Job, of a plausible solution to conflicts and alternatives which present themselves to the intelligence for appraisal and are thereafter fitted to a doctrine. It does not, in the Psalmist, exist to construct systems with the mathematician's pursuit of one proposition to the next, to the limit of the exploitability of the logic. It does not, in St. Paul, submit to the correctives by which we ordinarily test perception before bringing it to bear upon reality: evidence, plausibility, experiment. It subserves nothing, confirms nothing, mediates nothing. It is neither tidy nor homogeneous nor auxiliary. It is not even very dignified. It does not ask of logic: Am I congruous and consistent? of experiment: Am I demonstrable? of ethics: Am I desirable? of history: Am I real?—and straightway collapse when its incongruity or its fantasy has been established.

I do not mean to say that beliefs are not *interpretable* on occasion in all of these terms, or that the believer's passion has not been made to drive engines, detonate explosives, drag crosses, heap arguments, write epics, and contemplate values. On the contrary, it would be my contention that belief is the enabling genius of history that accomplishes both the work and the destiny of the world. There is nothing that belief in its sacred and secular guises cannot *do,* even, as with Job, to disavowing itself to reappropriate the full force of its passion. Our problem up to this point, however, has not been to suggest the *uses* of belief, but how belief, as a mode of being or an act of imagination, *inhabits* its subject and encompasses his reality.

But let us now put the question a second time. This time, let us engage belief as an activity, as *praxis*, rather than a *condition* of awareness. Let us ask: What can belief *do* for the sensibility of the believer? Taking our examples in turn again, we would have to say that the effect is the same in each case, though it may vary in the density and pressure of the outer event. Belief discovers the point at which will and assent are made one, casts out instinctual and intellectual fear, and then gives praise. Dante has given us the formula: "*La sua voluntate e nostra pace.*" In one case, the event will warrant the believer's praise and appear inevitable; in another, it will render praise unthinkable; in the third, it will render it absurd.

In every case, however, belief will appropriate its object with the entirety of its passion and *remove it from the event*. Even where the event offers plausible occasion for praise, as with the Psalmist, belief will straightway seek out the implausible remainder and convert itself into awe. If the event itself resists thanksgiving, as with Job, belief will overturn history, suspend logic, undo doctrine, in order to achieve praise. It will build on contradiction, in the center of cleavage, imbalance, illogic; it will be "all things to all men," like St. Paul; it will turn itself into imagination and fulfill itself at all costs to the limit of its creative entirety.

But is not belief then a mixed blessing? What of bias, fanaticism, prejudice, the furors of the fundamentalist? Are they not also modes of belief? How is one to distinguish between the "creative entirety" of the believer—the yea-saying monolith—and the monomania of the bigot? Is it not possible that the praiser, moving away from the event without the correctives of reality, logic, and consensual appraisal, may end up in fanaticism? Is it not possible that a belief which suspends thought, overturns history, and divinizes the ridiculous denies the dignity of the human condition?

Yes, it is possible. The axiom that must accompany our examination from the outset is: that beliefs, like radium and X-ray, disintegrate as well as penetrate. Concepts may lie still—but beliefs must keep operative; and, as William James has pointed out, belief—to which he gave the name of *option*—has a right to be called genuine only when it is "forced, living, and momentous." It is precisely on the word *living* again that I would like to rest the distinction which must be drawn between belief and bias, fanaticism and worship. It is the crucial word in James, as in Job, because *living* implies action which, whatever its inwardness, is explicitly productive and, in the deepest sense, contemporaneous. It is the *living* option which experiences, transforms, reimagines; which "beareth all things, believeth all things, hopeth all things, endureth all things." On the other hand, the option of the bigot is a dead option. In the "many mansions" of the Father, it is incapable of confronting either its own existence or any existence outside itself. It flinches before the Other. It is nerveless, unimpressionable, stopped.

6

It is time to ask a final question two ways: what is the importance of literature for belief? And of belief for literature? Let us consider the second half of the question first, and return a simpleminded answer: beliefs are important to literature because they create the occasion for the practice of literature and minister to its momentum. They inhabit its subject matter. For example, it is Milton's belief that the time has come to "justify" the ways of God to man in terms that will give stature and passion to the rational genius of his century and hasten a Reformation of the spirit: he "therefore" proceeds to set down twelve cantos of *Paradise Lost*. "Because" he is a convinced Christian, he chooses from the 99 conceivable projects competing for priority the story of our first parents from the Book of Genesis, and peoples his tale with the dizzying hierarchies of the Old and New Testaments. "Because" he is a Puritan, he stresses the redemptive power of individual labor in the sad finale of his fable and intimates that though Christ mediates and Grace is abundant, man must sue for it "running." His Eve, one may conjecture, is a consequence of his many public avowals on the subject of divorce, education, and marriage; and his Satan brings the well-known Miltonic passion for civil liberty—with the aid of seventeenth-century gunpowder— to the throne of Jehovah Himself. There is, moreover, a whole repertory of inherited "beliefs" which Milton, as a cultivated European, brought to bear on his theme from a lifetime of reading in Greek and Latin authors: ideas, techniques, myths, place names, allusions, allegiances. Doubtless, Milton "believed" that poetry was "simple, sensuous and passionate"; he "believed" in blank verse, free will, landscape gardening, heroic similes, the Reformation, twelve cantos, the deposition of Kings, and the abolition of prelates. And *Paradise Lost* is, from one point of view—admittedly a simplistic one—the result of belief operating on beliefs to induce belief.

However, as we have already noted, the believer's way is often an intractable and disorderly one. How can it be related to literature in this sense? How can we reconcile the selective processes of literature with the inspired muddle which the believer is pleased to invoke as his intuition? Here it is possible to make capital of all that is actually untidy, disjunct, and contradictory in the creative process of the artist and bring it to bear on the experience of the believer. For the creative act, despite its symmetrical façade, not only is characterized by conflicts and cross-purposes, labyrinthine blockages and collapses which open on the inchoate, but exists to provoke them: to make a virtue of its morbidity. For the artist at large in his medium, the way to knowledge is never a univocal one—it is never a public thoroughfare with all traffic proceeding on one-way lanes toward a quantifiable destination. It is an inalienable function of the artist, we learn from Keats, to heap doubt upon doubt, cleavage upon cleavage, to keep them in contradiction, and survive in the ensuing pandemonium: in this respect, the artist's way and the believer's way are the same. It was to this faculty that Keats — somewhat misleadingly—gave the name of "Negative Capability," which he defined as a state in which "a man is capable of being in uncertainties, mysteries, doubts, without any irritable reaching after fact and reason"; and he went on to observe that it was, above all things, "this quality which went to form a Man of Achievement, especially in literature, and which Shakespeare possessed enormously." For Blake, the equation could be expressed even more succinctly: "Without Contraries, is no Progression."

What, then, is the importance of literature for belief? In the first place, literature offers the believer a medium—linguistic, graphic, sonal, mimetic, symbolic—to which he can retire with all his doubts and contradictions intact, and bring them into expressive play. He can come to his art "ready like a strong man to run a race"; or he can come to it rocking, retching, and wrestling. In either case his medium will accept him without the forfeit of a single anxiety or certainty, and deliver him from the empirical life of contingency to the compositional life of the artifact. Like Praise, of which it is certainly a form, it will remove the artificer from the event with the entirety of its passion, and accomplish its autonomy at all costs. If it is important that two alternatives be kept in contradiction, to the immediate dismay of the intelligence, literature will keep them at bay while life rages for solutions. If the artist is beguiled to compromise with events, while his real misgivings lie sealed away in abandoned areas of his sensibility, his art will pursue him there and wait for an answer. If his mind is seemingly ready with all the wit of the ages, while his consent delays and denies, the resources of literature are there to disclose his confusions and give the lie to his bravado. In short, it is possible through the medium of literature for the artist to function with maximum fullness at two levels of awareness, as the vessel of a double disclosure: the beliefs which his will imposes on the appearance of things through the semiotic fiction of his medium, and the unruly intuitions which explode out of his psychic life.

For each of these needs, literature has its stock of expressive materials and precision tools: symbols and images, to build in darkness and transmit the divided commitment of the writer in metaphorical guise, unmediated by concession or the entrapments of consistency; drama, to find the moment of "option" when conflict is "forced, living and momentous"; fable, to bring it to rational sequence in time and space; statement, to ply back and forth between the abstract and the reifications of the particular; music, to measure and order and render it utterable; rhetoric, to refine, condense, insinuate, exaggerate, hallucinate, unite, enchant, disturb. Thus, literature can keep exact pace with the truth of the believer in both its singularity and its heterogeneity. It can bring belief to order, not by reducing life, but by invoking the unforeseeable abundance of things—"as though we were God's spies"— so that it contains both the contradiction which logic rejects, and the mystery of which the artist himself may remain unaware: the illumined half of cognition by whose light the artist brings his language to order, and the darkened half, in whose shadow the unconscious life constantly beckons to its encompassing eidolons.

(1985)

SUMMATIONS

SAUL BELLOW

EASING MYSELF INTO THIS TALK, I begin conveniently with Erskine Caldwell. A very good writer in his line, Caldwell (who died recently in his eighties) was asked some years ago by an interviewer whether he read much. The answer was no, he didn't read. When he was starting out in life he had to choose between reading and writing. If you were preparing to publish some fifty books of your own, you had no time to read the books of other people.

Caldwell, who succeeded admirably at his trade, came on as an uncomplicated cottonbelt populist. For his purposes, he knew all that he needed to know. His public was not terribly demanding. What he gave it was perfectly fine, so he zipped along, assisted by a cast of redneck sharecroppers who plowed with mules and drove flivvers, who prayed but also boozed and carried on like satyrs. These farmers were not so simple as they appeared; they were somewhat twisted, kinky, even decadent. It was precisely their back-country decadence that appealed to the readers and the theatergoers of New York. Bear in mind that *God's Little Acre* had a six-year Broadway run. Caldwell's hang-loose, informal, non-reading policy paid off.

More ambitious writers who do read widely, making a considerable effort to enter into a "higher," more advanced, more civilized sphere, often are a trouble to themselves, and also to us, their readers. A simplicity of just the right kind, as unpretentious servants of our art, would allow us to write as fluently and naturally as birds sing. To sit on a branch and utter pure notes (of unpremeditated art) would be bliss. At the same time, nobody wants to be a birdbrain, and so writers are for the most part involved in reading and study. Readers, furthermore, expect authors to be instructive, informative, edifying, revelatory, even prophetic, and writers put themselves out to meet these expectations. The public legitimately desires to be entertained, charmed, excited; to be relieved from unbearable monopolizing preoccupations and anxieties. It expects a new slant on things; it needs—considering the public now as a community—meaning; it requires purgation by pity and terror; it passionately hopes for health. Can all this be done by writers without thought, without the effort of study? Can it be done, to reverse the premises, *by* study?

I find that I have stated the Faustian question. I take no pleasure in being so ambitious. In fact, this huge craving to know, to be on top of everything, has produced such curious results in the modern world, has failed so dramatically, so operatically, that one wants, understandably, to avoid it. The idea of total mastery is repellent. The great Faustian or Napoleonic or world-historical view belongs to another age. I can sympathize with writers who still accept such a challenge, but the grand overview is not for me. This is no age for such ambitions. The writer of an earlier generation who tried hard to provide the overview-of-overviews seems to me to be a megalomaniac—the Leviathan who attempted to swallow up all the other fishes.

Yet I myself am a wide reader, a consumer of many books. I grew up that way. And I am able to tell you how precious a good book was to John Milton, how delicious reading was to Marcel Proust, or what Francis Bacon and many another lofty thinker said about the blessings of books, but I also react with a secret happiness when Plato throws suspicion on the poets—when I remember that Socrates sets a conversation above the written word, or when Nietzsche declares that the failure of his eyesight for a long time kept him from reading. Illness obliged him to think for himself—a lucky thing, he says, for he was freed from slavish studies and pointless scholarship.

I have, however, read a vast number of books, most of which it would have been better not to have read. No one warned me to avoid James Oliver Curwood, Zane Grey, Edgar Rice Burroughs, Frank Merriwell, Tom Swift, Irwin S. Cobb, *The Last Days of*

Pompeii, Lynd's *Middletown*, textbooks in sociology, Watson's *Behaviourism*. A certain number of useless books, of course, have to be read. That, alas, is part of the education of one's taste, of an untutored democratic self-education. There were also bad books that were taken to be good ones. I liked Walter Pater, for instance, for his style, and Lawrence's *Lady Chatterley's Lover*, which recommended sexual intercourse as the cure for every civilized ailment— I liked it, for the encouragement it gave to my inclinations. Both writers were attractive, both were all but useless to me.

But to get on with it, I was snared early by books.

I have a lively memory of riding through Caldwell's Georgia in a Greyhound in 1940. A chain gang doing road repairs held us up briefly. I was going from New York to Mexico City and planned to stop overnight in Augusta to visit my Uncle Max. I sat in a window seat holding a copy of Stendhal's *The Red and the Black*. Outside, a green landscape; the freshly turned soil was a deep red. The shackled convicts were black, the stripes they wore were black and yellow. My suitcase in the overhead rack contained more books than clothing.

Here was Jim Crow, here the forced labor I had read about in *The Nation* and other progressive weeklies, the guards in breeches holding shotguns, the sweating men pushed aside, making way for the bus. Julien Sorel was just then choosing between Matilde de la Mole, representing amour-propre, and Mme de Renal, the innocent, loving, natural woman whom he had tried to kill. At this moment Julien was in prison. There he found freedom from his artificial, complicated thoughts and feelings. He prepared himself philosophically for death. But suddenly I was distracted: a forced-labor gang, sweating blacks, picks, shovels, guns, shackles—prisoners of a very different sort. The bus crept over the ferrous soil of the humped road.

I was getting through America by reading. I don't know how else I would have done it. Could it be that only I, the hungry reader and intending writer, saw that chain gang as it should be seen— what, with a brain swollen with the stings of so many literary bees?

Or did my fellow passengers, looking out, see things more realistically, was their understanding more natural than mine? I can understand why Caldwell would turn away from reading. Reading would make him too different from the others, from the likes of these bus riders. His aim was to be one of those Americans for whom reality was unmixed, who riding on the highway saw, like everybody else, only the highway. As for me, I was under Stendhal's spell, but I too was there, and, being in Georgia, I belonged there. The Greyhound Line provided transportation; Random House made available the Modern Library Stendhal. My Uncle Max sold secondhand clothing to blacks. *He* had no notion what *they* were about, and it is improbable *they* took the slightest interest in him personally. What was I doing with what I saw? For me there were historical, perhaps cosmic, possibly arcane, personal reasons why I should wish to put it all together, somehow. There may have been people scattered about the world who would sympathize with my motives and appreciate the effort I was making. In every civilized country something in human nature would respond to this picture from Georgia, characteristically American, seen by an individual who could not claim to be a native observer (native in the sense that the other passengers were native). But I found justification in my belief that there was such a thing as human nature, which not even the most far-fetched exotic combinations offered by this American "new world" could unseat. I did not look to human nature as a sanctuary; nor did I believe it to be in all respects an attractive thing—a safe haven for the endangered. What I did assume was the psychic unity of humankind. But enough of this for the moment. I shall not enter into philosophical questions. What concerns me here is the formation of a writer's human overview. Here I can invoke Stendhal again. He believed that he had a philosophy through which he looked at the world, and thought that no writer could do without one. Without an organized point of view how would you know what you were looking at? One of Stendhal's biographers claims that Stendhal found what he needed in John Locke or in Locke's French interpreters. I am no expert in such matters, but I have read enough of Locke to know that he looked with a cold, unsparing eye on human affairs. The influence of Locke would not be a sentimental one. It was Rousseau who provided Stendhal with sentiments. And beyond the "big view" there was Stendhal's peculiar gift, his genius. Locke could never have written, would never have thought of writing, *The Red and the Black* or anything resembling it. But I mention this only in passing. Most of you—the readers among you—can readily put together a dozen literary world-summaries or theoretical frameworks in less time than it takes to work the *Times* Sunday crossword puzzle: what Balzac thought, how Dickens understood his world, or Zola, or, to move into the twentieth century, how D. H. Lawrence saw modern civilization, or T. S. Eliot; or, with more difficulty, a reader may sum up Franz Kafka or Thomas Mann, or Louis-Ferdinand Céline. If you had asked Céline about the passengers in the Georgia bus (or about me), he would have said we were a lot of self-absorbed bastards, cheaters, hypocrites, and con artists, typical of the little monsters you found in any modern country, forever thinking how to get the better of everybody, heads full of hambone fantasies, nickel-and-dime images, the male passengers obsessed with banging somebody, anybody, one of the ladies in the bus perhaps; the ladies for their part concerned with being banged, or getting money, or shopping for clothing, or domestic concerns (their lousy husbands, their upsetting kids). Occasionally a gleam of disinterestedness or of nobility might dart out of this gathering of Greyhound riders, but for the most part they would be dreaming some nihilistic nightmare, or evolving some pointless racket. When I say nihilism I mean that Céline denies that there is any reigning and acknowledged force holding human life together. Neither religion nor philosophy can help us now, he maintains. So it's down with Christianity, down also with the accepted and respected contemporary unifiers, guides, and apologists, with gurus, popes, professors, and "traditionalists," the pious tradition-loving respecters of founders and ancestors. Out with the saints, down with the heroes of history, away with Descartes, to hell with the politicians and the generals. As for democracy, the very word makes him vomit.

But these judgments, opinions, and prejudices, expressed so brilliantly, in so revolutionary and original a style, are generated by a rare intelligence and a certain amount of learning. And why should Céline denounce philosophers, teachers, highbrow journalists, ideologists, and the mental swindlers of modern France unless he was himself an intellectual? Certainly he is no philistine. He thinks. We all do. We think like anything. Most of us think idiotic things, but that is no deterrent. We keep busy—figuring everything out, computing, casing, angling, investigating. That we do it badly is no wonder. Most thoughts are dead to begin with. We are ill-educated, dependent on certified but shaky authorities, uninformed, misinformed, victims of disinformation. Disinformation begins at home. We practice self-disinformation to shield ourselves from intolerable realities, disfiguring, for defensive reasons, what the common-sense judgment of our less-threatened ancestors would have identified more correctly and bluntly. Our prepared or fabricated concepts and categories of thought, the concept kits created by bad teachers and worse "communicators," weaken our power to grasp the essentials. And perhaps we collaborate with "conceptualizers" from fear of the naked truth, which has become a threat.

In such circumstances, should writers "intellectualize" so extensively? Should they not instead distance themselves from intellectuals? They have tried that, too. At times they have been belligerently "anti-intellectual" (to Americans I need only cite the prominent case of Hemingway, the man of action who abominated "thinkers"), but there is no way to escape the modern "thought problem." Hemingway, the anti-intellectual, "the dumb ox," as W. Lewis described him in a book called "Men Without Art," was a sophisticated artist, soaked in thought and saturated with ideas. Think for instance of the nihilistic prayer in his extraordinary story "A Clean, Well-Lighted Place"—"Our nada who art in nada, nada be thy name." Like it or not, consciously or involuntarily, writers navigate by charted skies, and together with the rest of troubled humanity they depend on their inadequate powers of cognition. Modern writers are markedly orthodox in their views, faithful to a handful of ideologies and to fairly elementary interpretations of history dominated by a few romantic themes in Marxist, psychoanalytic, or Existentialist variations. "The good are attracted by men's perceptions and think not for themselves," said William Blake. He meant, of course, that the good were gullible, feeble, tame, that they loved safety more than truth and liberty. But Blake did not mean that the wicked were intellectuals. He meant that the wicked were sources of energy, and energy, he tells us, is delight. Intellectuals as a class seldom manifest high energy or give delight. They are not wicked in character but only in their effect on the rest of us.

It is clear that in human existence we see thought and anxiety as commutative terms. On the threshold of old age I seem to have become convinced that our democratic civilization, originating in the Enlightenment, is founded upon and sustained by certain abstractions and that for democratic man everything is analyzable by means of pre-thought thoughts. Not long ago I spoke with a psychologist—no simpleton, by the way—who was busy doing research on hope, and who was convinced that hope was a psycho-physiological phenomenon activated by a hope hormone. The volume of this hormone is high or low according to our optimistic or pessimistic projections or expectations. So in important respects what we anticipate controls our internal secretions. Our psychologist has lifted hope out of theology and taken possession of it in the name of physiology. This is entirely consistent with the outlook of a rational civilization whose revolutionary achievements in technology give it the confidence to claim that the only truths about human existence are scientific truths. This is a claim that may be traced to the Enlightenment abstractions on which modern democracies are founded.

Art can't quite come to terms with this. Art—I refer to the real thing—finds it hard to subordinate itself to this civilization of concepts: the ideas that rule us, that tell us with arbitrary authority what the universe is and what we human beings are. On the human question, usually without the conscious mental ability to oppose the dominant view, the imagination, subject to visions, cannot bring itself to agree. Visions and concepts disagree, and it is because of these disagreements that artists cannot be described as intellectuals. The divergence first manifests itself in differences of language, for the language of intellectuals is the common language of the cognitions, whereas the languages of art are individual. Their uniqueness is a guarantee that they are genuine. The speech of one artist is not interchangeable with the speech of another. Now, an artist will (as a rule) make a summation. Every reader's mind is a structure of "concepts," framed in mental "ready-mades." People who pick up a book will want, naturally, to see the writer's mental identity card, will want a sketch, at least, of his "summation." But what can such a summation signify? Is any writer capable of conceiving a fully satisfactory overview? Stendhal seems to have believed that he was following Locke, a Locke who would have been astonished at any attempt to connect him with the writing of such a book as *The Red and the Black*. *The Red and the Black* is the work of Stendhal the artist, not of Stendhal the disciple of Locke. Locke would never have had anything to do with so frivolous an enterprise.

It is not my intention to review any considerable number of literary overviews. I am going to limit myself to a small sample of modern writers in whose notions or world-digests we will, I hope, find some illumination.

I begin with a short statement by the Russian poet Mandelstam. He wrote, in an essay called "The Morning of Acmeism," "Given the enormous emotional excitement associated with works of art, it is desirable that talk about art be marked by the greatest restraint. The huge majority of people are drawn to a work of art only insofar as they can detect in it the artist's world view. For the artist, however, a world view is a tool and instrument, like a hammer in the hands of a stonemason, and the only thing that is real is the work itself." He is warning us that people crave cognitive statements. They seek abstractions, for the abstract is familiar; it is what they know best. There is therefore a contest between thought and imagination. Thought is the common realm; imagination, the unique one. Abstraction has become a communal passion, and community prefers what can be talked about—translated into "concept" or discourse. Not many people willingly give themselves to what is not adaptable to their familiar discursiveness. They do not habitually live in art. They seem aware that art will alter them whereas discourse does not threaten them with alteration. They prefer their world view to any unfamiliar state of being. And yet reality, true experience, lies in "unfamiliar" states of being.

With your permission I turn again to the Greyhound bus. I am riding through Georgia, reading *The Red and the Black*. We pass a chain gang with pickaxes, and I hover between the inner world of Julien Sorel and the contemporary American one. In Stendhal, I live the life of a young man from nowhere, Julien Sorel, who is upward bound, in imitation of Napoleon, improvising as he goes, a prodigy of rapid adaptation whose career culminates in a Napoleonic success. But Julien is a self-made man who in the end does not care for what he has made of himself.

The present time is June, 1940. The Nazis are in Warsaw, Paris has just fallen, Stalin has divided Europe with Hitler. I am absorbed in a novel written more than a century earlier. Under its influence I observe the chain gang. I make an effort to interpret the minds and feelings of my fellow passengers and try to find the level of their humanity. Of course I am weak and incompetent, as attested by the fact that I am doing something exotic—on a Greyhound bus I am reading a French author. But with this suspicion of unfitness there also comes a daring sense of liberty, an illumination. Gifted young men from the obscurest bottom of society can rise in the world despite their subjective complexity and singularity. Aristocrats of intellect and talent need not live at the level of their fellow bus passengers. Julien Sorel, from the town of Verrières, a reader of Rousseau and the Memoirs from St. Helena, takes on the Mayor of Verrières, M. de Renal, finding support for his outrageous ambitions in books. A comical, scheming, social-climbing bourgeois, the Mayor hires Julien to tutor his sons. Julien wins the affection of the boys and seduces Mme de Renal.

Were there, in America, such types as the bourgeois M. de Renal and his wife? We had Sinclair Lewis's *Babbitt*, we had H. L. Mencken's Oddfellows and Elks—"the booboisie"—but these I think were secondary or transitional categories. Our writers, familiar with modern French literature, attempted to reproduce the same types in the Midwest. Lewis must have had Mme Bovary in mind when he wrote *Main Street*. But *Main Street* did not have Flaubert's tragic force. We were not French. Flaubert described provincial life. From a French standpoint the U.S.A. was entirely provincial. From the radical European classics of the nineteenth century, an American might learn what it was to be a writer. But uncritical importation from Europe led us into error. The European literary artist defined himself largely by his bourgeois enemy and opposite. What we had this side of the Atlantic was not at all the same. Our class system resembled the European one only superficially. It was a mistake to follow European models and European summations too closely, for America, as it turned out, was developing human types peculiarly its own.

Permit me to give a few illustrations to support this claim. I begin with one of our national heroes, General Dwight Eisenhower. (Why not go to the very top?) Kenneth S. Davis, the historian, who wrote a biography of Ike, has recently published some of his personal observations and preparatory notes. Davis, who was with Eisenhower in Europe and knew him intimately, gives us his firsthand impressions of him. Some of these are deeply unsettling. "It is almost impossible," Davis says,

> to write a biography of any depth, any significant density, when its subject is a man who has no interior life. Eisenhower is a man whose whole mental life is involved in external strategy. If he cares about meanings, even historical ones, I am not aware of it. . . . Yet he is caught up in historical circumstances. In writing about him one is impelled to carry meanings to him. . . . Meaning, signifi-

cance is not rooted in him, it only adheres to him. . . . His significance is all external and he does nothing (practically) to determine
it. . . . He is in a heroic position without being himself a hero . . .
no creative will. There is no beyondness in him. . . . Eisenhower is
a mirror of democracy. He . . . mirrors events, colors them with his
personality but never, in the deep sense, causes them. SHAEF is
perhaps the greatest fact of this war, and SHAEF is certainly Ike's
creature. . . . History may yet write Eisenhower's special qualities
down as determining forces in the world stream.

We sense that Mr. Davis is apprehensive about the majestic
judgment of history. His personal observation of General
Eisenhower tempts him toward impiety. Can it be that a hero of
history should be without inner powers? Davis is impelled to carry
meaning *to* Ike because Davis is a writer in the traditional sense,
and where great events occur, his instinct is to attribute them to
personal greatness—the greatness of an Alexander or an Augustus,
who conquered the world and ruled over empires. Even a Hitler,
notwithstanding his shallow bourgeois traits, very nearly defeated
the civilized world. Some 50,000,000 people were destroyed in his
wars. History will grant him a weird creativity in evil. Ike, as time
goes by, will perhaps assume the form of a great professional, the
leading agent of America's technical and organizational miracles.
Organizational triumphs of such magnitude as the Normandy inva-
sion possibly require a kind of blankness or vacancy in their chief
agents. The general American behavioral-science view that human
beings have no innate determinate nature and are infinitely plastic
or malleable suits the purposes of a society pre-eminent in the production of capital machinery and commodities, the first in history
to inundate itself and the world in superabundance. What can it
profit such a society to think about the bourgeois character?
"Bourgeois," in the Romantic or Marxian sense, is not a term that
can be applied to the collective genius of American management.
In our high-tech U.S.A., a M. de Renal or a George Babbitt
means almost nothing. They are as remote today as Babylon or
Egypt. Instead of capitalism in its classic description we have a vic-

torious technology (the term is inadequate, but for the moment it will have to do), a *Great Enterprise* or *Force That Advances*. This Force has little use for the expanded selfhood we have been taught to associate with a high civilization, for individuality in its old forms. It takes little interest in selfhood, in our souls, or even in the souls of those who lead, or seem to lead, us. It intends us all, without exception, to be its agents and its instruments. Therefore Ike, who directed operations in the European Theater of War, lacked an *internal* theatre in which this struggle might be represented. But where could one expect to find such an internal theater? Let us take Davis's word for it that Ike received meaning; he did not give it. A leader like Churchill seemed capable of giving or expressing the meaning of the events in which he participated. But Churchill belonged to another civilization altogether. He himself was an original observer, a writer, and a psychologist. Eisenhower's historical role required that he clear himself of psychological traits so that he might make himself the instrument, the neutral medium, of the logistical tasks assigned to him.

From the nineteenth century we inherited the notion of a personal parity of individual capacities or intellect with the full complexity of the world. That world, revolutionized by ideas, could still be matched by individual powers. Balzac's de Rastignac challenges Paris, the City of Light (representing the world), to a duel; Dostoevsky's Raskolnikov is equally ready to take the world on—"one on one," in the American expression. This is the Napoleonic consciousness, which came forward to encircle the whole of civilization as an antagonist, an equal and opposite power. Nothing of this sort remains in the contemporary U.S.A. What is slowly taking form before our eyes is a revolutionary emptiness, a willing submission to the *Great Enterprise*.

In Ike as a type we see the personal challenge abandoned. Now collective intelligence in the form of production is the characteristic expression of a democracy. It may rule successfully; it may misrule disastrously. *The Force That Advances* eludes individual control.

We learn from historians of World War II that the American

military in England thought the subtle strategies proposed by the British a waste of time. Flood Europe with men and materiel, they said. Such a plan did not require a distinctive world-historical perspective. Churchill would have preferred a Mediterranean thrust against the "soft underbelly" of Europe. His plan would have prolonged the war deliberately by bleeding Germany and Russia to death. This would have extended the suffering of Europe by a year or two but it might also have destroyed Stalin. Liberal democracy and its technical civilization did not operate that way. It crossed the Channel, pushed across the Rhine, but it permitted Russia to create an empire in Eastern Europe.

Writers, or those who pass for writers, ought to concern themselves with these matters. They are not urged by the public—least of all the educated public—to do so. People seem sufficiently diverted by business, politics, sports, diseases, famines, and the terror of nuclear war, by the fever and giddiness of life. They may live day by day upon as many of these world elements as they care to ingest and therefore may not feel any great need for the arts. Current events are more exciting than any art. We are more moved by the millions paid for a de Kooning (a recent event) than by any painting. We are satisfied when writers add to the fever and the giddiness, for these express the preciousness, the sweet boundlessness of our needs—the intoxication of what we are, mingling with the pain of what we fail to be. When death comes, as it soon will, we will be nothing. Meanwhile, we spend our time talking about ourselves; we ourselves are, for the moment, *it*, the reason for it all, the name of the game, the object of universal flattery, and the very heart of a universal terror. Here and there writers—they seldom are American—make an effort to summarize our condition (the thing we refer to as civilization). Some of the summaries are suggestive. I propose to look at one or two of them now, not without repeating Mandelstam's indispensable warning: "The huge majority of people are drawn to a work of art only insofar as they can detect in it the artist's world view." That is to say, they are infatuated with cerebral statements and are happiest when they can reduce a work of art to its ideas. "For the artist, however, a world view is a tool . . . ," Mandelstam (vainly) insists, "and the only thing that is real is the work itself."

Having restated this indispensable warning, which artists themselves are apt to ignore, I direct your attention to the views of the Yugoslav writer Danilo Kis, an admirable novelist, the author of a powerful book, *A Tomb for Boris Davidovitch*. Like so many contemporary writers, Kis rigorously distinguishes between real subjects and superfluous ones. "This we need, while that must be dismissed." He tells us that the time for literary fabrication is past. The reader no longer believes in fabrications. In fiction they are unnecessary and also false. He says, "Modern times have shown Dostoevsky's famous catchword 'nothing is more fantastic than reality' to be more than a clever turn of phrase, that the fantastic quality of reality has been revealed to modern man as *fantastic reality*. . . ." He speaks oddly of occult forces at work about us and then he says, "So much accumulated evil and raw fantastic reality cannot be explained by historical or psychological factors alone." What he implies is that to seek for the causes of evil in our "subjectivity" is misleading. He refers to what Arthur Koestler called a modern schizopsychology, and the modern schizophysiology associated with it. In Kis's opinion psychology is incapable of dealing with man's paranoid behavior. Neither can behavior, he argues, be interpreted in terms of moral consistency. Allowed to speak for themselves, the facts cannot be dealt with by the writer "in the old way," because what lies behind those facts is a fantastic—i.e., a paranoid—reality, and this is what the writer has an obligation to put on paper.

Now, "paranoid" itself has become a buzzword. Yet it does direct our attention to something. An experience some writers nowadays frequently have is a surge of impatience, amounting at times to rage and nausea, with the terms used to explain human motives. To speak personally: they often outrage me with their falsity. What writers pursue now—or should pursue—is something lying behind the "concepts" and the appearances: signs and motions previously overlooked, a play of intentions, a shimmer in the looks of people that communicates impulses from a human hinterland unacknowledged by our modern enlightenment and its psychology, by the rational civilization that has brought us political and social gains and paid for them by sealing off our most significant impulses and powers. There are plenty of contemporary summations which agree in one way or another with the foregoing. A posthumous book by Harold Rosenberg, *The Case of the Baffled Radical*, speaks of "the transitional person of modern democracy." What Rosenberg says is that the "known" person against his "known" social background is no longer of interest to a modern reader. In nineteenth-century novels characters were as solid as nineteenth-century property. They were above all substantial, and their dense and palpable traits were classifiable and might be enumerated or inventoried like the assets of an estate. Contemporary social and personal facts resist this kind of treatment. Consider, as a variation on Rosenberg's judgment of what is peculiarly modern, the following statement by Borges. He writes, "The composition of vast books is a laborious and impoverishing extravagance. To go on for five hundred pages developing an idea whose perfect oral exposition is possible in a few minutes! A better course of procedure is to pretend that such books already exist, and then to offer a résumé, a commentary. . . . I have preferred to write notes upon imaginary books."

What such views have in common is a preference for the transitory, for summaries or résumés, for compression, fluidity, for flashing speed, for condensation. This is characteristic of the lives our contemporaries make for themselves. "The no-bio rule is a constant of this universe," writes Padgett Powell in his latest book. There shall be no more "life-histories." The author later adds, "These days, these characters, have at their center no center, no towardness." For the brainy ones this is still oppressive. But "those less burdened are capable of distracting themselves with central, self-important purpose . . . ." One must, to be "happy," "comprehend the beauty of failure, the glory of the fancy end run around importance." Freedom evidently is freedom from the ancient delusion that one's life matters. Only the gloomiest of idiots continue to take themselves seriously. The "saved" are sublimely indifferent. To have no "center" is their salvation and their bliss. Relief from traditional "seriousness" is welcome; we are tired of the exhausting task of fighting to maintain a personal center. But Mr. Padgett Powell also reminds me of Erskine Caldwell—the voice of Caldwell's successor is that of a more sophisticated populist.

On every side, American lives unfold, for which there is no accounting and to which former methods of presentation can never do justice. A few examples will make this quite clear: Mr. Armand Hammer, born of Russian parents, brought up in New York, trained as an M.D., goes to Russia shortly after the Revolution, meets leading Bolsheviks, wins their confidence, obtains a franchise to manufacture lead pencils, is commissioned to sell the treasures of the Hermitage for hard American currency. By such means he builds a private fortune and eventually acquires the Occidental Petroleum Co. This insignificant go-between becomes a billionaire and a great figure in both superpowers, living lavishly in California and in Moscow. Commuting in his own jet he enters Russia by all accounts without customs inspections. He has access to the White House and the Kremlin. At his own expense he sends medical specialists to Chernobyl when the reactor blows up. He writes about the lessons of Chernobyl on the Op Ed page of the *Times* in the accents of a statesman taking the view that the Russians after all are part of the civilized world community. He seems to be saying that Gorbachev's *glasnost* must be taken seriously.

A Jewish widow in a Midwestern city spends the millions her husband left her on Orthodox settlements in Israel. She is subsidizing a theocratic challenge to Zionism. If history had not disturbed her prewar Polish village she would have spent her life plucking chickens and arranging marriages. Now she dresses in Armani-designed clothing and commutes between Jerusalem and Cleveland Heights, where her heirs tie themselves in knots to prevent her spending their legacy. Of what underlies these historical and scientific wonders she hasn't the slightest idea.

From the White House a highly connected official accompanied by expert advisers flies to Teheran in a plane loaded with parts for Iranian tanks and rockets. His hope is to establish relations with a probably imaginary faction in the Iranian government, and to obtain the release of American hostages in Lebanon. As a gift for the Ayatollah he brings a Bible inscribed by the President, a brace of Colt pistols, and a key-shaped cake symbolizing the reopening of relations between Iran and the U.S. Later the emissary, Mr. McFarlane, evidently an honorable man, feeling disgraced, attempts suicide. The last we see of him is on the evening news, flanked by his wife and daughter, explaining himself in psychiatric jargon.

These actions and improvisations are in a sense diagrams of the mental history of the persons who perform them. They perhaps have a desire to present a life design others can grasp, and they tacitly assert that this is what human beings are in this day and age. I have emphasized the summations of writers, but the thought suggests itself that in the modern world many a life is an attempted summation; it accepts the challenge of interpreting our condition. Seemingly, people make an offering of their summation to one another, and to the world as well. Their message is: "I myself am a résumé, an example of what may be done with the strange compounds that make up my being." Thus it is possible that their behavior reveals a consciousness of an appropriate participation in contemporary life, and they apparently feel that they incarnate something of high significance. In this there is revealed a sense of form, perhaps even aesthetic form. People dart briefly into the foreground and do as much as can humanly be done—they exhibit their singularities, they establish themselves and thrive in our consciousness, and they behave with a kind of aesthetic obliquity, with precisely the kind of ellipsis we are best prepared to understand. They are "in the act." By the aesthetic dress of what they allege to be their life summary, these individuals, while actually serving the *Force That Advances*, are laying claim to the freedom of the artist. Celebrity, money—or even imaginary celebrity, power, and distinction—permit them to strike the posture of men and women who have freely created themselves. It also gives their ingenuity, their talents, an opportunity to come into play. Judged by the standard of art, however, this is poor stuff—these are summations of a very low order.

The artist is not necessarily bound by his summation, because as an artist he acts with freedom. His abstractions, his *cerebral* principles, will splinter and give way to the forces that make a work of art. Stendhal, who presents himself as a disciple of Locke, actually is a great wit and an ingenious interpreter of human behavior. He is *free* from the Enlightened ideas he holds. They are little more than a convenience to him. The most advanced ideas of an artist are, in the end, not declarations but questions. Shakespeare is free even from the ideas that tempt him most. He cannot be seduced by his own most powerful summations.

We can no longer derive our summations from the definitions of humankind set by enlightened democracy. These have been used up entirely. Those of us who are called, or call ourselves, artists must turn again to the sources of our permanent strengths, to the stronghold of the purest human consciousness. Only the purest human consciousness, art consciousness, can see us through this time of nihilism.

(1987)

MAGIC AND SPELLS

HUGH KENNER

A POET'S REACH EXTENDS FROM THEN TO NOW; from a time of great power to what we're pretty well used to. It's from Then that lightnings are fetched: from archaic intimations that Words are not for arranging lightly; that they may be dangerous; have force; command invisible legions; may explode. Such feelings descend from a foretime of charms and curses. Studying and teaching literature as we do, we are apt to handle it as casually as chemists do poisons. It lies there—does it not?—inert on the page, twitching occasionally when disturbed by an editor. Otherwise it's quiescent. But that's a deceptive quiet.

I've told elsewhere a story I'll retell here, about one of the last poets who could feel sure what being a poet meant. His name was, more or less, Michael O'Govern—"more or less" because I'm transliterating from the Irish—and he offers us what Maire Cruise O'Brien calls "a scientific experiment" to confirm the authenticity of his calling. As he tells it in a poem he wrote in Irish, he was out walking, and a tribe of rats surrounded him, meaning to attack. That appears to be the habit of Irish rats. As for what happened next, here is a bit of his Irish in Mrs. O'Brien's translation:

> . . . They were no melodious words I spoke . . .
> But the psalmody of sorcery
> > Which I did not learn at school.
>
> When I lifted my head from the book
> > The rout fell silent. . . .
> Whatever power was in that quatrain
>
> > Which was as ancient as the rock
> I saw them flee in terror
> > Under the overhang of the stones.

What O'Govern spoke from "the book"—which would have been a manuscript, not something bound—was the rat charm, *Artha na bhFrancach*, and "This charm," Mrs. O'Brien advises us, "if recited in the proper manner by a properly qualified person, has the effect of banishing all rodents from the immediate vicinity." But "if spoken by an illegitimate operator . . . not only will it not work, but the rats will turn upon the would-be exterminator and tear him limb from limb!" So when his rats left, O'Govern had demonstrated his poetic credentials beyond doubt.

Now, reflect that what you have just heard me narrate is not a piece of remote folklore. It happened in the twentieth century. Maire Cruise O'Brien lives at this moment—I have spoken with her myself—and Michael O'Govern was someone she knew as a child. So late did one definition of the poet's role linger. The job of the poet is to speak efficacious words. By long tradition, one of the tests is rats; when the bard Senchen Torpest spoke quatrains against rodents who'd eaten his dinner, ten of them dropped dead from the rafters. That was about A.D. 600, in Gort, in the West of Ireland, and we know Shakespeare heard of it from *As You Like It*, III.ii, where Rosalind speaks of an Irish rat "berhymed." I've wondered if Shakespeare's informant may not have been Spenser; if so, then we've three bards in confluence. Browning likewise heard of the Pied Piper of Hamelin, who had similar powers though his charm wasn't worded. We are stirring among Paleolithic roots.

Notice that the charm needs two things. It needs "a properly qualified person," and it needs the efficacious words. The qualification, by Irish usage, tends to be hereditary. The words, however, had to be learned, and there was provision for learning them.

They were learned by careful and long apprenticeship. The young bard learned the charm against rats, and the charm that makes antlers spring from someone's head, and the one that brings offenders out in blisters, and the one that makes their cattle sicken. He learned—or she learned, inheritors of the gift being not infrequently women—the many intricate systems of meter and assonance, and ways to tense those against natural rhythms of speech, and the art of singing it all to stringed music. These matters were even learned in bardic schools, of which we know little save that they existed and were likely not much like State U. Poetry Workshops. There they learned, too, something akin to the language of the gods—the *Berla na bhFiled*, poets' tongue, which put them in touch with power but could bewilder such mortals as the king who said, "That is a very good poem, for the man who could understand it." Poems are addressed to Powers; we but overhear; hence "obscurity."

The bard's job, put simply, was to praise the king's friends, curse the king's enemies. Those the bard praised prospered; those the bard cursed sickened. People correspondingly esteemed the bard, who wherever he went was fed and honored and looked after. In the remote West, where they grow up speaking Irish, they are said to esteem the bard to this day—such a bard as Michael O'Govern. That man lived, Mrs. O'Brien also informs us, amid "the essential charmlessness of poverty." He would have fared better before there was a shortage of kings. Still, there were compensations; O'Govern was untroubled by rats.

In Greece, "Orpheus with his lute made trees," also tamed birds and beasts. As he strummed the lute he sang some *epaoide* or other. An *epaoide* is a song (*aoide*) not just released into the air but aimed in a certain direction, with a certain intent. That is what *epi* says, with a force we catch when we say "lay a trip on." Likewise, in Rome they said *in* for *epi, cantare* for *aoide*, and came up with *incantare*: incant, enchant. (For an English cognate try "bewitch.") One time an *epaoide* was sung over wounded Odysseus, to stanch the flow of dark blood. The scholar who isolates this information (Lain Entralgo, in *The Therapy of the Word*) connects Plato's bureaucratic nervousness about poets with the fact that an *epode* (as it was later spelt) could as easily harm as heal—a force that can kill Irish rats cries for regulating—and reminds us how even for hardheaded Aristotle metered words, perhaps uttered in song, could have an effect that deserved a medical name: *katharsis*, purification.

Magical power, cathartic or just blighting, could even locate itself in single words, words you spoke with caution if at all. "Abracadabra" was a word of that kind; so was "Jesus." They could degenerate into gibberish, the way the English inn called "God Encompasseth Us" became "Goat and Compasses," a much safer phrase for casual uttering, or the way "Eeny Meeny Miney Moe" may preserve some phonemes of a pre-Christian Germanic incantation never meant for kiddies to fool with. There's an Anglo-Saxon spell of seven lines to ward off theft; it begins

> *Luben luben niga*
> *Efith Efith niga*

and if you get no sense from those syllables, be assured that the Evil One does. We're not as far as we may think from a twentieth-century poet writing

> *Shantih Shantih Shantih*

A Scandinavian Edda cites "Beech-runes, Help-runes, Love-runes, and great Power-runes, for whomsoever will, to have for charms, pure and genuine, till the world falls in ruins." It is not in ruins yet, and meanwhile on what do the fortunes of the Hallmark Company rest save a belief, however vestigial, that rhymes will bring our friends cheer and maybe good luck? As for our enemies, we no longer send them rhymed curses; but in the old days of the Comic Valentine we affected to. The curse—the insulting rhyme sent to the ugly woman, the graceless boy—is no longer felt to be in good taste, maybe out of a lingering fear lest it still may be efficacious. In a time of massive lawsuits we've grown cautious.

The tradition of the efficacious word survives too. Each Valentine's Day, as everyone knows, these words include Love and Hearts and Flowers; and the rather surprising reason is that in Provençal, Europe's first language of secular poetry, these were sonorous words that rhymed. Love was *amor*, and Heart was *cor*, and Flower was *flor*. They sound and chime through innumerable troubadour melodies; they recur like charms. So, in their affinity of sound it was possible to intuit something magical, and Dante even lets us watch him avoid them while he makes Provençal for lustful

Arnaut Daniel to speak in Purgatory and turns the speech not on the magic words but on rhymes that evoke them, *plor, folor, valor, dolor*: weep, folly, Power, pain. When Petrarch imitated troubadour effects in Italian he had at his disposal Italian words sounding rather like them. Then in one of literary history's great landslides the Petrarchan Tradition lapsed into English, and the magic intertwining of sound was lost; for the words we must use in English do not sound in the least like one another. They stay linked, though, Love, Heart, Flower: and are linked today on any cliché Valentine. For that is one definition of a cliché, that it guards complications no longer understood, like *flor, cor, amor*. The heart, we're now taught, is a pump, and love gets called a glandular illusion; but *cor* and *amor* rhyme still, and Love and Heart, and the Valentine industry prospers, florists and all.

Language is very stubborn, very conserving; the route from Then to Now is signposted by equivalences we have been unwilling to give up. Consider, for instance, all the taboo words—what until quite recently were the unprintable words, though even *The New York Times* will likely be printing them before long, and the *Times* of London gave in long ago. "Hocus pocus" was once "Hoc est corpus," the most efficacious words in Christendom, the very words of consecration, too dangerous for an Elizabethan mountebank's rigmarole. "Hocus pocus" is that powerful phrase rendered, as we now say, printable; it's analogous in that way to "Darn!" and "Gee!" But you were thinking of the reproductive and excretive words, the ones the great *Oxford English Dictionary* excluded even when its editors could have adduced Chaucer. True, such words are not without interest. One of them, which Robert Browning found in Chaucer, he misunderstood completely, supposing it to be part of a nun's habit though Chaucer was referring to pudenda. So Browning put "Nuns in twats" in a rhyming position (the rhyme was "bats") in the time of Victoria herself. Less squeamish lexicographers might have saved him.

But observe a far more interesting order of delicacy: the kind that drove Victorian novelists to vague talk of the year 18-- in the city of B-----. That's a manifestation of something little studied, a recurrent skittishness about the specific. Whole aesthetic systems have derived from it, notably the Augustan Grandeur of Generality: as when the moping Owl does to the Moon complain and Gray's idiom creates a generic Owl, distanced and soothingly emblematic. So when

> Sweepings from butchers' stalls, dung, guts, and blood,
> Drowned puppies, stinking sprats, all drenched in mud,
> Dead cats, and turnip-tops, come tumbling down the flood

they show off Swift's counter-Augustan decorum of the indecorous, which amounts to a relentless naming, naming.

Again we may be in the domain of the blessing and the curse: since you didn't know what powers you might be wielding when you specified, it was generally safest not to. It seems not irrelevant, either, that Augustan norms came into coherence along with the publishing industry. Men have always been freer to say than to write, to write than to print. As with Wilde's fox-hunters—the unspeakable hallooing in pursuit of the uneatable—"unspeakable" is but a word that amusingly exaggerates, but whenever we say "unprintable" we mean it. Somehow, when fixed in space, even written in sand like the signs that enabled conjuration but still more when frozen in the eerie finality of type, words accrete disquieting power, not least their power to make you hear your own voice saying them. To excuse our constraining what gets into print we often say we are protecting children. Yet we're far less cautious about what we say in their earshot. No, such taboos go with subliminal fears. (Those fears are the iron bars we need poets to bend.)

Thus printing from the day it was invented has been vaguely connected with magic, especially by its practitioners; there is no more effective censor than the man who sets type and declines to set *that*. Ezra Pound in 1916 used a Greek word, *phaloi*, meaning the spikes on helmets, and Robert McLehose & Sons, who are still in business, declined to have any hand in printing that word. It was too much like another Greek word with *two* l's. (Fifty-five years later Messrs. McLehose got a mild comeuppance when ironic destiny had them typesetting *The Pound Era*, a book in which I quoted the offending line.)

But I digress; the hero of the story I want to tell now is James Joyce, whose *Dubliners* in 1907 contained several instances of the word "bloody"—then a taboo word—and some other offences we'll come to. A Dublin publisher, Maunsell & Co., dithered and temporized, adducing "bloody," not mentioning that they were even at that moment publishing the collected works of J. M. Synge, whose *Playboy of the Western World* used "bloody" four times. For "bloody" was a pretext. What really bothered Maunsell & Co. was that Joyce had specified several Dublin pubs by name, and while he'd compromise on "bloody" with infinite regret, for those pubs he declined absolutely to substitute fictional equivalents. He needed them, he said, to map his character's progress round the city. Also, if you knew Dublin, you knew what class of establishment each one was, and that conveyed information too.

In vain did Joyce protest that nothing unseemly went on in any of the pubs; people drank and talked, that was all. He even offered to drive round the city with Maunsell's manager, obtaining written permission from each pubkeeper. Maunsell's manager was having none of that. Threatened over breach of contract, he grudgingly did have the book typeset and printed; then the printer saved him by a fit of rectitude amid which the sheets of all 1,000 copies were guillotined. Who paid for the mess I don't know, but *Dubliners* went unpublished until 1914.

What it all led to was, of course, *Ulysses*, the most specifying novel in history. Hundreds and hundreds of establishments—pubs, plumbers, haberdashers, hatters, tailors, butchers, bakers, printers even—got named and even located by exact address: a very orgy of naming, a defiance of taboo. For it was a taboo. No one could have told you why, but one just didn't do such things. *Ulysses* had to be published in Paris, typeset in Dijon, by innocent Frenchmen who didn't know the meaning of the words they were profaning. The four-letter words in *Ulysses* are surprisingly few. The real

taboo it broke was the taboo against specifying: a taboo related to
the fear some peoples have of being photographed, or the fear that
whatever you speak lightly of you tempt. Cross your fingers.
Knock wood. And if you're a star athlete, contrive to stay off the
cover of *Sports Illustrated*.

That naming wields power seems an immemorial intuition.
You're careful about naming God; in some traditions you never
name Him at all. And you call up a spirit—Faust did it—by recit-
ing all the names by which he's known. Otherwise put: you catch
him in a net you weave out of all your quarry's attributes. Hence
Shelley's procedure in his *Ode to the West Wind*, a poem in which
he implores a daemon to possess him. To summon the Wind (a
Spirit, from *spiritus*, breath) Shelley, always counting the numinous
numbers, expends three stanzas on a litany of its seven powers:

> —thou breath of Autumn's being . . .
> —thou from whose unseen presence . . .
> —thou who chariotest . . .
> —thou on whose stream . . .
> —thou dirge . . .
> —thou who didst waken . . .
> —thou for whose path . . .

And having obtained the Destroyer-and-Preserver's presence, he
states, Faust-like, his terms of equivocal surrender:

> . . . Be thou, Spirit fierce,
> My spirit! Be thou me, impetuous one!
>
> Drive my dead thoughts over the universe
> Like withered leaves to quicken a new birth!
>
> And by the incantation of this verse,
>
> Scatter, as from an unextinguished hearth
> Ashes and sparks, my words amongst mankind!

Yes, "incantation," for what he's after is power, a daemon's traditional fief: power over somnolent mankind that tends to prefer
(according to another poet)

> Earth in forgetful snow, feeding
> A little life with dried tubers.

Unabashed by Faust's discovery that by such a bargain the Spirit gets control over you, Shelley is impetuously confident that *he'll* somehow command *it*: "Be thou me, impetuous one!" Punctilious in ritual, he prints his lines in threes, and by cunningly co-opting Dante's *terza rima* ensures that four rhymes of the five in each 14-line part will occur three times.

But back to Ireland, whence I've fetched many examples because they seem connected with an Irish intuition more direct— I do not say more primitive—concerning words and their efficacy than we are likely to find in cultures where words have become chiefly instrumental: are items to be paid for by the hundred, or sprayed onto pages by haphazard. I have seen a Dubliner so little cowed by printer's doings that he made his living setting type; nevertheless when I showed him something to read dodging into another room to read it, quite as though reading under the eyes of another was an act not quite decent. There's a deep awe underlying that, awe presumably of communing with the letter that abides. And here's William Butler Yeats, in his circumlocutory manner of 1898, making a poem called "The Fish" into one fine intricate ceremonious sentence, a deed that could only have been worked out on paper; and listen to the ending it builds to:

> Although you hide in the ebb and flow
> Of the pale tide when the moon has set,
> The people of coming days will know
> About the casting out of my net,
> And how you have leaped times out of mind
> Over the little silver cords,
> And think that you were hard and unkind,
> And blame you with many bitter words.

Those "many bitter words" from the lips of posterity: behold there his ultimate weapon, the harshest threat he can wield.

They will know of my casting and casting, your leaping and leaping, and the poem contains posterity too, endlessly reprobat-

ing as though in an echo chamber. In short, we are in the presence of a Curse, the most ceremonious and decorous of all
rhymed Irish Curses.

Irish Curses don't generally mince words. Here's Douglas
Hyde's English version of a nineteenth-century one:

> May none of their race survive,
>> May God destroy them all,
> Each curse of the psalms in the holy books
>> Of the prophets on them fall.
>>>> Amen.
>
> Blight skull, and ear, and skin,
>> And hearing, and voice, and sight,
> Amen! before the year be out,
>> Blight, Son of the Virgin, blight.
>>>> Amen!

And here's the thrust of James Stephens's reprobation of the bar-
maid who wouldn't bring him an unpaid-for glass:

> May the devil grip the whey-faced slut by the hair,
> And beat bad manners out of her skin for a year. . . .
> May she marry a ghost and bear him a kitten, and may
> The High King of Glory permit her to get the mange.

After such vigors Yeats may sound positively pallid, and it's true
that by a decade after "The Fish" he was striving to inoculate his
language with a directness that could blister folk who "fumble in
the greasy till." Still, listen to "The Fish" once more:

> Although you hide in the ebb and flow
> Of the pale tide when the moon has set,
> The people of coming days will know
> About the casting out of my net,
> And how you have leaped times out of mind
> Over the little silver cords,
> And think that you were hard and unkind,
> And blame you with many bitter words.

There's almighty condescension in that "although" clause—all very well to keep dodging, but just you wait—and a powerful threat where a fish is least likely to notice it, in "The people of coming days will know." For how will they know? They will know because I am a poet, and have the power not only of wielding the Curse but of doing something old Irish bards didn't aspire to, something I inherit from Renaissance poets who had it from Latin ones, the power of framing words not only efficacious but durable, words that will reach into coming days, to let posterity know about bad behavior. Not marble nor the gilded monuments of princes shall outlive this powerful rhyme. More: I am able to count on the moral sensitivity of the people of coming days, on their command of many bitter words and on their awareness that these are called for; I am able to count on that because the nutriment of the people of coming days will include a body of poetry such as mine: poetry to lift the will and sharpen the vision and see to it that they remember what needs remembering. "The Fish" draws energies from Then, for channeling through Now to Henceforward. It's unlikely, moreover, that its Fish is a mere fish, not when the net is woven of silver cords. A woman who won't be wooed? A poem that won't be written? This poem's generality is not its least unnerving feature. Let whatever exists anywhere near a Poet be wary.

A case was decided just a few months back in favor of a woman who felt her reputation destroyed because she had known a poet; whereafter not even a poem but a television dramatization of a novel by the poet had damaged her to a degree that only huge sums could redress. The bitter words she felt blamed by were a scriptwriter's. I'll name none of the names lest I bring down a curse on myself; but you know who I mean. That the case was expensively settled out of court means that no one with however rational a head felt secure in defying the power over judges' minds of what even dead poets are capable of. I'm not privy to judges' minds, but the precedent is sobering. An awesome Then reaches into judicial Now. In prehistory they'd have thought it all quite intelligible.

Charms and spells tend to be asyntactic; they string words together. Now, it's a tenable generalization, that with language you can do essentially two things: tell stories, make lists. You can say, "The king died, and then the queen died of grief," which is E. M. Forster's example of a story, or you can say, minimizing the busy-work of syntax,

> They went up the King mountain,
> straight trunks of pine and cypress
> they cut and brought there,
> hewed pillars and rafters
> carved beam-horns ornate
> contrived pillars and sockets
> to the inner shrine, perfect
> that his ray come to point in this quiet

which ends Ezra Pound's version of the last of the Confucian Odes, and may sound like a narrative but is actually a list of actions, "cut," "brought," "hewed," "carved," "contrived," and all to a quasi-magical purpose:

> that his ray come to point in this quiet

That it's analyzed into "lines" for the reading eye is an aspect of its status as a list. Poems, it may be, are essentially lists: if only of their own lines, which we find we have an itch to number. And listing is specific naming; it touches on the very specificity by which the Irish publisher was dismayed when James Joyce named those pubs eight decades ago. It was to preserve lists that writing itself was invented; the oldest writings we have from whatever civilization always turn out to be lists: of storehouse inventories—six jars, one measure of oil—or of the ships that sailed against Troy. One explanation is that stories are easy to remember but lists are not and require recording. But another might be that lists are so dangerous they require a distancing technology: as it were, handling with tongs. For a list is a distilled and concentrated naming. Even a storehouse list will have meant taxes for somebody.

To think of the poem as a list is to gain a new respect for its hidden power. A poem specifies, specifies. It does what can stir deep fear: it names, names, names.

> From Val Cabrere, where two miles of roof to San Bertrand
> so that a cat need not set foot in the road
> where now is an inn, and bare rafters,
> where they scratch six feet deep to reach pavement
> where now is a wheat field, and a milestone
> an altar to Terminus, with arms crossed
> back of the stone
> Where sun cuts light against evening,
> where light shaves grass into emerald . . .

—Pound again, and the indictment of what lost its *vertù* and vanished mounts up in a listing of remnants; five lines of nine affirm the list structure in beginning with "where."

A blessing is a list of delights; a curse, a list of misfortunes. A story soothes with suggestions that one thing follows smoothly from another. A list, staccato, bespeaks the discontinuity of the unforeseeable, the not necessarily welcome. Here's a list to keep us slightly on edge, from tart ingratiating Marianne Moore. It's the opening stanza of *Virginia Britannia*. (I'll quote a version she'd not yet had second thoughts about. She did tend to get scared of what she'd first rashly printed, and one might ponder that.)

> Pale sand edges England's Old
> Dominion. The air is soft, warm, hot
>   above the cedar-dotted emerald shore
> known to the redbird,
>   the red-coated musketeer,
>   the trumpet-flower, the cavalier,
> the parson, and the
>   wild parishioner. A deer-
>   track in a church-floor
> brick, and Sir George Yeardley's
> coffin-tacks and
> tomb remain. The now tremendous vine-
> encompassed hackberry
>   starred with the ivy flower,

shades the church tower;
And "a great sinner lyeth here" under
  the sycamore.

And what is that a list *of*? A list of what's left. The Old
Dominion is England's no more; edged by "pale sand," it never
quite was, and the heat was un-English and still is. The "cedar-dot-
ted emerald shore," that's distinctly North American, and so is the
redbird. But the "red-coated musketeer"— he's smuggling himself
into belonging, abetted by the color he shares with a native bird.
The cavalier and the parson, they were English immigrants. The
"wild parishioner"? A red Indian surely, fellow to that deer-track.
But "Sir George Yeardley" is no American name, and reference to
"a great sinner" is not phrased in the American grain. As for "ivy
flower" rhyming with "church tower," that comes from the world
of Gray's *Elegy*; John Slatin acutely remarks how we half expect a
moping owl complaining to the moon.

This landscape, in short, has been diligently composed by past
hands, in a way that once made English immigrants feel at home,
and it now offers welcome to English poetic effects. (In that vein,
reconstructed Williamsburg is as depressing a place as I know.) But
such effects don't include the mockingbird, who makes his entry
three stanzas later:

Observe the terse Virginian,
  the mettlesome gray one that drives the
      owl from tree to tree and imitates the call
  of whippoorwill or
      lark or katydid—the lead-
      gray lead-legged mocking bird with head
  held half away, and
      meditative eye as dead
      as sculptured marble
  eyes. Alighting noiseless-
  ly it muses
  in the semi-sun, on tall thin legs,
  as if it did not see,
      still standing there alone

> on the round stone-
> topped table with lead cupids grouped to
> form the pedestal.

"Terse," he's an imitator, even of larks; and he ends up like a marble sculpture on a round table amid lead cupids. He's caught by old forms? He looks as awkward as Hawthorne or Poe. I must leave off quoting; I'll remark, though, that this whole strange long poem, tirelessly listing, listing, never leaves off tensing Then against Now, the Old Dominion where colonists made shift to make it seem like home, the New World state where twentieth-century visitors encounter the shock of the new amid pleasing reminders of the old. The pull of the newcomers' Old is nearly deadly: a pull into contrivance, into inauthenticity, into what Norton Anthologies condition us to receive as Poetry (which Marianne Moore famously "disliked"). Throughout *Virginia Britannia* her abrupt rhymes and broken lines struggle to affirm some putatively still older, more native, poetic. Wrestling with ghosts that (as William Carlos Williams kept affirming) never did get embodied—a chunk of the continent even got called New England—it's the most disturbing perhaps of all her poems.

For the New World was Old to its old chthonic spirits, whose outrage is what keeps the air "soft, warm, hot"; is what fragments the stanzas into heterogeneity. Intruders here, Europeans are uneasy, never really at home.

> . . . a collector's vagaries metamorphosed into possessions
> I would heap at the door if I could, to interpret
> my lost predilections and repeat my identity.

> Nicky and Judy and Eddy and Robert and Dusty—
> deliver my things from the vandals!

> The Creek jostles its darknesses under the ice.
> Below is a roaring, a grating of angles and edges, a
> slobber, a drowning.

> The boiler-room readies its column of blood in the
> shaken thermometer and sets forth on the torrent.

What have we ever possessed?

I wait for the tomb-robbers.

And that's Ben Belitt, a list poet if ever there was one, in the collection he calls *Possessions*; I've omitted the poem's list of "Egyptian possessions" (as from a tomb). "The Creek" is literal; his house abuts a potential torrent. And "Deliver my things from the vandals": that is a Spell. Recall those spells against rats. (And it's worked so far.)

For a native poetic, to be a poetic at all, must rely on certain continuities: on the List, on the Curse and the Blessing, on the deep tradition of efficacious words. Its power, like the Irish bard's, stems from an authority of naming, and edgy meditations on *Then* and *Now* cannot but draw their strength from an older, less articulate *Then* such as no poem, maybe, can permit itself to take explicit stock of. The deeps of language are nearly inarticulate, what we can say with it today no more an enhancement of what got said in caves than a snapshot improves on the strong bulls of Lascaux. If we understand more than the cave dwellers, it's partly by our partial understanding of them. We say more, therefore; more complicated things, with no need to pretend that our speech carries greater authority. Its strength draws still on the shaman's resources: rhythm and surprise, the unnerving force of naming, the curse, the blessing, the enforced claim on attention. *Then* sleeps, unsleeping, within the force of *Now*, and only triviality can pretend that by its analytic habits magic has at last been superseded.

(1987)

THE BARBER OF KASBEAM:
NABOKOV ON CRUELTY

RICHARD RORTY

IN AN AFTERWORD TO *Lolita*, Vladimir Nabokov wrote a notorious passage, one which is often quoted against him. It reads as follows:

> . . . *Lolita* has no moral in tow. For me a work of fiction exists only in so far as it affords me what I shall bluntly call aesthetic bliss, that is a sense of being somehow, somewhere, connected with other states of being where art (curiosity, tenderness, kindness, ecstasy) is the norm. There are not many such books. All the rest is either topical trash or what some call the Literature of Ideas, which very often is topical trash coming in huge blocks of plaster that are carefully transmitted from age to age until somebody comes along with a hammer and takes a good crack at Balzac, at Gorki, at Mann.[1]

Nabokov's insistent aestheticism has led many people to compare him unfavorably with writers who seem to care more about human solidarity—writers like George Orwell, who said that "every line of serious work" which he had done since 1936 "has been written, directly or indirectly, *against* totalitarianism and *for* democratic Socialism."

Although Nabokov despised Orwell's work, and Orwell, had he read it, might well have despised Nabokov's, we need not choose sides. Both men, unfortunately, tried to make their own talents definatory of "the novel" or "writing" or "literature." But we should eschew definitions, and indeed discussion, of such gawky topics as these. We should not try to specify the aim of fiction, or the point of writing, or the task of the writer.

If we firmly reject such notions, we can begin to reconcile Orwell and Nabokov. We can say that the pursuit of private perfection is a perfectly reasonable aim for some writers—writers like

Plato, Heidegger, Proust, and Nabokov, who share certain talents. Serving human liberty is a perfectly reasonable aim for other writers—people like Dickens, Mill, Dewey, Orwell, Habermas, and Rawls, who share others. There is no point in trying to grade these different pursuits on a single scale by setting up factitious kinds called "literature" or "art" or "the novel"; nor is there any point in trying to synthesize them. There is nothing called "the aim of writing" any more than there is something called "the aim of philosophizing." Both Orwell and Nabokov, unfortunately, got enmeshed in attempts to excommunicate people with talents and interests different from their own. This has obscured a lot of similarities between the two men, resemblances which should not be obscured by philosophical quarrels conducted in terms of shop-worn oppositions like "art vs. morality," or "style vs. substance."

One resemblance was that both Nabokov and Orwell were political liberals. They shared pretty much the same political credo, and the same reactions to the same political events. More important, however, they both met Judith Shklar's criterion of a liberal: somebody who believes that cruelty is the worst thing we do. Cruelty was, I would claim, the topic of the best work of both. Nabokov wrote about cruelty from the inside, helping us see the way in which the private pursuit of aesthetic bliss can produce cruelty. Orwell, for the most part, wrote about cruelty from the outside, from the point of view of the victims, thereby producing what Nabokov called "topical trash"—the kind of book which helps reduce future suffering and serves human liberty. But, at the end of his last book, in his portrait of O'Brien, Orwell does the same thing as Nabokov: he helps us get *inside* cruelty, and thereby helps articulate the dimly felt connection between art and torture.

I cannot, here, say more about Orwell. But I shall offer you a reading of Nabokov which, I hope, may predispose you to accept the sort of reconciliation between the two men which I have been suggesting. I shall try to present him in a way which brings together three of his most characteristic traits: his perversely insistent aestheticism, his fear of being led into cruelty by that aestheticism, and his preoccupation with immortality. This last trait is best exemplified by the epigraph to *Invitation to a Beheading*: "*Comme un fou se croit Dieu, nous nous croyons mortels.*" "We believe ourselves to be mortal, just as a madman believes himself to be God."

I begin with his aestheticism as it appears in his literary criticism. Consider his lecture on Dickens's *Bleak House*. At one point in that lecture he quotes at length from the chapter in which Dickens describes the death of the boy Jo. This is the chapter whose coda is the famous paragraph beginning "Dead, your Majesty! Dead, my lords and gentlemen!" and ending "And dying around us every day." That paragraph is a call to action if anything in Dickens is. But Nabokov tells us that the chapter is "a lesson in style, not in participative emotion."[2]

If Nabokov had said "as well as" instead of "not," nobody would have disagreed. By saying "not" he maintains his stance as someone who is concerned with nothing but "aesthetic bliss," someone who thinks that "the study of the sociological or political impact of literature has to be devised mainly for those who are by temperament or education immune to the aesthetic vibrancy of authentic literature, for those who do not experience the telltale tingle between the shoulder blades" (LL 64). Nabokov has to pretend, implausibly, that Dickens was not, or at least should not have been, interested in the fact that his novels were a more powerful impetus to social reform than the collected works of all the British social theorists of his day.

Nabokov should not have insisted that there is some incompatibility, some antithetical relation, between Housmanian tingles and the kind of participative emotion which moved liberal statesmen, such as his own father, to agitate for the repeal of unjust laws. He should just have said that these are two distinct, non-competitive, goods. Nabokov is quite right when he says "That little shiver behind is quite certainly the highest form of emotion that humanity has attained when evolving pure art and pure science" (LL 64)— for this claim simply spells out the relevant sense of the term "pure." But that claim seems quite compatible with saying that the ability to shudder with shame and indignation at the unnecessary death of a child—a child with whom we have no connection of family, tribe, or class—is the highest form of emotion that humanity has attained while evolving modern social and political institutions.

Nabokov does not try to defend his assumption that social reform does not have the same claim on our attention as pure art and pure science. He gives no reasons for doubting that people as gifted as Dickens have sometimes been able to do quite different things in the same book. It would have been much easier to admit that *Bleak House* aroused participative emotions which helped change the laws of England, and also made Dickens immortal by having been written so as to keep right on producing tingles between the shoulder blades long after the particular horrors of Dickens's century had been replaced by new ones. Yet Nabokov insists over and over again that the latter accomplishment—the effect produced by style as opposed to that produced by participative emotion—is all that matters. He never makes clear what scale of importance he is using, or why we should insist on a *single* scale. It is hardly *evident* that "pure art and pure science" matter more than absence of suffering, or even that there is a point in asking which matters more—as if we could somehow rise above both and adjudicate their claims from a neutral standpoint.

I share Nabokov's suspicion of general ideas when it comes to philosophers' attempts to squeeze our moral sentiments into rules for deciding moral dilemmas. But I would take the lesson of our failure to find such rules to be that we should stop talking in a quasi-metaphysical style about "the task of the writer" or "what ultimately matters" or "the highest emotion," stop working at the level of abstraction populated by such pallid ghosts as "human life," "art," or "morality," and stay at a middle range. We should stick to questions about what works for particular purposes. We should say that Orwell shares some important purposes with Dickens (producing shudders of indignation, arousing revulsion and shame) and Nabokov shares others (producing tingles, aesthetic bliss).

But Nabokov does not want to be reconciled. He wants

Dickens and himself to count as members of an elect from which Orwell—and other objects of his contempt, such as Balzac, Stendhal, Zola, Gorki, Mann, Faulkner, and Malraux—are forever excluded. We get an important clue to his motives from a passage in which he explains why he reads Dickens as he does:

> As is quite clear, the enchanter interests me more than the yarn spinner or the teacher. In the case of Dickens, this attitude seems to me the only way of keeping Dickens alive, above the reformer, above the penny novelette, above the sentimental trash, above the theatrical nonsense. There he shines forever on the heights of which we know the exact elevation, the outlines and the formation, and the mountain trails to get there through the fog. It is in his imagery that he is great [LL 65].

The fog in question is the one which Dickens has described in the opening chapter of *Bleak House*. As Nabokov says, Dickens uses the London fog to revivify a standard trope: the legal miasma which rises from proceedings in Chancery. Nabokov wants us to treat Dickens's attacks on the evil of the Chancery system—and more generally his portrayal of conflicts between what Nabokov, putting the words in shudder quotes, calls "good" and "evil"—as merely "the skeleton" of *Bleak House*. He congratulates Dickens on being "too much of an artist" to make this skeleton "obstrusive or obvious." Writers without Dickens's ability, the people who write "topical trash," do not know how to put flesh on the "moral" skeleton of their work. So, to mix the two metaphors, heaps of such piled up skeletons—the novels of Orwell and Mann, for example—form the fog-bound, boggy foothills of literature. For lack of precise imagery, writers who can give lessons in participative emotion but not in style fail to achieve immortality.

Two things should be noticed about the passage I have just quoted. The first is that Nabokov is writing about Dickens not for the sake of the students in his class, nor for the sake of the educated public, but *solely* for Dickens's sake. He wants to do a favor for one of his few peers. He wants him to have the immortality he deserves. When he says, for example, that Edmund Wilson's treatment of Dickens in *The Wound and the Bow* is "brilliant" but that the "sociological side" of Dickens is "neither interesting nor important," he is saying that literary criticism of the sort which Wilson did brilliantly creates the same kind of particularly thick fog as was created by particularly brilliant members of the Chancery Bar. By pointing out the mountain peak above the fog, and by tracing the trails that reach it, he is rescuing Dickens from people like Wilson, rescuing him from the creeping miasma of historical time and mortal chance.

The second thing to notice is that Nabokov's concern with Dickens's immortality was a corollary of his own intense, lifelong preoccupation with the question of whether he might survive death, and thereby meet his parents in another world. Such survival, and such meetings, suddenly appear, in the last lines of *Invitation to a Beheading*, as the point of that novel. They are also the topic of a canto of John Shade's poem "Pale Fire," and of the magnificent closing sentences of *Lolita*:

> And do not pity C.Q. (Clare Quilty). One had to choose between him and H.H. (Humbert Humbert), and one wanted H.H. to exist at least a couple of months longer, so as to have him make you live in the minds of later generations. I am thinking of aurochs and angels, the secret of durable pigments, prophetic sonnets, the refuge of art. And this is the only immortality you and I may share, my Lolita.

In this latter passage, as in many others, Nabokov is talking about immortality in the "literary" sense—the sense in which one is immortal if one's books will be read forever. But elsewhere, especially in his autobiography, he talks about immortality in the ordinary theological and metaphysical sense—the chance of somehow surviving death, and of thus being able to meet dead loved ones in a world beyond time.[3] He makes no bones about his own fear of death:

> Over and over again, my mind has made colossal efforts to distinguish the faintest of personal glimmers in the impersonal darkness on both sides of my life. That this darkness is caused merely by the

walls of time separating me from the free world of timelessness is a belief I gladly share with the most gaudily painted savage.[4]

Over and over again, Nabokov tried to tie this highly unfashionable concern for metaphysical immortality together with the more respectable notion of literary immortality. He wanted to see some connection between creating tingles, creating aesthetic bliss, being an artist in the sense in which he and Joyce and Dickens were artists and Orwell and Mann were not, and freeing oneself from time, entering another state of being. He is sure that there is a connection between the immortality of the work and of the person who creates the work—between aesthetics and metaphysics, to put it crudely. But, unsurprisingly, he is never able to say what it is.

The best example of this gallant, splendid, and foredoomed attempt is one of Nabokov's few attempts to work in the uncongenial medium of general ideas. This is his essay called "The Art of Literature and Common Sense," in which he offers the same generalized protest against general ideas as we find in Heidegger (in such essays as "On the Essence of Truth"). Heidegger and Nabokov agree that common sense is a self-deceptive apologia for thoughtlessness and vulgarity. They offer the same defense of the unique and idiosyncratic irony. They both reject the Platonist and democratic claim that one should only have beliefs which can be defended on the basis of widely shared premises. The theme of Nabokov's essay is what he calls "the supremacy of the detail over the general" (LL 373). His thesis is that "the capacity to wonder at trifles—no matter the imminent peril—these asides of the spirit, these footnotes in the volume of life are the highest forms of consciousness, and it is this childishly speculative state of mind, so different from common sense and its logic, that we know the world to be good" (LL 374).

Here we are not told merely, and tautologically, that "pure art and pure science" culminate in such tingling trifles. We are told that these tingles are "the highest forms of consciousness." That claim is ambiguous between a moral and a metaphysical interpretation. It can mean that tingles are what is most worth striving for, or it can mean the sort of thing Plato meant, that this form of consciousness is higher in that it gets us in touch with the non-temporal, that it gets us out of the flux and into a realm beyond time and chance. If one took the claim only in its moral sense, then one could plausibly reply that this was certainly what it behooved people like Nabokov to strive for, but that other people with other gifts—people whose brains are not wired up to produce tingles, but who are, for example, good at producing shudders—might reasonably strive for their own form of perfection. But Nabokov wanted to absolutize the moral claim by backing it up with the metaphysical claim. He wanted to say that idiosyncratic imagery, of the sort he was good at, rather than the kind of generalizing ideas Plato was good at, is what opens the gates of immortality. Art, rather than mathematics, breaks through the walls of time into a world beyond contingency.

The trouble with the essay is, once again, that Nabokov runs together literary with personal immortality. If only the former is at stake, then, indeed, Plato was wrong and Nabokov, Heidegger, and Derrida are right. If you want to be remembered by future generations, go in for poetry rather than for mathematics. If you want your books to be read rather than respectfully shrouded in tooled leather, you should try to produce tingles rather than truth. What we call common sense—the body of widely-accepted truths—is, just as Heidegger and Nabokov thought, a collection of dead metaphors. Truths are the skeletons which remain after the capacity to arouse the senses—to cause tingles—has been rubbed off by familiarity and long usage. After scales are rubbed off a butterfly's wing, you have transparency, but not beauty—formal structure without sensuous content. Once the freshness wears off the metaphor, you have plain, literal, transparent language—the sort of language which is ascribed not to any particular person but to "common sense" or "reason" or "intuition," ideas so clear and distinct you can look right through them. So if, like Euclid's or Newton's or J. S. Mill's, your metaphors are socially useful and become literalized, you will be honored in the abstract and forgotten in the particular. You will have become a name, but ceased to be a person. But if, like Catullus, Baudelaire, Derrida, and Nabokov, your works (only, or also) produce tingles, you have a chance of surviving as more than a name. You might be, like Landor and Donne, one of the people whom some future Yeats will hope to dine with, at journey's end.

However, although all this is quite true, it has no bearing on the suggestion that literary immortality is connected with personal immortality—the claim that you will actually be out there, beyond the walls of time, waiting for dinner guests. As Kant pointed out, and as Nabokov ruefully admitted (SM 14), nothing *could* lend plausibility to that claim. Waiting, like everything else one can imagine doing, takes time. But even if we dismiss the metaphysical claim we still need to take seriously a further claim Nabokov makes—that it is in "this childishly speculative state of mind" that "we know the world to be good."

Nabokov thinks that "goodness" is something irrationally concrete, something to be captured by imagination rather than intellect. He inverts Plato's divided line so that *eikasia*, rather than *nous*, becomes the faculty of moral knowledge. He says:

> From the commonsensical point of view the "goodness," say, of some food is just as abstract as its "badness," both being qualities that cannot be perceived by the sane judgment as tangible and complete objects. But when we perform the necessary mental twist which is like learning to swim or to make a ball break, we realize that "goodness" is something round and creamy, and beautifully flushed, something in a clean apron with warm bare arms that have nursed and comforted us . . . [LL 375].

In the same essay he brings together this idea of the good as something "real and concrete" with his sense of solidarity with a "few thousand" others who shared his gifts:

> . . . the irrational belief in the goodness of man . . . becomes something much more than the wobbly basis of idealistic philosophies. It becomes a solid and iridescent truth. This means that goodness becomes a central and tangible part of one's world, which world at

first sight seems hard to identify with the modern one of newspaper editors and other bright pessimists, who tell you that it is, mildly speaking, illogical to applaud the supremacy of good at a time when something called the police state, or communism, is trying to turn the globe into five million square miles of terror, stupidity, and barbed wire. . . . But within the emphatically and unshakably illogical world which I am advertising as a home for the spirit, wars are unreal not because they are conveniently remote in physical space . . . . but because I cannot imagine (and this is saying a good deal) such circumstances as might impinge upon the lovely and lovable world which quietly persists, whereas I can very well imagine that my fellow dreamers, thousands of whom roam the earth, keep to these same irrational and divine standards during the darkest and most dazzling hours of physical danger, pain, dust, death [LL 373].

I interpret these two passages as making an important psychological point: that the only thing which can let a human being combine altruism and joy, the only thing that makes either heroic action or splendid speech possible, is some very specific chain of associations with some highly idiosyncratic memories. Freud made the same point, and Freud was the one man Nabokov resented in the same obsessive and intense way that Heidegger resented Nietzsche—the resentment of a precursor who may already have written all one's best lines. This psychological thesis binds Hume, Freud, and Nabokov, and sets them over against Plato and Kant. But it is not a metaphysical claim about the "nature" of "goodness," nor an epistemological claim about our "knowledge" of goodness. Being impelled or inspired by an image is not the same as knowing a world. We do not need to postulate a world beyond time which is the home of such images in order to account for their occurrence, or for their effects on conduct.

Yet only if he could somehow have squeezed some metaphysics out of his two soundly anti-Platonic claims—the one about the nature of literary immortality and the other about the nature of moral motivation—would Nabokov have been able to hook up the utilization of his own gifts with the nature of things. Only then could he see his special gifts as putting him in an epistemologically privileged position, in a position to be aware of the secret that, as gaudily painted savages believe and as Cincinnatus C. eventually realized, time and causality are merely a vulgar hoax. Only if he can make such a hook-up will he be able to defend his claim that Dickens's interest in social reform was merely a great artist's foibles, and his suggestion that Orwell deserves no thanks for his services to human liberty.

The collection of general ideas which Nabokov assembled in the hope of convincing himself that time and causality were hoaxes is an odd, inconsistent mixture of Platonic atemporalism and anti-Platonic sensualism. It is an attempt to combine the comforts of old-fashioned metaphysics with the up-to-date antimetaphysical polemic common to Bergson and Heidegger. Like the systems of general ideas which ironist theorists construct in order to attack the very idea of a general idea, it is what Stanley Fish calls a "self-consuming artifact." Still, such fragile and unbalanced devices, with their artful combination of dogma and irony, have the same iridescence as John Shade's poem, "Pale Fire." Like that poem, Nabokov's system is the shadow of waxwing, just before it smashes itself against the walls of time.

Why did Nabokov want such a device? Why did he stick his neck out that way? I think there were two reasons, neither of which had anything to do with fear of death. The first, and most important, was an oversize sense of pity. His eccentrically large capacity for joy, his idiosyncratic ability to experience bliss so great as to seem incommensurable with the existence of suffering and cruelty, made him unable to tolerate the reality of suffering. Nabakov's capacity to pity others was as great as Proust's capacity to pity himself — a capacity which Proust was, amazingly, able to harness to his attempt at self-creation. Bliss began early for Nabokov, and he had no occasion for self-pity and no need for self-creation. The difference between Proust's novel and Nabokov's novels is the difference between a *Bildungsroman* and a crescendo of ever more fervent pledges of the same childhood faith. Nabokov seems never to have suffered a loss for which he blamed himself, never to have despised, distrusted, or doubted himself. He did not *need* to struggle for autonomy, to forge a conscience in the smithy of his soul, to seek a self-made vocabulary. He was a hero to both his parents and a hero to himself—a very lucky man. He would have been merely a self-satisfied bore if it were not that his brain happened to be wired up so as to make him able continually to surprise and delight himself by arranging words into iridescent patterns.

But the other side of this capacity for bliss was an inability to put up with the thought of intense pain. The intensity of his pity brought him to the novel which has aroused most protest among his admirers: *Bend Sinister*. In this novel, the eight-year-old son of Adam Krug is tortured to death by madmen because his folder has been misfiled by the inexperienced bureaucrats of a revolutionary government. Nabokov does not attempt to portray Krug's pain. More than that, he refuses to countenance the reality of a pain that great. So, as in *Invitation to a Beheading*, he translates the hero to another "realm of being." In the earlier novel, Cincinnatus rises as soon as his head has been chopped off, watches the scaffold and spectators dissolve, and then "makes his way in that direction where, to judge by the voices, stood beings akin to him." In *Bend Sinister*, Nabokov saves Krug from the realization of what has happened by what he calls "the intervention of an anthropomorphic deity impersonated by me."[5] Nabokov says he "felt a pang of pity for Adam and slid towards him along an inclined beam of pale light—causing instantaneous madness, but at least saving him from the senseless agony of his logical fate" (pp. 193–91). Krug's author steps through "a rent in his [Krug's] world leading to another world of tenderness, brightness, and beauty" (p. 8). Nabokov's toying with general ideas about immortality, with the idea that there was a rent in his and our worlds like that in Krug's, was a further expression of the same pity which saved Cincinnatus and Krug.

But there is a second reason which needs to he taken into account. This is that Nabokov seems never to have allowed himself social hope. He was the son of a famous liberal statesman who was

assassinated when his son was twenty-two. His father's circle—
which included, for example, H. G. Wells, whom Nabokov met at
his father's table—had had no time for metaphysics because their
hopes were centered on future generations. They exemplified the
substitution of hope for future generations for hope of personal
immortality. Nabokov seems to have had no trace of the former
hope. Perhaps he had it once, and abandoned it as a result of his
father's murder. Perhaps he never had it, having recognized early on
that he and his father had antithetical, if equally great, gifts, and that
he would betray himself by attempting even the slightest imitation
of someone he loved so fiercely. Whatever the reason, he always
repudiated any interest in political movements. In *The Gift,* Fyodor
walks down the streets of Berlin in the 1920s and notices that "three
kinds of flags were sticking out of the house windows: black-yel-
low-red, black-white-red, and plain red: each now meant something, and funniest of all, this something was able to excite pride or
hatred in someone." Noticing the flags induces a meditation on
Soviet Russia, which ends when Fyodor thinks

> Oh, let everything pass and be forgotten—and again in two
> hundred years' time an ambitious failure will vent his frustration
> on the simpletons dreaming of a good life (that is if there does
> not come *my* kingdom, where everyone keeps to himself and
> there is no equality and no authorities—but if you don't want it,
> I don't insist and don't care).[6]

Nabokov had no idea—who does?—about how to bring about
a state with no equality and no authorities, and he gave up on the
modern liberal idea of working for a future in which cruelty would
no longer be institutionalized. In this respect, he was a throwback
to antiquity, a period in which such social hope was so obviously
unrealistic as to be of little interest to the intellectuals. His other-
worldly metaphysics are what one might imagine being written by
a contemporary of Plato, writing in partial imitation of, and partial
reaction against, the *Phaedo*—a contemporary who did not share
Plato's need for a world in which he could not feel shame, but did
need a world in which he would not have to feel pity.

If, however, Nabokov's career as a novelist had climaxed with the creation of Fyodor Godunov-Cherdyntsev, Cincinnatus C., and Adam Krug, we should not be reading him as often or as much we do. The characters I just mentioned are known because they were created by the author of two others—Humbert Humbert and Charles Kinbote. These two are the central figures of Nabokov's books about cruelty—not the "beastly farce" common to Lenin, Hitler, Gradus, and Paduk, but the special sort of cruelty of which those who are capable of bliss are also capable. These books are reflections on the possibility that there can be sensitive killers, cruel aesthetes, pitiless poets—masters of imagery who are content to turn the lives of other human beings into images on a screen, while simply not noticing that these other people are suffering. Nabokov's uneasiness at the unstable philosophical compromise which he had worked out, and what must have been at least occasional doubts about his refusal to think in terms of human solidarity, led him to write his best books about the possibility that he was mistaken. Like the honest man he was, Nabokov wrote his best books to explore the possibility that his harshest critics might, after all, be right.

What his critics were suggesting was that Nabokov was really Harold Skimpole. Skimpole, the charming aesthete in *Bleak House*, brings about Jo's death—an action beautifully described by Nabokov as "the false child betraying the real one" (LL 91). Skimpole claims the privileges of the child and of the poet. He views everyone else's life as poetry, no matter how much they suffer.[7] Skimpole sees his having taken five pounds to betray Jo's whereabouts to Tulkinghorn's agent as an amusing concatenation of circumstances,[8] a pleasant little poem, the sort of thing John Shade calls "some kind of link-and-bobolink, some kind of correlated pattern in the game." By claiming not to grasp concepts like "money" and "responsibility," Skimpole tries to exonerate himself from living off the charity and the suffering of others.

It is clear from his autobiography that the only thing which could really get Nabokov down was the fear of being, or having been, cruel. More specifically, what he dreaded was simply not having noticed the suffering of someone with whom one had been in contact (SM 86–87). It hurt Nabokov horribly to remember the pain he might unthinkingly have caused to a schoolmate, or a governess. It must have terrified him to think that he might be Skimpole after all. The intensity of his fear of cruelty seems to me to show that we should read *Pale Fire* as about two of Nabokov's own personae. On the one side there is John Shade, who combines Nabokov's private virtues with a Jarndyce-like patience for his monstrous friend, the false child Kinbote. On the other is Kinbote himself, whose central characteristic is his inability to notice the suffering of anyone else, especially Shade's own, *but who is a much better writer than Shade himself.*

Nabokov's greatest creations are obsessives—Kinbote, Humbert Humbert, and Van Veen—who, though they write as well as their creator at his best, are people whom Nabokov himself loathes— loathes as much as Dickens loathed Skimpole. Humbert is, as Nabokov said, "a vain and cruel wretch who manages to appear "touching" (SM 94)—manages it because he can write as well as Nabokov can. Like Kinbote, Humbert is exquisitely sensitive to everything which affects or provides expression for his own obsession, and entirely incurious about anything that effects anyone else's. These characters dramatize, as it has never before been dramatized, the particular form of cruelty which Nabokov worried most about—incuriosity.

Before giving examples from the novels of this sort of incuriosity, let me offer another sort of evidence to back up the claim I have just made. Remember Nabokov's rapid definition of the term "art" in the passage about "aesthetic bliss" I cited at the outset. Writing what he knew would be the most discussed passage of what he knew would become his most widely-read manifesto, the "Afterword" to *Lolita*, he parenthetically identifies art with the compresence of "curiosity, tenderness, kindness, and ecstasy." Notice that "curiosity" comes first.

Nabokov is, I think, trying to jam an ad hoc and implausible moral philosophy into this parenthesis, just as he is trying to jam metaphysical immortality into the phrase "other states of being" which he uses to define "aesthetic bliss." If curiosity and tenderness are the marks of the artist, if both are inseparable from ecstasy—so that where they are absent no bliss is possible—then there is no distinction between the aesthetic and the moral. The dilemma of the liberal aesthete is resolved. All that is required to act well is to do what artists are good at—noticing things that most other people do not notice, being curious about what others take for granted, seeing the momentary iridescence and not just the underlying formal structure. The curious, sensitive artist will be the paradigm of morality, because he is the only one who always notices everything.

This view is, once again, an inverted Platonism: Plato was right that to know the good is to do it, but he gave exactly the wrong reason. Plato thought that "knowing the good" was a matter of grasping a general idea, but actually knowing the good is just sensing what matters to other people, what their image of the good is—noticing whether they think of it as something round and creamy and flushed, or perhaps as something prism-shaped, jewel-like, and glistening. The tender, curious artist would be the one who, like Shade and unlike Skimpole or Kinbote, has time for other people's fantasies, not just his own. He would be a non-obsessed poet, but nonetheless one whose poems could produce ecstasy.

But Nabokov knew quite well that ecstasy and tenderness are not only separable, but tend to preclude each other—that most non-obsessed poets are, like Shade, second-rate. This is the "moral" knowledge that his novels help us acquire, and to which his aestheticist rhetoric is irrelevant. He knows quite well that the pursuit of autonomy is at odds with feelings of solidarity. His parenthetical moral philosophy would be sound only if it were true that, as Humbert says, "poets never kill." But, of course, Humbert does kill—and, like Kinbote, Humbert is exactly as good a writer, exactly as much of an artist, capable of creating exactly as much iridescent ecstasy, as Nabokov himself. Nabokov would like the four characteristics which make up art to be inseparable, but he has to face up to the unpleasant fact that writers can obtain and produce ecstasy while failing to notice suffering, while being incurious about the people whose lives provide their material. He would like to see all the evil in the world—all the failures in tenderness and kindness—as produced by non-poets, by generalizing, incurious vulgarians like Paduk and Gradus. But he knows that this is not the case. Nabokov would desperately like artistic gifts to be sufficient for moral virtue, but he knows that there is no connection between the contingent and selective curiosity of the autonomous artist and his father's political project—the creation of a world in which tenderness and kindness are the human norm. So he creates characters who are both ecstatic and cruel, noticing and heartless, poets who are only selectively curious, obsessives who are as sensitive as they are callous. What he fears most is that one cannot have it both ways—that there is no synthesis of ecstasy and kindness.

The two novels of his acme spell out this fear. The remarkable thing about both novels is the sheer originality of the two central characters—Humbert and Kinbote. No one before had thought of asking what it would be like to be a Skimpole who was also a genius—one who did not simply toss the word "poetry" about but who actually knew what poetry was. This particular sort of genius-monster—the monster of incuriosity—is Nabokov's contribution to our knowledge of human possibilities. I suspect that only someone who feared that he was executing a partial self-portrait could have made that particular contribution.

Let me offer some further evidence for this interpretation of the two novels by citing another remark from the "Afterword" to *Lolita*. Nabokov is listing "the nerves of the novel . . . the secret points, the subliminal co-ordinates by means of which the book is plotted" (p. 315). Among these secret points, he tells us, is "the barber of Kasbeam (who cost me a month of work)." This barber appears in only one sentence, viz.:

> In Kasbeam a very old barber gave me a very mediocre haircut: he babbled of a baseball-playing son of his, and, at every explodent, spat into my neck, and every now and then wiped his glasses on my sheet-wrap, or interrupted his tremulous scissor work to produce

faded newspaper clippings, and so inattentive was I that it came as a
shock to realize as he pointed to an easelled photograph among the
ancient gray lotions, that the moustached young ball player had
been dead for the last thirty years [p. 211].

This sentence epitomizes Humbert's lack of curiosity—his
inability to notice anything which is irrelevant to his own obsession—and his consequent inability to attain a state of being in which
"art," as Nabokov has defined it, is the norm. This failure parallels a
failure described earlier in the book, one which occurs when
Humbert transcribes from memory the letter in which Charlotte
proposes marriage to him, and adds that he has left out at least half
of it, including "a lyrical passage which I more or less skipped at the
time concerning Lolita's brother who died at two when she was
four, and how much I would have liked him" (p. 68).

This is one of only two passages in the book in which Lolita's
dead brother is referred to. The other is one in which Humbert
complains that Charlotte rarely talks about her daughter—the only
subject of interest to him—and in particular that she refers to the
dead boy more frequently than to the living girl (p. 80). Humbert
mourns that Lolita herself never referred to her pre-Humbertian
existence in Humbert's presence. But he did once overhear her
talking to a girlfriend, and what she said was: "You know what's so
dreadful about dying is that you are completely on your own" (p.
282). This leads Humbert to reflect that "I simply did not know a
thing about my darling's mind," and that "quite possibly, behind
the awful juvenile clichés, there was in her a garden and a twilight,
and a palace gate—dim and adorable regions which happened to
be lucidly and absolutely forbidden to me, in my polluted rags and
miserable convulsions."

Continuing this meditation on possibilities which had not previously occurred to him, Humbert remembers an occasion on
which Lolita may have realized that another of her girlfriends had
"such a wonderful fat pink dad and a small chubby brother, and a
brand-new baby sister, and a home, and two grinning dogs, and
Lolita had nothing" (p. 285). It is left to the reader to make the

connection—to put together Lolita's remark about death with the fact that she once had a small chubby brother who died. This, and the further fact that Humbert does not make the connection himself, is exactly the sort of thing Nabokov expects his ideal readers— the people whom he calls "a lot of little Nabokovs"—to notice. But, ruefully and contemptuously aware that most of his readers will fall short, he tells us in his "Afterword" what we have missed.

Consider the impact of being told this on the reader who only then remembers that the death of a child is Nabokov's standard example of ultimate pain—the occasion for John Shade's poem "Pale Fire" as well as the central event in *Bend Sinister*. It dawns on this reader that he himself was just as inattentive to that month-long sentence, and to that dead moustached son, as Nabokov suspected he had been. The reader, suddenly revealed to himself as, if not hypocritical, at least cruelly incurious, recognizes his *semblable*, his brother, in Humbert and Kinbote. Suddenly *Lolita* does "have a moral in tow." But the moral is not to keep one's hands off little girls but to notice what one is doing, and in particular to notice what people are saying. For it might turn out, it very often does turn out, that people are trying to tell you that they are suffering. Just insofar as one is preoccupied with building up to one's private kind of sexual bliss, like Humbert, or one's private aesthetic bliss, like the reader of *Lolita* who missed that sentence about the barber the first time around, people are likely to suffer still more.

Turning from *Lolita* to *Pale Fire*, we can see Shade as having been given all of Nabokov's own tenderness and kindness and curiosity, but Kinbote as getting all the ecstasy. Shade's poem about the death of his daughter is not nearly as good a poem as *Pale Fire* is a novel. That is because the rest of the novel, Kinbote's commentary, gives us something Shade could not—it surrounds the ordinary suffering of an elderly mortal man with glimpses of Zembla, glimpses of what Humbert Humbert called "a paradise whose skies were the color of hell-flame." Kinbote is a marvel of self-involvement, a man who knows himself to be (except in his dreams) utter-ly heartless, but he is much more imaginative than Shade. Psychotics are, after all, a lot more imaginative than the rest of us. In Humbert and Kinbote Nabokov managed to create two sociopaths who, unlike most real-life psychotics, managed to write their own case histories, and to do so knowing exactly how those histories would sound to normal ears.

Kinbote is very curious indeed about anything which at all affects his own desires for boys or for glory. He is bored and annoyed by everything else. He is enraged that Shade has dared to write about his own daughter's death and the joy of his own marriage rather than about "the glory of Zembla," about Kinbote's merry minions and his miserable wife. Yet Shade's poem without Kinbote's commentary would be merely wistful. It is the counterpoint between the poem and the commentary which makes the poem itself memorable. Shade's tenderness and kindness are made visible by Kinbote's remorseless pursuit of the sort of ecstasy which necessarily excludes attention to other people. We are more likely to notice the joys or the sufferings of one person if our attention is directed to it by the surprising indifference of another person. Just as the misery of the peasantry is made visible by the conspicuous consumption of the nobles, or the hovels of the blacks by the swimming pools of the whites, so the death of Shade's daughter is made more vivid by Kinbote's dismissal of it than in Shade's own remembrance. Hegel's point was sound: the thesis will escape our notice, after a bit of time has passed, unless it catches the reflection, the pale fire, of the brand-new, shiny antithesis.

To put the point in some of Nabokov's favorite terms of praise, Kinbote is crueler, cooler, and dryer—and thus a better writer—than Shade. Shade's verse, by his own confession, is written below freezing-point. In his poem he remarks that his own reputation, among literary critics, is always "one oozy footstep" behind Robert Frost's. Kinbote for once glosses a line with due respect to its author's interests, and speaks for Nabokov, when he says, "In the temperature of charts of poetry high is low, and low high, so that the degree at which perfect crystallization occurs is above that of tepid facility" (*Pale Fire*, p. 136). Kinbote understands what Shade is getting at here because, as befits two aspects of a single creator, Shade and Kinbote have a lot in common. Shade realizes this. Cruel as he may be, Kinbote is not vulgar enough to be physically brutal, and to Shade that matters a great deal (p. 145). Shade's knowledge that "without . . . Pride, Lust and Sloth, poetry might never have been born" (p. 150) lets him be indulgent about Kinbote's delusions, as he would not have been indulgent with anyone who brought about physical harm. He treats Kinbote as a fellow-artist in whom, as in Swift and Baudelaire, the mind sickened before the body collapsed (p. 111). The two men share the same view of tyrants and fools—of people like Monsieur Pierre, Gradus, and Paduk, whose brutality they take to stem from their underlying vulgarity. This vulgarity consists in being obsessed with general ideas rather than with particular butterflies, words, or people.

But although Kinbote is, in a general way, aware of the danger of general ideas, he himself has some very bad ones, whereas Shade really does manage to forswear them all. One of Kinbote's worst ideas is aestheticism, the belief that there is something called "literary technique" or "poetic gift": a practical ability which floats free of the contingencies of an individual poet's life. This is why what he has to do for immortality is to find a good poet, tell the poet all about himself, and then wait to be glorified in imperishable verse. He expects Shade to "merge the glory of Zembla with the glory of his verse" (p. 144), because, as Shade tells him, he thinks that "One can harness words like performing fleas and make them drive other fleas" (p. 144). This idea that somehow language can be separated from authors, that literary technique is a godlike power operating independently of mortal contingencies, and in particular from the author's contingent notion of what goodness is, is the root of "aestheticism" in the bad sense of the term, the sense in which the aesthetic is a matter of form and language rather than of content and life. In this sense of the term, Nabokov the novelist had no interest in being an aesthete, even if Nabokov the theorist could think of no better account of his own practice.

Nabokov has often been read as an aesthete in this sense, and in particular as someone whose work stems from, and illustrates, the Barthian view that language works all by itself.[9] Nabokov the theorist and generalizer encourages such a reading, but that reading ignores the point which I take to be illustrated by Nabokov's best practice: the point that only what is relevant to our sense of what we should do with ourselves or for others is aesthetically useful.

One can uphold this point while agreeing with Barthes and his fellow textualists that the point of novels or plays or poems is not to represent human emotions or situations "correctly." Literary art, the non-standard, non-predictable, use of words, cannot be gauged in terms of accuracy of representation because such accuracy is a matter of conformity to convention, and the point of writing well is precisely to break the crust of convention. But the fact that literary merit is not a matter of reinforcing a widely-used final vocabulary, not a matter of success in telling us what we have always known but could not express satisfactorily, should not obscure the fact that literary language is, and always will be, parasitic on ordinary language, and in particular on ordinary moral language. Further, literary interest will always be parasitic on moral interest. In particular, you cannot create a character without thereby making a suggestion about how your reader should act.

I can sum up my reading of Nabokov by saying that he needed to defend himself against the charge of infidelity to his father's project by some general ideas about the function of "the writer," views which connect this function both with his own special gifts and with his own special fear of death. This led him to create a private mythology about a special elite—artists who were good at imagery, who never killed, whose lives were a synthesis of tenderness and ecstasy, who were candidates for literal as well as literary immortality, and who, unlike his father, placed no faith in general ideas about general measures for the general welfare. This was the mythology in which he fruitlessly attempted to enfold Dickens and upon which he relied whenever he was asked, or asked himself, what he had done for the relief of human suffering. But Nabokov also knew perfectly well that his gifts, and artistic gifts generally, neither had any special connection with pity and kindness nor were able to "create worlds." He knew as well as John Shade did that all one can do with such gifts is to sort out one's relations to this world—the world in which ugly and ungifted children like Shade's daughter and the boy Jo are humiliated and die. Nabokov's best novels are the ones which exhibit his inability to believe his own general ideas.

(1988)

NOTES

1. Vladimir Nabokov, *Lolita* (Harmondsworth: Penguin, 1980). p. 313. References to this book will henceforth he parenthetical, to page numbers in this edition..

2. Vladimir Nabokov, *Lectures on Literature*, ed. Fredson Bowers (New York: Harcourt Brace Jovanovitch, 1980), p. 94. This book will henceforth be cited parenthetically as "LL."

3. Vladimir Nabokov, *Speak, Memory: An Autobiography Revisited* (New York: Pyramid Books, 1968), pp. 14, 37, 57, 87, 103. Henceforth this book will be cited parenthetically as "SM".

4. Ibid., p.14.

5. Vladimir Nabokov, *Bend Sinister* (Harmondsworth: Penguin, 1974), p. 11. Cited parenthetically below by page number.

6. Vladimir Nabokov, *The Gift* (Harmondsworth: Penguin, 1980), p. 370.

7. Charles Dickens, *Bleak House* (New York: Signet Books, 1964), pp. 445, 529.

8. See Nabokov's discussion of this passage at LL, p. 90

9. David Rampton and Ellen Pifer both begin their excellent revisionist books on Nabokov by citing, and deploring, a lot of such readings, and by emphasizing the "moral" side of Nabokov. I have learned a great deal from both of these books, and in particular from Rampton's discussion of *The Gift*.

Collective Violence and Sacrifice in Shakespeare's *Julius Caesar*

René Girard

THE THEATER deals with human conflict. Curiously, dramatic criticism discusses the subject very little. Can we automatically assume that Shakespeare shares the commonsense view according to which conflict is based on differences? Can we assume that tragic conflict is due to the different opinions or values of the various protagonists? This is never true in Shakespeare. Of two persons who do not get along, we say: *they have their differences.* In Shakespeare the reverse is true: the characters disagree because they agree too much.

Let me explain this paradox. Why does Brutus hate Caesar? Most people will answer that they stand on opposite sides in a meaningful political struggle. This is true in the sense that Brutus is a sincere Republican and that Caesar's popularity makes him a real threat to the Republic, but the reason for Brutus' hatred of Caesar lies elsewhere.

To understand this hatred we must start from its opposite, which is the love of Brutus for Caesar. Yes, Brutus loves Caesar dearly. He says so and we can believe him; Brutus never lies.

To Brutus, Caesar is what we call today a role model and much more; he is an incomparable guide, an unsurpassable teacher. To a Roman with political ambition—and Brutus' ambition is great, being patterned on Caesar's—Caesar is the unbeatable champion and therefore an insurmountable obstacle. No one can hope to equal him and become another Caesar, and this is what Brutus really wants to be. Far from excluding hatred, Brutus' love for Caesar necessarily leads to it. Caesar is Brutus' rival because he is his model, and vice versa. The more Brutus loves Caesar, the more he hates him, and vice versa. This ambivalence must be defined not in Freudian but in mimetic terms.

I call the desire of Brutus mimetic or mediated desire. Everything Brutus wants to have and to be, he owes to Caesar; far from having differences with Caesar, he has none, and that is why he hates him. He is like a lover who sees the woman he loves in the arms of another man. The woman here is Rome herself. And Brutus loves that woman because Caesar loves her. My erotic comparison is not psychoanalytical; it is inspired by Shakespeare's comedies, which are as full of mimetic desire as the tragedies.

Mimetic desire is the mutual borrowing of desire by two friends who become antagonists as a result. When mimetic rivalry becomes intense, tragic conflict results. Intense conflict and intense friendship are almost identical in Shakespeare. This paradox is a source of linguistic effects that should not be dismissed as pure rhetoric. They are highly meaningful. *Beloved enemy* is no rhetorical expression; it is exactly what Caesar is to Brutus.

When mimetic rivalry escalates beyond a certain point, the rivals engage in endless conflicts which undifferentiate them more and more; they all become *doubles* of one another. During the civil war, Brutus sounds increasingly authoritarian and majestic, just like Caesar. In order to be Caesar, Brutus acts more and more like Caesar. After the murder, in his speech to the Romans, Brutus imitates the terse prose style of Caesar. The shout that rises from the crowd, "Let him be Caesar," is enormously meaningful. Sincere Republican though he is, Brutus unconsciously turns into a second Caesar, and this must be interpreted less in terms of individual psychology than as an effect of the worsening mimetic crisis. Caesar is a threat and, in order to restore the Republic, he must be eliminated, but whoever eliminates him, *ipso facto*, becomes another Caesar, which is what Brutus secretly desires, anyway, and so do the people themselves. The destruction of the Republic is this very process; no single man is responsible for it; everybody is.

The political genius of Rome is the ability of its Republican institutions to accommodate the kind of rivalry that exists between Brutus and Caesar. This is true but only up to a point. The Republic is a *cursus honorum*, and as long as rival ambitions keep each other in check, liberty survives. Rival ambitions can become so intense, however, that they no longer tolerate one another. Instead of competing within the limits of the law, the rival leaders turn violent and treat each other as enemies. They all accuse each other of destroying Republican institutions and this false excuse quickly becomes the truth of the situation. All of them together are destroying the Republic.

We cannot say that these leaders have their differences; they all want the same thing; they all copy each other; they all behave in the same way; what Shakespeare portrays is no conflict of differences, but a plague of undifferentiation.

The very first lines of the play suggest that the populace itself partakes of this leveling process. The common people show up on the Forum without the insignia of their profession, reflecting the undifferentiation at the top. The Roman Republic is unraveling from top to bottom:

> Hence! home, you idle creatures, get you home!
> Is this a holiday? What! know you not,
> Being mechanical, you ought not to walk
> Upon a labouring day without the sign
> Of your profession? (I.i.1–5)

These Romans are not soldiers but their regular organization resembles the military, and their departure from tradition recalls the confusion of ranks in the Greek army, such as Ulysses describes in *Troilus and Cressida*, the "choking" or "neglection" of Degree. The word Degree means the differential principle thanks to which the cultural and social order is what it is. In the eyes of Shakespeare, the end of the Roman Republic is an historical example of such a crisis.

I think that Shakespeare conceives that crisis exactly as all traditional societies do; his genius does not contradict and yet transcends traditional wisdom. The reason why the mimetic crisis exacerbates more and more is the peculiar logic that it obeys, the logic abundantly exemplified in *Julius Caesar*, the logic of mimetic rivalry and mimetic contagion. The more mimetic desire there is, the more it generates, the more attractive it becomes as a mimetic model.

A conspiracy is a mimetic association of murderers; it comes into being at an advanced but not yet the most advanced stage of a mimetic crisis. Shakespeare dedicates his first two acts to the genesis of the conspiracy against Caesar, and he treats the subject in full conformity with the logic of mimetic desire.

The instigator of the conspiracy is Cassius and his maneuvers are dramatized at length. Once the conspiracy has become a reality, Brutus accepts leading it, but its real father is Cassius, who is the dominant figure at the beginning. Cassius plays the same role as Pandarus, the erotic go-between, at the beginning of *Troilus and Cressida*; he works very hard at instilling in his associates his own desire to kill Caesar.

Cassius' mimetic incitement is very similar to what we have in many comedies, except for the fact that the people he manipulates are mimetically seduced in choosing not the same erotic object as their mediator but the same victim, a common target of assassination.

The conspiracy originates in the envious soul of Cassius. Envy and mimetic desire are one and the same. Caesar portrays the man as a self-tortured intellectual unable to enjoy sensuous pleasures. Unlike his modern posterity, this early prototype of *ressentiment*— Nietzsche's word for mimetic envy—has not yet lost all capacity for bold action, but he excels only in the clandestine and terroristic type exemplified by the conspiracy.

Cassius reveals his envy in everything he says. Unable to compete with Caesar on Caesar's ground, he claims superiority in small matters such as a swimming contest that he once had with the great man. Had it not been for himself, Cassius, his rival, who helped him across the Tiber, Caesar would have drowned. Cassius refuses to worship a god who owes him his very life.

Cassius' invidious comparisons, his slanted anecdotes, and his perpetual flattery of Brutus are worthy of Pandarus and, therefore,

they recall Ulysses, the political counterpart of the "bawd" in
Troilus and Cressida:

> Brutus and Caesar: what should be in that "Caesar"?
> Why should that name be sounded more than yours?
> Write them together, yours is as fair a name;
> Sound them, it doth become the mouth as well;
> Weigh them, it is as heavy; conjure with 'em,
> "Brutus" will start a spirit as soon as "Caesar."
> Now in the names of all the gods at once,
> Upon what meat doth this our Caesar feed
> That he is grown so great? (I.ii.142–150)

A little later, Cassius resorts to the language of Ulysses with
Achilles in *Troilus and Cressida*, also for the purpose of stirring up
mimetic rivalry in a man obsessed by a successful rival. The two
plays are very close to each other from the standpoint of their
mimetic operation.

The second man recruited for the conspiracy is Casca; he is superstitious in the extreme. He describes a violent but banal equinoctial
storm in terms of supernatural signs and portents exclusively.
Shakespeare does not believe in astrology and, in order to refute
this nonsense authoritatively, he resorts to no less a man than
Cicero, who contradicts Casca's interpretation. This is the philosopher's only invention in the play.

The mimetic seducer, Cassius, is no more superstitious than
Cicero; his famous saying on the subject shows it:

> The fault, dear Brutus, is not in our stars,
> But in ourselves, that we are underlings.
>   (I.ii.140–141)

Cassius does not believe in astrology, but, for the purpose of
seducing Casca into the conspiracy, he can speak the language of
astrology. Instead of deriding his interlocutor's irrationality, he tries
to channel it in the direction of Caesar. What he condemns in
Casca is his failure to blame Caesar for the terrifying storm:

> Now could I, Casca, name to thee a man
> Most like this dreadful night,
> That thunders, lightens, opens graves and roars
> As doth the lion in the Capitol—
> A man no mightier than thyself, or me,
> In personal action, yet prodigious grown,
> And fearful, as these strange eruptions are.
>   (I.iii.72–78)

Cassius never mentions Caesar by name because he wants Casca to name him first; this credulous man will believe that he discovered Caesar's evil influence all by himself. Casca finally comes up with the right name:

> 'Tis Caesar that you mean; is it not, Cassius?

Cassius literally hypnotizes Casca into believing that Caesar is responsible for the bad weather. If someone must be *most like this dreadful night*, why not Caesar, the most powerful man in Rome? Seeing that Cassius seems angry rather than afraid, Casca feels somewhat reassured and, in his eagerness for more reassurance, he makes the other man's anger his own; he eagerly espouses Cassius's quarrel against Caesar.

Casca's decision to join the murderers is more disturbing than Brutus' because, unlike Brutus, the man is obsequious with Caesar and totally unconcerned with abuses of power and other political niceties. He is petty and envious but not talented enough to feel jealous of such a towering figure as Caesar. His real personal rivals belong to a lower type. If Cassius had directed his mimetic urge toward someone else, Casca would have chosen the someone else. His participation in the conspiracy has nothing to do with what Caesar is or might become; it rests entirely on his own mimetic suggestibility, stimulated by fear. Caesar is being turned into what we call a scapegoat, and Shakespeare insists on all the scapegoat signs that designate him to the crowd: his lameness, his epileptic fear, and even a bad ear, an incipient deafness that Shakespeare seems to have invented all by himself. The other physical infirmities are in

Plutarch, and Shakespeare emphasizes them because he understands their importance in the overall scheme of victimization.

After Brutus and Casca, we witness the recruiting of a third citizen into the conspiracy, Ligarius. The man is so susceptible to mimetic pressure, so ready for conspiratorial mischief that, although very ill, as soon as he understands that the gathering around Brutus must have some violent purpose, he throws his bandages away and follows the leader.

Ligarius does not know the name of his future victim and he does not even want to know. Brutus gives no indication that he finds this behavior shocking; his equanimity is as disturbing as Ligarius's irresponsibility. This virtuous Republican sees nothing wrong, it seems, in a Roman citizen's blindly surrendering his freedom of choice into the hands of another:

> LIGARIUS: Set on your foot,
> And with a heart new fir'd I follow you
> To do I know not what; but it sufficeth
> That Brutus leads me on.
>
> BRUTUS: Follow me then.
> (II.i.331–334)

The times are nasty, and normally law-abiding Romans are more and more easily swayed in favor of murder, less and less selective regarding the choice of their victims. Being part of the crisis, the genesis of the conspiracy is itself a dynamic process, a segment of an escalation in which the murder of Caesar comes first, then the murder of Cinna, and finally the ever-intensified violence that leads to Philippi. Instead of putting an end to the crisis, the murder of Caesar speeds up its acceleration.

Let us make the mimetic significance of what we read quite explicit. The intensification and diffusion of mimetic rivalry has turned all citizens into hostile carbon copies of one another, mimetic *doubles*. At first these *doubles* are still paired in conformity with the

mimetic history that they have in common; they have been fighting for the same objects and, in this sense, they truly "belong" to
one another. This is the case with Brutus and Caesar. Conflicts are
still "rational" to the extent at least that each *double* is truly entitled
to call his antagonist "his own."

This element of rationality is still present in the case of Brutus.
It seems that Brutus would not have to be recruited at all, since he
really hates Caesar, but he is a law-abiding citizen and, were it not
for the mimetic incitement of Cassius, his hatred, intense as it is,
would never become homicidal.

When the crisis gets worse, this last element of rationality dis-
appears. When mimetic effects constantly intensify, the disputed
objects disappear or become irrelevant. The mimetic influx must
find some other outlet and it affects the choice of the only entities
left inside the system, the *doubles* themselves. Mimetic contamination determines more and more the choice of antagonists.

At this advanced stage of the mimetic crisis, many people can
exchange their own *doubles*, their own mimetic rivals, for the *double*
of someone else. This is what Casca does. The someone else is
Cassius, a mediator of hatred and no longer a mediator of desire.
This is a new stage in the process of violent undifferentiation. The
more "perfect" the *doubles* are as *doubles*, the easier it becomes to
substitute one for another.

With each of the three Roman citizens successfully recruited
for the conspiracy, this kind of substitution becomes easier and we
go down one more notch in regard to these individuals' ability to
think by themselves, to use their reason, and to behave in a
responsible way.

It is less a matter of individual psychology than the rapid
march of mimetic desire itself. As the conspiracy becomes larger,
the job of attracting new members becomes easier. The combined mimetic influence of those already attracted makes the
chosen target more and more attractive mimetically. As the crisis
worsens, the relative importance of *mimesis* versus rationality
goes up.

We have reached a point when dual conflicts give way to associations of several people against a single one, usually a highly visible individual, a popular statesman—Julius Caesar, for instance.
When a small number of people clandestinely get together for the
purpose of doing away with one of their fellow citizens, we call
their association a *conspiracy*, and so does Shakespeare. Both the
process and the word are prominently displayed in *Julius Caesar*.

Whereas the *mimesis* of desire means disunity among those who
cannot possess their common object together, this mimesis of conflict means more solidarity among those who can fight the same
enemy *together* and who promise each other to do so. Nothing
unites man like a common enemy but, for the time being, only a
few people are thus united, and they are united for the purpose of
disturbing the peace of the community as a whole. That is why the
conspiratorial stage is even more destructive of the social order than
the more fragmented enmities that preceded it.

The forming of a conspiracy is a sinister threshold on the road
to civil war, significant enough to call for a solemn warning which
the author paradoxically places in the mouth of the conspiracy's
own reluctant leader, Brutus. There is logic in this paradox, however, since Brutus' purpose is to defend threatened Republican
institutions. Brutus himself is aware that his violent medicine could
be as bad as the disease and even worse; it could make the recovery
of the patient impossible and, indeed, it will. Even though Brutus
feels that he must join the conspiracy, this great defender of traditional institutions is horrified by the historical sign that the forming
of a conspiracy constitutes:

BRUTUS: O Conspiracy!
   Sham'st thou to show thy dang'rous brow by night,
   When evils are most free? O then, by day
   Where wilt thou find a cavern dark enough
   To mask thy monstrous visage? Seek none,
       Conspiracy!
   Hide it in smiles and affability;
   For if thou path, thy native semblance on,

Not Erebus itself were dim enough
To hide thee from prevention.
                                        (I.i.77–85)

The conspiracy is said to have a monstrous visage and it certainly does in the usual Shakespearean sense of uniting contradictory features in some kind of artificial mimetic unity, something which happens only at the most advanced stages of the mimetic crisis.

We should not believe that, because he represents the conspiracy harshly, Shakespeare must feel political sympathy for Caesar. At first sight, no doubt, Caesar seems more generous and kind than his opponents. Whereas Brutus hates Caesar as much as he loves him, Caesar's love is free from hatred. But Caesar can afford to be generous; neither Brutus nor any other Roman can be an obstacle to him anymore. This is not enough to demonstrate that Caesar stands above the mimetic law.

On the morning of the murder, Caesar first follows the advice of his wife, who is terrified because she has been dreaming of his violent death, and he decides not to go to the Senate; but then Decius reinterprets the dream for him and he goes to the Senate after all. It takes only a few words of ambiguous flattery to change Caesar's mind. He has become a mimetic weathervane.

The more the dictator rises above other men, the more autonomous he subjectively feels and the less he is in reality. At the supreme instant, just before falling under the conspirators' blows, in a strange fit of exaltation, he hubristically compares himself to the North Star, the one motionless light in the firmament. His self-sufficiency is no less deceptive than the erotic "narcissism" of certain characters in the comedies.

The more intense our mimetic pride, the more fragile it becomes, even in a physical sense. Just like the crowd and the conspirators themselves, Caesar is an example of what happens to men caught in the crisis of Degree. His common sense has left him, just as it will leave Brutus a few moments later. Because of the crisis, the quality of all desires is deteriorating. Instead of feeling neurotically inferior, as his unsuccessful rivals do, Caesar feels neurotically superior. His symptoms look completely different, but solely because of his position inside a fragile mimetic structure; underneath, the disease is the same. If Caesar had found himself in the same position relative to some man as Brutus does relative to him, he, too, would join a conspiracy against that man.

Brutus wants the murder to be as discreet, orderly, and "nonviolent" as it possibly can. Unfortunately for the conspiracy, he himself proves incapable of abiding by his own rule. Losing his sang-froid in the hot blood of his victim, Brutus gets carried away in the most dangerous fashion at the most crucial instant, right after the murder. He suggests to the conspirators that they should all bathe their arms in Caesar's blood *up to the elbows* and smear their swords with his blood.

Needless to say, our blood-spattered conspirators do not make a favorable impression. But they make a very strong one and they provide the already unstable populace with a potent mimetic model, a model which many citizens will imitate even and especially if they reject it most violently. The subsequent events tell the whole story. After listening to Brutus, then to Mark Antony, the crowd reacts by collectively putting to death an unfortunate bystander, Cinna, in a grotesque parody of what the conspirators themselves have done. The crowd becomes a mirror in which the murderers contemplate the truth of their action. They wanted to become mimetic models for the people and they are, but not the kind that they intended.

When they kill Cinna, the people mimic Caesar's murder but in a spirit of revenge, not of Republican virtue. Mimetic desire is perceptive, and it will immediately detect any discrepancy between the words and the deeds of its models; it will always pattern itself on what these models do and not on what they say.

Cinna is the first totally uninvolved and perfectly innocent victim. He is a poet and he has nothing to do with the conspirator named Cinna; he politely says so to the crowd. His only connection to Caesar's murder is a fortuitous coincidence of names. He even happens to be a friend of Caesar's and he mentions the fact, but to no avail; one anonymous shout comes from the mob: "Tear him to pieces."

A mob never lacks "subjective" and "objective" reasons for tearing its victims to pieces. The more numerous these reasons, the more insignificant they really are. Learning that Cinna is a bachelor, the married men in the mob feel insulted. Others resent the poet in this harmless individual and one more shout is heard: "Tear him for his bad verse!" Obediently, mimetically, the mob tears the wrong Cinna to pieces.

When it was first organized, the conspiracy against Caesar was still an unusual enterprise that required a rather lengthy genesis; once Caesar is murdered, conspiracies sprout everywhere and their violence is so sudden and haphazard that the word itself, *conspiracy*, no longer seems right for the spontaneous enormity of the disorder. Violent imitation is responsible for this as for everything else and that is the reason we have a single continuous process instead of the discontinuous synchronic patterns that the structuralists want to discover everywhere, in a misguided denial of history.

The general trend is clear: it takes less and less time for more and more people to polarize against more and more victims, for flimsier and flimsier reasons. A little earlier, Ligarius' indifference to the identity of his victim was still an exceptional phenomenon; after Caesar's murder, this indifference becomes commonplace and the last criteria disappear in the selection of victims. *Mimesis* learns fast and, after only one single try, it will do routinely and automatically what seemed almost unthinkable a moment before.

The contagion is such that the entire community is finally divided into two vast "conspiracies" that can only do one thing: go to war with each other; they have the same structure as individual doubles; one is led by Brutus and Cassius and the other by Octavius Caesar and Mark Antony. Shakespeare sees this civil conflict not as an ordinary war but as the total unleashing of the mob:

> Domestic fury and fierce civil strife
> Shall cumber all the parts of Italy;

Blood and destruction shall be so in use,
And dreadful objects so familiar,
That mothers shall but smile when they behold
Their infants quartered with the hands of war;
All pity chok'd with custom of fell deeds;
And Caesar's spirit, ranging for revenge;
With Ate by his side, come hot from hell,
Shall in these confines with a monarch's voice
Cry "Havoc!" and let slip the dogs of war,
That this foul deed shall smell above the earth
With carrion men, groaning for burial.

(III.i.263–275)

Just as Brutus, in Act II, solemnly proclaimed the advent of the fearful conspiracy, Mark Antony informs us in this soliloquy that an even worse stage of the crisis has arrived; his name for it is: *domestic fury* or *fierce civil strife*. As each new stage of the crisis is reached, Shakespeare has someone make a rather formal and impersonal speech about it. These speeches do not really tell us anything about the character who utters them; they are unnecessary to the plot; they are speeches about the various stages in the mimetic crisis.

Domestic fury and fierce civil strife culminate in the battle of Philippi, which Shakespeare does not treat as a banal military encounter but as the climactic epiphany of the mimetic crisis, the final explosion of the mob that gathered after the murder of Caesar, when the conspiracy began to metastasize.

As Peter S. Anderson observed, in this battle no one is really where he should be; everything is dislocated; death is the sole common denominator ("Shakespeare's *Caesar*: The Language of Sacrifice," *Comparative Drama*, 3, pp. 5–6). Instead of a few victims killed by still relatively small mobs, thousands of people are killed by thousands of others who are really their brothers and do not have the faintest idea of why they or their victims should die.

At Philippi, total violence is unleashed and it seems that the point of no return has been reached. No hope remains and yet, in the very last lines of the play, all of a sudden, peace returns. This is no ordinary victory, no mere overpowering of the weak by the strong. This conclusion is a rebirth of Degree; it concludes the mimetic crisis itself.

The return to peace seems rooted in the suicide of Brutus. How could that be? In two very brief but majestic speeches, the victors, Mark Antony and Octavius Caesar, eulogize Brutus. Mark Antony speaks first:

> This was the noblest Roman of them all:
> All the conspirators save only he,
> Did what they did in envy of great Caesar;
> . . . .
> His life was gentle, and the elements
> So mix'd in him that Nature might stand up
> And say to all the world: "This was a man!"
> (V.v.68–75)

This famous tribute is not quite truthful; Brutus was free only from the basest kind of envy. This truth is sacrificed to the new spirit now blowing, a spirit of reconciliation.

Sensing a political master stroke, Octavius Caesar consecrates the new Brutus by granting full military honors to him. By absolving Brutus of envy, Mark Antony and Octavius Caesar sanctify his political motives. Only the loving side of his ambivalence toward Caesar remains visible; we remember the words of Brutus after he killed Caesar: "I slew my best lover"; we remember his words before he killed himself:

> Caesar, now be still,
> I killed not thee with half so good a will.
> (V.v.50–51)

It seems that both Caesar and Brutus accepted giving their lives for the same cause, in a mysterious consummation that makes *Pax Romana* possible once again.

Up to that point, unanimity had eluded both parties; neither the Republicans nor their opponents could achieve it. Caesar's death was divisive: one part of the people united against Caesar and around Brutus while another part united against Brutus and around Caesar. If Brutus and Caesar become one in death, then all the people can unite *against* and *around* the same double-headed god.

To Brutus, this posthumous apotheosis would seem the ultimate derision, the supreme betrayal. It makes him a junior partner in the enterprise that he was desperately trying to prevent, the creation of a new monarchy. But the real Brutus no longer matters; a mythical figure has replaced him inside a newly emerging structure of meaning. According to this new vision, the Roman Emperor is both an absolute monarch and the official protector of the Republic, its only legitimate heir.

Caesar's murder has become the *foundational violence* of the Roman Empire.

What does it mean for violence to be foundational? Mimetic theory has its own interpretation of this and it throws a great deal of light on what Shakespeare is doing. Mimetic theory believes in the reality of the mimetic crises portrayed by Shakespeare, and, from their nature, as well as from a great many other clues, it speculates that these crises, in primitive societies, must be concluded by unanimous mimetic polarizations against single victims or a few victims only; this hypothetical resolution is the original sacrifice, and I call it *foundational murder, foundational violence.*

This original sacrifice means that human communities unite around some transfigured victim. There is nothing genuinely transcendental or metaphysical about the foundational murder. It is similar to mimetic polarizations of the conspiracy type except for one difference, crucial no doubt from a social viewpoint but in itself minor: it is unanimous. Unanimity means that the people suddenly find themselves without enemies, and, lacking fuel, the spirit of vengeance becomes extinguished. The unanimity is the automatic end-product of the mimetic escalation itself; it can almost be predicted from the constantly increasing size of the mimetic polarizations that precede it. Shakespeare sees the importance of this question and that is why the rivalry of Brutus and

Mark Antony first takes the form of rival speeches in front of the Roman mob. The real battle is a battle for the interpretation of Caesar's murder.

The conclusion is not the only reason for defining the origin and substance of sacrifice as I just did. There are many indications in Julius Caesar that Shakespeare espoused this idea.

I see a first reason in the references to the collective expulsion of the last king of Rome, Tarquin. Both Cassius and Brutus invoke this event as a precedent *and a mimetic model* for the murder they contemplate; here is what Brutus says in his soliloquy of Act II.i:

> Shall Rome stand under one man's awe? What, Rome?
> My ancestors did from the streets of Rome
> The Tarquin drive when he was call'd a King.
> (II.i.52–54)

Initially, the violence against Tarquin was an illegal act, one more violence in a violent escalation, just as Caesar's murder is when it is committed, but Tarquin's expulsion met with the unanimous approval of the people and it put an end to a crisis of Degree; instead of dividing the people along factional lines, it united them and new institutions sprang from it. It is the real foundation of the Republic.

Brutus sees the murder of Caesar as a ritual sacrifice ordained by the murder of Tarquin. He says so in his great speech to the conspirators:

> Let's be sacrificers but not butchers, Caius,
> . . . .
> Let's kill him boldly but not wrathfully;
> Let's carve him as a dish fit for the gods.
> (II.i.166–173)

Brutus interprets sacrifice as a re-enactment of the foundational violence, the expulsion of Tarquin, with a different victim, Caesar. The sole purpose is to rejuvenate the existing order. This is the definition of sacrifice according to mimetic theory, the re-enactment of the foundational violence. The coincidence between mimetic theory and Shakespearean tragedy is perfect.

In connection with this foundational violence, another passage of *Julius Caesar* which I already mentioned is essential, Calphurnia's dream. If we go back to it and to its reinterpretation by Decius, we can see immediately that it is more than a prophecy of Caesar's murder; it is a literal definition of its foundational status at the end of the play.

First, let us read Caesar's initial account:

> She dreamt to-night she saw my statue,
> Which, like a fountain with a hundred spouts,
> Did run pure blood; and many lusty Romans
> Came smiling and did bathe their hands in it.
> And these does she apply for warnings and portents
> And evils imminent, and on her knee
> Hath begg'd that I will stay at home to-day.

One of the conspirators, Decius Brutus, immediately reinterprets the dream:

> This dream is all amiss interpreted,
> It was a vision fair and fortunate.
> Your statue spouting blood in many pipes,
> In which so many smiling Romans bath'd,
> Signifies that from you great Rome shall suck
> Reviving blood, and that great men shall press
> For tinctures, stains, relics, and cognizance.
> This by Calphurnia's dream is signified.
>
> (II.ii.76–90)

The author found Calphurnia's dream in Plutarch, as well as her terrified reaction to it, but, as far as I know, Decius' reinterpretation is a pure invention of Shakespeare's and there are very few in this play. From the point of view of our foundational violence, it is the essential text.

The two texts together are a superb definition of the foundational murder, the original sacrifice, a definition that takes its mimetic ambivalence into account. The two interpretations seem to contradict each other, but in reality they are both true. The first corresponds to what Caesar's murder is at first, during the play, a source of extreme disorder, and the second to what the same murder becomes in the conclusion, the source of the new imperial order. Brutus' death triggers this transformation but its role is secondary. It is the first ritual sacrifice of the new order, ordained to a new divinity, Caesar himself. Ironically, Brutus, who wanted to sacrifice Caesar to the Roman Republic, is the one who ends up carved as a dish fit for the gods, and the real god is Caesar. Caesar is a god because his murder is the paramount event, the pivot upon which the violence of the crisis slowly revolved in order to generate a new Roman and universal Degree.

There is a question the critics have always asked regarding the composition of *Julius Caesar:* why did Shakespeare locate the murder of Caesar in the third act, almost at the precise center of the play, instead of locating it at the conclusion, as a more conventional playwright would have done?

Can a play in which the hero dies in the wrong place be a real tragedy; in other words, can it be satisfactory as entertainment? Is it not the juxtaposition of two plays rather than a single one, a first tragedy about Caesar's murder and a second one about the murderers?

The answer is clear: *Julius Caesar* is centered neither on Caesar nor on his murderers; it is not even about Roman history but about collective violence itself. The real subject is the violent crowd. *Julius Caesar* is the play in which the violent essence of the theater and of human culture itself are revealed. Shakespeare is the first tragic poet and thinker who focuses relentlessly on the foundational murder.

Shakespeare is not interested primarily in Caesar, or in Brutus, or even in Roman history. What fascinates him obviously is the exemplary nature of the events he portrays; he is obviously aware that the only reason why collective violence is essential to tragedy is that it has been and it remains essential to human culture as such. He is asking himself why the same murder that cannot reconcile the people at one moment will do the trick a little later; how the murder of Caesar can be a source of disorder first, and then a source of order; how the sacrificial miscarriage of Brutus can become the basis for a new sacrificial order.

To shift the murder from the conclusion to the center of this play means more or less what it means for an astronomer to focus his telescope on the enormously large but infinitely distant object he is studying. Shakespeare goes straight to what has always been the hidden substance of all tragedy and he confronts it explicitly.

Tragedy is a by-product of sacrifice; it is sacrifice without the immolation of the victim, an attenuated form of ritual sacrifice, just as ritual sacrifice itself is a first attenuation of the original murder. Like the great tragic poets of Greece but much more radically, Shakespeare turns sacrifice against itself, against its own sacrificial and cathartic function, and he uses it for a revelation of the foundational murder.

Julius Caesar was written in such a way, however, that it can be read and performed sacrificially and cathartically. Traditional interpretations and stage performances almost invariably turn the play into some kind of monument to the glory of both the Republic and the Empire, of ancient Rome as a whole. Shakespeare wrote the play at two levels, the traditional one which is sacrificial, and the anti-sacrificial one which I am trying to formulate.

If we consider the amount of collective violence in this play, even in purely quantitative terms, we will see that collective violence and sacrifice are its real subject. Not counting Philippi, three instances of collective violence are either displayed on the stage or prominently mentioned: the murder of Caesar, the lynching of the unfortunate Cinna, and the expulsion of Tarquin.

Of the three, Caesar's murder is the most important, of course, and no fewer than three different interpretations of it play a significant role in the play; first, we have the Republican sacrifice of Brutus, before the murder occurs, then we have this same murder as total disorder, and then, finally, this same deed becomes the founding of a new order, the original sacrifice from which great Rome shall suck reviving blood. There is not one thing in this play that does not lead to the murder if it occurs before it, and that does not proceed from the murder if it occurs after it. The murder is the hub around which everything revolves. Who said that this play lacks unity?

The dramatic process I have described contradicts all political interpretations of *Julius Caesar*. Political questions are all of the same differential type: which party does Shakespeare favor in the civil war, the Republicans or the monarchists? Which leader does he like better, Caesar or Brutus? Which social class does he esteem, which does he despise, the aristocrats or the commoners? Shakespeare feels human sympathy for all his characters and great antipathy for the mimetic process that turns them all into equivalent *doubles*.

Political answers are one of the ways in which our insatiable appetite for differences satisfies itself. All differentialism, pre-structuralist, structuralist, or post-structuralist, is equally unable to grasp the most fundamental aspect of Shakespearean dramaturgy, conflictual undifferentiation. We can see this in the fact that the most opposite political views can be defended with equal plausibility and implausibility. The case for a Shakespeare sympathetic to the Republic and hostile to Caesar is just as convincing, or unconvincing, as the case for the reverse political view.

Undecidability is the rule in Shakespeare as in all great mimetic writers, but it does not stem from some transcendental property of *écriture*, or from the "inexhaustible richness" of great art; it is great art, no doubt, but carefully nurtured by the writer himself who deals with human situations mimetically.

One of the errors generated by the twentieth-century love affair with politics is the widespread belief that the mob-like propensities of the crowd in *Julius Caesar* must reflect contempt for the common man, a distressingly "conservative" bias on the part of Shakespeare himself.

His pleasantries about the foul-stinking breath of the multitude seem deplorable to our democratic prudishness, but this sentiment had not yet been invented circa 1600. The mob-like propensities of the plebeians are even less significant because all social classes are similarly affected, not only in *Julius Caesar*, but in the other Roman plays and in all crises of Degree, really. Ligarius and Casca, two aristocrats, are no less prone to irrational violence than the idle workers in the first lines of the play.

The crisis turns not only the lower classes into a mob but the aristocrats as well, via the conspiracy, or via their degrading idolatry of Caesar. Our preoccupation with class struggle distorts our appreciation not only of Shakespeare but of tragic literature in general. Our virtuous defenders of the proletariat see only the symptoms that affect their protégés.

Marxism confuses tragic undifferentiation with a vain striving for political neutrality. If Shakespeare does not lean in one direction, he must necessarily lean in the other, even if he pretends that he does not. So goes the reasoning. According to this view, politics is so intrinsically absorbing, even the politics of fifteen hundred years ago, that not even Shakespeare can be even handed in his treatment of it; his apparent impartiality is only a devious way of playing politics.

Shakespeare does not try to be "impartial." We must not see the practical equivalence of all parties in conflict as a hard-won victory of "detachment" over "prejudice," as the heroic triumph of "objectivity" over "subjectivity," or as some other feat of epistemological asceticism that historians of all stripes should either emulate or denounce as a mystification.

Mimetic reciprocity is the structure of human relations for Shakespeare, and his dramatization of it is no painstaking obligation, but his intellectual and aesthetic delight. In his approach to a great historical quarrel, the objects in dispute, momentous as they seem to us, interest him much less than mimetic rivalry and its undifferentiating effects.

Like "true love" in the comedies, politics in *Julius Caesar* is always a direct or indirect reflection of what is taking place on some mimetic chessboard. Caesar's politics of imperial reconciliation are a move on this chessboard, and so is Brutus' defense of republicanism. Even the poetry of Shakespeare is inseparable from this undifferentiation, which tends to *confound contraries*, as Shakespeare would say, and to generate countless metaphors and other figures of speech.

I do not want to imply that political questioning is always out of place in Shakespeare. Until the mimetic logic that erases differences is established, it is premature; after this logic is in place, to inquire about the political significance of the logic itself is not only legitimate but imperative.

The perpetual "plague on both your houses" in Shakespeare must not be void of political significance. When I read *Julius Caesar* I see no utopian temptation, but I also see an author more nauseated with the aristocratic politics of his time than critics usually believe. I see more satire than most critics perceive. I see an antipolitical stance in Shakespeare that suggests a rather sardonic view of history. On political subjects, he reminds me of two French thinkers who are themselves closer to one another than it appears, Montaigne and Pascal. But Shakespeare's mimetic vision, which is artistic form as well as intellectual insight, always takes precedence over other considerations.

(1989)

THREE IN A BED: FICTION, MORALS, AND POLITICS

NADINE GORDIMER

THREE IN A BED: it's a kinky cultural affair. I had better identify the partners.

Politics and morals, as concepts, need no introduction, although their relationship is shadily ambiguous. But fiction has defining responsibilities that I shall be questioning all through what I have to say, so I shall begin right away with the basic, dictionary definition of what fiction is supposed to be.

Fiction, says *The Oxford English Dictionary*, is "the action of feigning or inventing imaginary existences, events, states of things." Fiction, collectively, is prose novels and stories. So poetry, according to the *OED*, is not fiction. The more I ponder this, the more it amazes me; the more I challenge it. Does the poet not invent imaginary existences, events, states of things?

If I should ask you, in this erudite and literary gathering, to give examples of the powers of the poets' invention of imaginary existences, events, the poets' matchless evocation of "states of things," all drawn just as the prose writers' is, from life—the fact of life—as the genie is smoked from the bottle, you could fill the rest of the evening with quotations. If fiction is the supra-real spirit of the imagination, then poetry is the ultimate fiction. In speaking of fiction, I should be understood to be including poetry.

What is politics doing in bed with fiction? Morals have bedded with storytelling since the magic of the imaginative capacity developed in the human brain—and in my ignorance of a scientific explanation of changes in the cerebrum or whatever, to account for this faculty, I believe it was the inkling development that here was somewhere where the truth about being alive might lie. The

harsh lessons of daily existence, coexistence between human and
human, with animals and nature, could be made sense of in the
ordering properties of the transforming imagination, working upon
the "states of things." With this faculty fully developed, great art in
fiction can evolve in imaginative revelation to fit the crises of an
age that comes after its own, undreamt of. *Moby Dick* can now be
seen as the allegory of environment's tragedy: we have sought to
destroy the splendid creature that is nature, believing we could survive only by "winning" a battle with nature; now we see our death
in the death of nature, brought about by ourselves. But the first
result of the faculty of the imagination was, of course, religion.
And from the gods (what a supreme feat of the imagination they
were!), establishing a divine order out of the unseen, came the secular, down-to-soil-and-toil order of morals, so that humans could
somehow live together, and in balance with other creatures.

Morals are the husband or at least the live-in lover of fiction.
And politics? Politics somehow followed morals in, picking the
lock and immobilizing the alarm system. At first it was in the dark,
perhaps, and fiction thought the embrace of politics was that of
morals, didn't know the difference. And this is understandable.
Morals and politics have a family connection. Politics' ancestry is
morality—way back, and generally accepted as forgotten. The
resemblance is faded. In the light of morning, if fiction accepts the
third presence within the sheets, it is soon in full cognizance of
who and what politics is.

Let me not carry my allegory too far. Just one generation further. From this kinky situation came two offspring, Conformity
and Commitment. And you will know who fathered whom.

Until just two years ago I would have said that the pressures to
write fiction that would conform to a specific morality, whether
secular or religious, long had been, still could be, and were, safely
ignored by writers. The Vatican still has its list of proscribed
works, but in most countries one assumed there was freedom of
expression as far as religion was concerned. (The exception was
perhaps in certain American schools.) Blasphemy? A quaint taboo,

outdated, like the dashes that used to appear between the first and last letters of four-letter words. Where censorship was rigidly practiced, in Eastern Europe, the Soviet Union, and South Africa, for example, the censors were concerned with what was considered politically subversive in literature, not with what might offend or subvert religious sensibilities. This was true even in my own country, South Africa, where the Dutch Reformed Church with a particular form of Calvinistic prudery had twisted religion to the service of racism and identified the church, including its sexual morality based on the supposed "purity" of one race, with the security of the state. A few years ago an actor in South Africa could not get away with exclaiming "My God!" on the stage, and *Jesus Christ Superstar* was banned; by 1989 savage satire of the church and its morality was ignored. As for sexual permissiveness, full frontal nudity in films was not snipped by the censor's scissors.

But in holding this illusion about freedom of expression in terms of religious and sexual morality, I was falling into the ignorance Islam finds reprehensible in the Judeo-Christian-Atheist world (more strange bedfellows)—that world's ignorance of the absolute conformity to religious taboos that is sacred to Islam. And here Islam was right; I should have known that this kind of censorship was not evolving into tolerance, least of the rights of non-Muslim countries to grant their citizens the freedom of disbelief, but was instead becoming an international gale force of growing religious fanaticism. Then came the holy war against *The Satanic Verses* in which the enemy was a single fiction, a single writer, and the whole might and money of the Islamic world was deployed in the *fatwa*: death to Salman Rushdie.

Now I and other writers were stunned to know that situations where religious persecution is turned on its head, and religion persecutes freedom—not only freedom of expression but a writer's freedom of movement, finally a writer's *right to life itself*—are back with us. Now in a new decade, with freedoms rising, we see that while a writer becomes president in one country, another writer is being hounded to death throughout the world. We see how a religion has the power to terrorize, through its followers, throughout the world. Political refugees from repressive secular regimes can seek asylum elsewhere; Salman Rushdie has nowhere to go. Islam's edict of death takes terrorist jurisdiction everywhere, contemptuous of the laws of any country.

Pre-Freudian hypocrisy, puritan prudery may be forgotten. The horror of what has happened to Salman Rushdie is a hand fallen heavily on the shoulder of fiction: pressures to write in conformity with a specific morality still can arrive, and pursue with incredible vindictiveness, even if this is unlikely to happen to most writers.

Am I positing that morals should be divorced from fiction? That fiction is free of any moral obligation? No. Fiction's morality lies in taking the freedom to explore and examine morals, including moral systems such as religions, with unafraid honesty.

This has not been an easy relationship, whether in the ghastly extreme of Salman Rushdie's experience or, say, that of Gustave Flaubert,[1] who, commenting on the indecency case against *Madame Bovary* after he won it in 1857, wrote of the establishment of spurious literary values and the devaluation of real literary values such a case implies for fiction: "My book is going to sell unusually well. . . . But I am infuriated when I think of the trial; it has deflected attention from the novel's artistic success . . . to such a point that all this row disquiets me profoundly. . . . I long to . . . publish nothing; never to be talked of again."

The relationship of fiction with politics has not had the kind of husbandly/fatherly authoritarian sanction that morals, with their religious origins, lingeringly has. No literary critic I know of suggests that *moralizing* as opposed to "immorality" has no place in fiction, whereas many works of fiction are declared "spoiled" by the writer's recognition of politics as as great a motivation of character as sex or religion. Of course, this lack of sanction is characteristic of an affair, a wild affair in which great tensions arise, embraces and repulsions succeed one another, distress and celebration are confused, loyalty and betrayal change place, accusations fly. And whether the fiction writer gets involved with politics initially through his/her convictions as a citizen pushing within against the necessary detachment of the writer, or whether by the pressure of seduction from without, the same problems in the relationship arise and have to be dealt with in the fiction as well as in the life.

For when have writers not lived in times of political conflict? Whose Golden Age, whose Belle Epoch, whose Roaring Twenties were these so-named lovely times?

The time of slave and peasant misery, while sculptors sought perfect proportions of the human torso? The time of revolutionaries in Czar Alexander's prisons, while Grand Dukes built mansions in Nice? The time of the hungry and unemployed, offered the salvation of growing Fascism while playboys and -girls danced, balancing glasses of pink champagne?

When, overtly or implicitly, could writers evade politics? Even those writers who have seen fiction as the pure exploration of language, as music is the exploration of sound, the babbling of Dada and the page-shuffling attempts of Burroughs have been in reaction to what each revolted against in the politically imposed spirit of their respective times; literary movements which were an act—however far out—of acknowledgment of a relationship between politics and fiction.

It seems there is no getting away from the relationship. On the one hand, we live in what Seamus Heaney[2] calls a world where the "undirected play of the imagination is regarded at best as luxury or licentiousness, at worst as heresy or treason. In ideal republics . . . it is a common expectation that the writer will sign over his or her venturesome and potentially disruptive activity into the keeping of official doctrine, traditional system, a party line, whatever. . . ." Gerard Manley Hopkins felt obliged to abandon poetry when he entered the Jesuits "as not having to do with my vocation"; a submission of the imagination to religious orthodoxy exactly comparable to that demanded of writers, in many instances in our epoch, by political orthodoxies.

We are shocked by such clear cases of creativity outlawed. But things are not always so drastically simple. Not every fiction writer entering a relation with politics trades imagination for the hair shirt of the party hack. There is also the case of the writer whose imaginative powers are genuinely roused by and involved with the spirit of politics as she or he personally experiences it. This may be virtually inescapable in times and places of socially seismic upheaval. Society shakes, the walls of entities fall; the writer has known the evil, indifference, or cupidity of the old order, and the spirit of creativity naturally pushes toward new growth. The writer is moved to fashion an expression of a new order, accepted on trust as an advance in human freedom that therefore also will be the release of a greater creativity.

"Russia became a garden of nightingales. Poets sprang up as never before. People barely had the strength to live but they were all singing"—so wrote Andrey Bely[3] in the early days of the Russian Revolution. One of Pasternak's latest biographers, Peter Levi,[4] notes that Pasternak—popularly known to the West on the evidence of his disillusioned *Dr. Zhivago* as the anti-Communist writer—in his young days contributed manifestos to the "infighting" of the day." In his poem to Stalin[5] he sang:

> We want the glorious. We want the good.
> We want to see things free from fear.
> Unlike some fancy fop, the spendthrift
> of his bright, brief span, we yearn
> for labour shared by everyone,
> for the common discipline of law.

This yearning is addressed by writers in different ways, as fiction seeks a proper relation with politics. In the Soviet Union of Pasternak's day, some fell into what the Italian contemporary writer Claudio Magris,[6] in a different context, calls with devastating cynicism "a sincere but perverted passion for freedom, which led . . . into mechanical servitude, as is the way with sin." The noble passion deteriorated to the tragically shabby, as in the 1930s the Writers' Union turned on itself to beat out all but mediocrity mouthing platitudes, driving Mayakovsky to suicide and turning down Pasternak's plea to be granted a place where he would have somewhere other than a freezing partitioned slice of a room in which to write and live. Yet Pasternak had not abandoned belief—never did—in the original noble purpose of revolution. When Trotsky asked why he had begun to abstain from social themes, Pasternak wrote to a friend, "I told him, *My Sister, Life* [his then recent book] was revolutionary in the best sense of the word. That the phase of the revolution closest to the heart . . . the *morning* of the revolution, and its outburst [is] when it returns man to the *nature* of man and looks at the state with the eyes of *natural* right."[7] But for him the writing of this period had become, by the edicts of the State and the Writers' Union, "a train derailed and lying at the bottom of an embankment." And in this choice of an image there is a kind of desperate subconscious assertion of the creativity so threatened in himself and his fellow writers, since trains, perhaps symbolic of the pace at which passes, fleetingly, the meaning of life the writer must catch, recur so often in his work.

Yeats's "terrible beauty" of the historic moments when people seek a new order to "return man to the nature of man, a state of natural right" does not always make politics the murderer of fiction. The Brechts and Nerudas survive, keeping that vision. But the relation, like all vital ones, always implies some danger. The first dismaying discovery for the writer is once again best expressed by Magris's[8] cynicism: "The lie is quite as real as the truth, it works upon the world, transforms it"; whereas the fiction writer, in pursuit of truth beyond the guise of reasoning, has believed that truth, however elusive, is the only reality. Yet we have seen the lie transforming; we have had Goebbels. And his international descendants, practicing that transformation on the people of a number of countries, including the white people of my own country, who accepted the lie that apartheid was both divinely decreed and secularly just, and created a society on it.

To be aware that the lie also can transform the world places an enormous responsibility on art to counter this with its own transformations. The *knowledge* that the writer's searching and intuition gain instinctively contradicts the lie.

> We page through each other's faces
> we read each looking eye. . . .
> It has taken lives to be able to do so

writes the South African poet Mongane Wally Serote.[9] We may refuse to write according to any orthodoxy, we may refuse to toe any party line, even that drawn by the cause we know to be just, and our own, but we cannot refuse the responsibility of what we know. What we know beyond surface reality has to become what—again in Serote's[10] words—"we want the world to know"; we must in this, our inescapable relation with politics, "page for wisdom through the stubborn night."

At its crudest and most easily identifiable, the stubborn night is politically inspired censorship, and still, in some countries—read the pages of index on censorship—imprisonment and torture. But even in countries—like this one—where no writer is locked up or beaten for his fiction, and censorship is minimal and open to challenge by the law, fiction is threatened by the power of the lie. Orwell alerted us to the insidious destruction of truth in the distortion of what words mean; but 1984 is long passed, and he is remembered more for the cute cartoon movie of an animal farm than for a prophetic warning about the use of language. Harold Pinter[11] spoke recently of

a disease at the very center of language, so that language becomes a permanent masquerade, a tapestry of lies. The ruthless and cynical mutilation and degradation of human beings, both in spirit and body . . . these actions are justified by rhetorical gambits, sterile ter- minology and concepts of power which stink. Are we ever going to look at the language we use, I wonder? Is it within our capabili- ties to do so? . . . Does reality essentially remain outside language, separate, obdurate, alien, not susceptible to description? Is an accu- rate and vital correspondence between what is and our perception of it impossible? Or is it that we are obliged to use language only in order to obscure and distort reality—to distort what is—to distort what *happens*—because we fear it? . . . I believe it's because of the way we use language that we have got ourselves into this terrible trap, where words like freedom, democracy and Christian values are still used to justify barbaric and shameful policies and acts.

The writer has no reason to be if for him or her reality remains outside language. An accurate and vital correspondence between what is and the perception of the writer is what the fiction writer has to seek, finding the real meaning of words to express "the states of things," shedding the ready-made concepts smuggled into language by politics. All very fine in theory, yes—but how would you refer, in a novel, to the terms "final solution," coined by the Nazis, the term "Bantustans," coined by a South African government in the sixties to cover the dispossession of blacks of their citizenship rights and land, the term "constructive engagement" coined by the government of the U.S.A. in the seventies in its foreign policy toward apartheid—how would you do this without a paragraph of explanation (which has no place in a novel) of what these counterfeits of reality actually were?

The false currency of meaning jingles conveniently in our vocabularies; but it is no small change. It becomes accepted values, for which writers bear responsibility. Every fiction writer has to struggle to expose them by discarding them, for the reader, in favor of the reality of the "states of things," since generally journalism—supposed to be "fact" as opposed to "fiction"—won't. Here, on the primal level of language itself, by which we became the first self-questioning animals, able to assess our own behavior, is where fiction finds its footing in relation to politics.

My own country, South Africa, provides what can be cited as the paradigm of problems of the full development of the relationship, from there; the wild affair, embraces and repulsions, distress and celebration, loyalty and betrayal. Perhaps echoes of the debate at present in progress over what post-apartheid fiction will be, ought to be, have reached you. Of course, the very term "post-apartheid" fiction reveals the acceptance that there has been and is such an orthodoxy as "apartheid" or, more accurately, "anti-apartheid" fiction. In the long struggle against apartheid, it has been recognized that an oppressed people need the confidence of cultural backing. Literature, including fiction, became what is known as "a weapon of struggle," and the current debate among us now is

between those who—perceiving that the cost was the constraint of
the writer's imaginative powers within what was seen narrowly as
relevant to the political struggle—think the time has come for
writers to release themselves if they are to be imaginatively equal to
the fullness of human life predicated for the future, and others who
believe literature still must be perceived as a weapon in the hands
and under the direction of the liberation movement come to
power in a future democracy.

The revolutionary and writer Albie Sachs, with the undeniable
authority of one who lost an arm and the sight of one eye in that
struggle, has gone so far as to call, even if half seriously (nothing has
been able to damage his lively humor!), for a five-year ban on the
slogan "culture is a weapon of struggle."

But, of course, there are some writers who have been—I adapt
Seamus Heaney's[12] definition to my own context—"guerrillas of
the imagination": in their fiction serving the struggle for freedom
by refusing any imposed orthodoxy of subject and treatment, but
furthering the struggle by attempting to take the unfettered creative
grasp of the complex "states of things" in which, all through people's lives, directly and indirectly, in dark places and light, that
struggle has taken place.

Since I am bound to be asked about this later, in relation to my
own fiction, I had better answer for myself now. As a citizen, a
South African actively opposed to racism all my life, and as a sup-
porter and now member of the African National Congress, in my
conduct and my actions I have submitted voluntarily and with self-
respect to the discipline of the liberation movement.

For my fiction, I have claimed and practiced my integrity to
the free transformation of reality, in whatever forms and modes of
expression I need. There, my commitment has been and is to
make sense of life as I know it and observe it and experience it. In
my few ventures into non-fiction, my few political essays, my
political partisanship has no doubt showed bias, perhaps a selectivi-
ty of facts. But then, as I have said before, and stand by: nothing I
write in such factual pieces will be as true as my fiction.

So if my fiction and that of other writers has served legitimately the politics I believe in, it has been because the imaginative transformations of fiction, in the words of the Swedish writer Per Wästberg,[13] "help people understand their own natures and know they are not powerless."

"Every work of art is liberating," he asserts, speaking for all of us who write. That should be the understanding on which our fiction enters into any relationship with politics, however passionate the involvement may be. The transformation of the imagination must never "belong" to any establishment, however just, fought for and longed for. Pasternak's[14] words should be our credo:

> When seats are assigned to passion and vision
> On the day of the great assembly
> Do not reserve a poet's position:
> It is dangerous, if not empty.

(1990)

NOTES

1. *Letters of Gustave Flaubert 1830–1857*, selected, edited, and translated by Francis Steegmuller (Cambridge: The Belknap Press of Harvard University Press, 1990), p. 224.

2. Seamus Heaney, *The Government of the Tongue* (London: Faber & Faber, 1988), p. 96.

3. Quoted in Peter Levi, *Boris Pasternak* (London: Century Hutchinson Publishing, Hutchinson, 1990), p. 142.

4. Ibid., p. 77.

5. Quoted in Evgeny Pasternak, *Boris Pasternak: The Tragic Years, 1930–60* (London: Collins/Harvill, 1990), p. 38.

6. Claudio Magris, *Inferences From A Sabre*, trans. Mark Thompson (Edinburgh: Edinburgh University Press, Polygon, 1990), p. 63.

7. Quoted by Peter Levi, *Boris Pasternak*, p. 100.

8. Magris, *Inferences*, p. 43.

9. Mongane Wally Serote, *A Tough Tale* (Kliptown Books, 1987), p. 7.

10. Ibid.

11. Harold Pinter, broadcasting on the British Channel 4 TV program "Opinion," May 31, 1990.

12. Seamus Heaney, "Osip & Nadezhda Mandelstam," *The Government of the Tongue*, p. 73.

13. Per Wästberg, addressing PEN International Writer's Day conference, June 2, 1990. Wästberg, former International President of PEN, is a distinguished Swedish novelist and journalist, and former editor of *Dagens Nyheter*.

14. Quoted in *Pasternak*, p. 159.

Dylan the Durable?
On Dylan Thomas

SEAMUS HEANEY

DYLAN THOMAS IS BY NOW as much a case history as a chapter in the history of poetry. Mention of his name is enough to turn on a multi-channel set of associations. There is Thomas the Voice, Thomas the Booze, Thomas the Debts, Thomas the Jokes, Thomas the Wales, Thomas the Sex, Thomas the Lies—in fact there are so many competing and revisionist inventions of Thomas available, so many more or less corrective, reductive, even punitive versions of the phenomenon, that it is with a certain tentativeness that one asks about the ongoing admissibility into the roll-call of Thomas the Poet.

Yet it was very much Thomas the Poet that my generation of readers and listeners encountered in our teens. He died at the age of thirty-nine in New York, immediately because of a wrongly prescribed dose of morphine, but inevitably because of years of spectacular drinking, and he died at the height of his fame, at the moment when print culture and the electronic media were perfecting their alliance in the promotion of culture heroes. Indeed, to recollect that moment is to have second thoughts about any easy condescension toward the role of the media in these areas. The records of Dylan Thomas reading his own poems, records which were lined up on the shelves of undergraduate flats all over the world, were important cultural events. They opened a thrilling line between the center and the edges of the English language collective. For all of us young provincials, from Belfast to Brisbane, the impact of Thomas's performance meant that we had a gratifying sense of access to something that was acknowledged to be altogether modern, difficult, *and* poetry.

Later, of course, there were second thoughts, but Dylan
Thomas will always remain part of the initiation of that first 11+
generation into literary culture. He was our Swinburne, a poet of
immense, immediate impact who swept us off our ears. And yet
nowadays he has become very much the Doubted Thomas. This
evening, therefore, I want to ask which parts of his *Collected Poems*
retain their force almost forty years after his death. In the present
climate of taste, his rhetorical surge and mythopoeic posture are
unfashionable, and his bohemianism is probably suspect as a form
of male bonding, which only makes it all the more urgent to ask if
there is not still something we can isolate and celebrate as Dylan
the Durable.

Dylan Thomas was both a uniquely gifted writer and a recognizable type. Within the sociology of literature, he was a Welsh
version of what Patrick Kavanagh called in the Irish context a
"bucklepper," which is to say, one who leaps like a young buck.
The bucklepper, as you might guess, is somebody with a stereotyp-
ical sprightliness and gallivanting roguery, insufficiently self-aware
and not necessarily spurious, but still offering himself or herself too
readily as a form of spectator sport. Thomas's Welshness, his high
genius for exaggeration and for entertaining (which was genuine
and genuinely beloved), his immense *joie de vivre* and his infectious
love of poetry, the intoxication (in every sense) of his presence—all
of this qualified him as a fully developed specimen of the bucklep-
ping tribe, an image of the Celt as perceived by the Saxon, a principle of disorder and childish irresponsibility complementary to the
earnest, gormless routines and civility of Albion. But the clamorous
spectacle of writers such as Brendan Behan or Dylan Thomas
quickly becomes, according to Kavanagh, a way of getting credit as
an artist without having to produce the art. In fact, the very con-
ventionality of Thomas's anti-conventional behavior contributed to
his being too easily slotted and accommodated. He was inevitably
co-opted by the literary establishment on both sides of the Atlantic
as the in-house bohemian, and no matter how sympathetic we may
find his masquerade as the lord of misrule, no matter how attractive

his recklessness and his mockery of fiscal and social rectitude may at times appear, it is still regrettable to think of his acting out the allotted role so predictably. Indeed, one of one's regrets about Thomas is that he did not follow the example of a far sturdier interloper from the Celtic realms, the example, that is, of W. B. Yeats himself. Yeats in the 1890s punted into the scene on the Celtic current, but once in the swim he used his mystique to initiate a counter-cultural move within English poetry itself. But Thomas never did have that kind of ambition.

In the end, Thomas's achievement rests upon a number of strong, uniquely estranging, technically original, and resonant poems, including one of the best villanelles in the language, and it is to these that I am going to direct my attention. His "play for voices," *Under Milk Wood,* is of course an idyllic romp, as if *The Joy of Sex* were dreamt under the canvas at a Welsh Eistedfodd. It will always occupy an honorable place in that genre which Graham Greene usefully christened "entertainments," as will his many broadcast talks and stories. But the poems are his indispensable achievement. They promote his melodramatic apprehension of language as a physical sensation, as a receiving station for creaturely imitations, cosmic process, and sexual impulses. But they also manage to transform such unremarkable obsessions into a mighty percussive verse. No history of English poetry can afford to pass them over. Others may have written like Thomas, but it was never vice-versa. Call his work Neo-Romantic or Expressionist or Surrealist, call it apocalyptic or overrated or an aberration, it still remains *sui generis*, a body of real poems that are fit though few.

Thomas himself was good at recognizing and describing the real thing although unfortunately he rarely paused to do so. Vernon Watkins, however, brought out the best in him. Here is Thomas, at twenty-three years of age, writing to Vernon Watkins about poems which Watkins has sent him:

Poems. I liked the three you sent me. There is something very unsatisfactory, though, about 'All mists, all thoughts' which seems—using the vaguest words—to lack a central strength. All the words are lovely but they seem so *chosen*, not struck out. I can see the sensitive picking of words, but not the strong inevitable pulling that makes a poem an event, a happening, an action perhaps, not a still life or an experience *put down*. . . . They (the words) seem, as indeed the whole poem seems, to come out of the nostalgia of literature. . . . A motive has been rarefied; it should be made common. I don't ask you for vulgarity, though I miss it; I think I ask you for a little creative destruction, destructive creation.

This is the voice of somebody who knows what the demands are. There's a wonderful sureness about the passage, an authority that comes from the writer's knowing what it feels like to have composed something true and knowing the difference between it and all imitations, however worthy. What Thomas is talking about here is the *élan* which distinguishes the most powerfully articulated metrical verse. Yeats's "Sailing to Byzantium," Pope's "Epistle to Arbuthnot," the prologue to Marlowe's *Tamburlain*—these and other moments of passionate utterance in English poetry do not depend upon what Thomas fondly but critically terms "the nostalgia of literature." They are literary, certainly, in that all of them take a self-conscious pleasure in stepping it out correctly, showing their prosodic paces and their rhyming heels; but they are not what Thomas calls nostalgic, the poems I mention are not concerned with "effects." Like all definitive poems, they spring into presence and stand there, as Czeslaw Milosz says, blinking and lashing their tails. They break the print-barrier, as it were, and make their sonic boom within the ear. All of which can be said without exaggeration of "Before I Knocked and Flesh Let Enter," an early Thomas poem about incarnation in both the biological and the theological sense of the term. Eternal life enters and exits the womb, and in crossing that threshold twice, it double-crosses it, as the poem says. The poem speaks out of a moment that could either be the moment of the Christian annunciation or the moment when the sperm fertilizes the ovum and the spirit of life knocks to be admitted through the door of the flesh:

> Before I knocked and flesh let enter,
> With liquid hands tapped on the womb,

I who was shapeless as the water
That shaped the Jordan near my home
Was brother to Mnetha's daughter
And sister to the fathering worm.

I who was deaf to spring and summer,
Who knew not sun nor moon by name,
Felt thud beneath my flesh's armour,
As yet was in a molten form,
The leaden stars, the rainy hammer
Swung by my father from his dome.

I knew the message of the winter,
The darted hail, the childish snow,
And the wind was my sister suitor;
Wind in me leaped, the hellborn dew;
My veins flowed with the Eastern weather;
Ungotten I knew night and day.

As yet ungotten, I did suffer;
The rack of dreams my lily bones
Did twist into a living cipher,
And flesh was snipped to cross the lines
Of gallow crosses on the liver
And brambles in the wringing brains.

My throat knew thirst before the structure
Of skin and vein around the well
Where words and water make a mixture
Unfailing till the blood runs foul;
My heart knew love, my belly hunger;
I smelt the maggot in my stool.

And time cast forth my mortal creature
To drift or drown upon the seas
Acquainted with the salt adventure
Of tides that never touch the shores.
I who was rich was made the richer
By sipping at the vine of days.

I, born of flesh and ghost, was neither
A ghost nor man, but mortal ghost.

> And I was struck down by death's feather.
> I was a mortal to the last
> Long breath that carried to my father
> The message of his dying christ.
>
> You who bow down at cross and altar,
> Remember me and pity Him
> Who took my flesh and bone for armour
> And doublecrossed by mother's womb.

Dylan Thomas died long before men landed on the moon, before we saw our planet from that perspective, profiled like the green-webbed x-ray of a fetus's head. But even though he missed those photographs of earth, round and gelid with oceans, translucent like a cell under the microscope, this poem offers a corresponding superimposition of images, of the microcosm and macrocosm. Thomas listens in for the potential at the first place in the sperm and the ovum, but he also lets himself go as far as his metrical sound waves can reach across aural space. Even if there is something Godawful about the maggot in the stool, there is still something superbly forthright about the verse itself, a sense of the poet going head-on and barehanded at the task in front of him. There is no sense of him hovering over a word choice or taking a bow because of some passing felicity. There are, of course, several flourishes, yet these high-flown phrases like "the rainy hammer," "the vine of days," "death's feather," "the fathering worm," and so on go sweeping past like eddies on a big flow. They aren't set out for our admiration: instead, they are going swiftly about their business. The words, to quote the letter to Watkins, are "struck out" rather than "chosen."

There is, of course, always a temptation to caricature this early poetry as a kind of tumescent fantasia, but to take that line too glibly is to demean a real achievement. One must beware of confusing the subject with what the poet makes of it. At twenty, Thomas knew about art as a making and a discipline and was writing to Charles Fisher: "I like things that are difficult to write and difficult to understand. I like 'redeeming the contraries' with secretive images; . . . But what I like isn't a theory, even if I stabilize into dogma my own personal affections." We might say, therefore, that in the case of "Before I Knocked" and "The Force that through the Green Fuse drives the Flower" and "A Process in the Weather of the Heart" and in the early poems generally, affections and impulses have been stabilized not into dogma but in the form. Work has been done. Imaginative force has moved a load of inchoate obsession into expressed language: something intuited and reached for has had its contours and location felt out and made manifest.

Thomas himself was often given to speaking of the process of composition as one of bringing the dark to light, although in his case, the creative work of hauling forth the psychic matter and discovering its structure probably has more to do with the story of Caedmon than with the practices of Freud. In his *Ecclesiastical History*, the Venerable Bede recounts the brief and simple tale of the calling of the poet Caedmon, an event that is set near the monastery at Whitby. Caedmon, the cowherd, found it impossible to contribute any improvised verses when it was his turn to take the harp and keep the banquet lively. But he always managed to find a way of dodging these crises by contriving to be at his yard-work when the harp was being passed. He would be out among the cattle, busy being busy. Then, one night when he was in the byre stalls as usual, he fell asleep and an angel appeared and commanded him to sing the creation of the world; and he did so, in the poem known ever since as Caedmon's Hymn, a poem dictated in a dream and entered into the language as a marvel and a bewilderment. Caedmon wrote, "It is meet that we worship the Warden of heaven, / The might of the maker, His purpose of mind," and I am reminded of that hymn every time I read the last sentence of Thomas's "Note" to his *Collected Poems*. "These poems," Thomas declared there, "with all their crudities, doubts, and confusions, are written for the love of Man and in praise of God, and I'd be a damn' fool if they weren't."

To his contemporaries, however, Thomas was not the Caedmon of Cwdomkin Drive but its Rimbaud, and his status as *enfant terrible* combined with the opacity of his writing to give the nickname a certain appropriateness. Rimbaud's famous conjunction of the vowels with colors corresponded to Thomas's helplessly physical relationship with his medium, and the French poet's readiness to let the id menace the proprieties and categories of literal sense would have been congenial to him also. He went at full tilt into the sump of his teenage self, filling notebooks with druggy, bewildering lines that would be a kind of fossil fuel to him for years to come. For composition to be successful, Thomas had to be toiling in the element of language like a person in a mudbath; the hydraulic passage into and through the words was paramount, the strain of writing palpably muscular. "I think (poetry) should work from words, from the substance of words and the rhythm of substantial words set together, not towards words." So he wrote to Charles Fisher in the letter I have already quoted, and in doing so played a variation on a theme that was preoccupying him at the time, namely the difference between working *out* of words, as he called it, and working *toward* them. He blames John Clare for working toward them, not out of them, "describing and cataloguing the objects that met his eyes. . . . He could not realize," said Thomas, "that the word is the object." How far this is fair to John Clare or how good it is as linguistic theory is not the point: what it does is to clue us in to Thomas's need for an almost autistic enclosure within the phonetic element before he could proceed. Probably the most famous of his utterances about the physicality of writing is in the letter where he tells Pamela Hansford Johnston that the greatest description of the earthiness of human beings is to be found in John Donne's *Devotions*, where the body is earth, the hair is a shrub growing out of the land, and so on. He continues as follows:

All thoughts and actions emanate from the body. Therefore the description of a thought or an action—however abstruse it may be—can be beaten home by bringing it on to a physical level. Every idea, intuitive or intellectual, can be imaged and translated in terms of the body, its flesh, skin, blood, sinews, veins, glands, organs, cells and senses. Through my small bone island I have learnt all I know, experienced all, and sensed all.

There is something about this passage that might be called Egyptian. Thomas, on the evidence here, would have been completely at home in a world where the cycles of life manifested themselves in the mud and floods of the Nile and the god of the dead was Anubis—a doghead, so to speak; and creation myths involving the almost glandular collusion of the elements would have suited him down to the ground. So the Caedmon comparison should take in not only the note of praise in each poet, but should extend to the inescapable physical conditions in which each of them labored: the body heat of Thomas's imaginings corresponding to the reek of the byre and the breath of the beasts. And perhaps it should extend also to the language they both used, insofar as the stress and alliteration of Caedmon's Anglo-Saxon are still clearly audible in the following early creation song by Thomas:

> The force that through the green fuse drives the flower
> Drives my green age; that blasts the roots of trees
> Is my destroyer.
> And I am dumb to tell the crooked rose
> My youth is bent by the same wintry fever.
>
> The force that drives the water through the rocks
> Drives my red blood; that dries the mouthing streams
> Turns mine to wax.
> And I am dumb to mouth unto my veins
> How at the mountain spring the same mouth sucks.
>
> The hand that whirls the water in the pool
> Stirs the quicksand; that ropes the blowing wind
> Hauls my shroud sail.
> And I am dumb to tell the hanging man
> How of my clay is made the hangman's lime.
>
> The lips of time leech to the fountain head;
> Love drips and gathers, but the fallen blood
> Shall calm her sores.

And I am dumb to tell a weather's wind
How time has ticked a heaven round the stars.

And I am dumb to tell the lover's tomb
How at my sheet goes the same crooked worm.

When I thought of Dylan Thomas as the subject of this lecture, I intended to stress the positive metrical power of these early poems, and had hoped to find in them an echo still traveling outward from Christopher Marlowe's mighty line. In my recollection, Thomas's poems retained a turning, humming resonance, as if they had a purchase at one and the same time on the hub of the iambic pentameter and the circulation of the blood itself. Remembered fragments conspired to strengthen this impression. "I see the boys of summer in their ruin / Lay the gold tithings barren. . . ." You intoned that and you felt again in your bones and joints a trace of the purchase it had on you at your first reading. The words did indeed "thud beneath the flesh's armour," so much so that they constituted a kind of Finneg-onan's wake. Still I wanted to be able to praise a poetry of such fullness, to commend without reservation the heave of positive gesture, to feel that the recurrent obscurity and bravura of the poems were a small price for the authentic power that produced them. What I was wanting, in fact, was a return to poetic Eden. In my mind, Thomas had gradually become the locus of a longed-for, prelapsarian wholeness, a state of the art where the autistic and the acoustic were extensive and coterminous, where the song of the self was effortlessly choral and its scale was a perfect measure and match for the world it sang in.

Even so, I would still like to be able to affirm Thomas's kind of afflatus as a constant possibility for poetry, something not superannuated by the irony and self-knowledgeable tactics of the art in postmodern times. I would like to stand up for the kind of fine contrary excess that had preceded Thomas in the poetry of Hart Crane and succeeded him in poems like Geoffrey Hill's "Genesis" and Sylvia Plath's "Ariel." I would like to discover in the largeness of his voice an implicit ethic of generosity that might be worth emulating because of its inclusiveness and robustness.

But too often in the *Collected Poems* the largeness of the utterance is rigged. The poet is under the words of the poems like a linguistic body-builder, flexing and profiling. Too often what he achieves is something Martin Dodsworth called "redundancy" rather than intensity, a theatrical verve, a kind of linguistic hype. The generosity promoted by poems such as "In the White Giant's Thigh" turns out to be a kind of *placebo,* and the robustness of "Lament" becomes more and more an embarrassingly macho swagger. All in all, what his work begins to lose after the dark "Egyptian" mode of *Eighteen Poems* is a quality that might be called "tonal rectitude," taking tone in the radically vindicating sense attributed to it by Eavan Boland in an essay in *Poetry Nation.* Boland is writing there about Elizabeth Bishop—in particular about Bishop's tone, and this leads her to meditate as follows upon the primacy of tone in general:

> Poetic tone is more than the speaking voice in which the poem happens; much more. Its roots go deep into the history and sociology of the craft. . . . Even today, for a poet, tone is not a matter of the aesthetic of any one poem. It grows more surely, and more painfully, from the ethics of the art. Its origins must always be in a suffered world rather than a conscious craft.

This last sentence is a wonderful formulation of what we seek from any poet's undermusic. The power of the final chorus of *Doctor Faustus* or the opening lines of *Paradise Lost* or the whole somnambulant utterance of a late Wallace Stevens poem such as "The River of Rivers in Connecticut" has not to do simply with their author's craft. The affective power in these places comes from a kind of veteran knowledge which has gathered to a phonetic and rhythmic head, and forced an utterance. It is, for example, the undermusic of just such veteran knowledge that makes Emily Dickinson devastating as well as endearing and makes the best of John Ashbery's poetry the common, unrarefied expression of a disappointment that is beyond self-pity.

The gradual withdrawal of a suffered world and the compensatory operations of a conscious craft weaken much of Thomas's poetry and rob it of emotional staying power as well as "tonal rectitude." The snowscape of a later poem like "A Winter's Tale," for example, is meant to be a visionary projection, but it rather suggests a winter-wonderland in the Hollywood mode. It is too softly contoured, too obligingly suffused with radiance and too repetitive the—verbal equivalent of a Disney fantasia:

> It is a winter's tale
> That the snow blind twilight ferries over the lakes
> And floating fields from the farm in the cup of the vales,
> Gliding windless through the hand folded flakes,
> The pale breath of cattle at the stealthy sail,
>
> And the stars falling cold,
> And the smell of hay in the snow, and the far owl
> Warning among the folds, and the frozen hold
> Flocked with the sheep white smoke of the farm house cowl
> In the river wended vales where the tale was told.

This displays a genius for lyricizing, for setting forth to good advantage its own immediacy and naïvety and textures. And as the poem goes sweeping forward for the whole of its twenty-six stanzas, one move forward for every two moves back—in keeping with the swirling motions of its blizzard world—Thomas does rise to the technical occasion. He meets the demands of a difficult rhyme scheme (ABABA) that also involves from time to time the deployment of internal rhyme and the manipulation of end-of-line assonance—and he does it so resourcefully that it almost feels like an injustice to question the poem's excellence and blame it for having just *too* much of the craftsman's effort about it. Yet the demand for more matter, less art, does inevitably arise. The tone is a rhetorical pitch framed for the occasion. The reader is tempted to quote Thomas's letter to Vernon Watkins against Thomas himself and to say "all the words are lovely but they seem so chosen. . . . I can see the sensitive picking of words, but not the strong, inevitable pulling. . . ." For example, in the second stanza above, in those lines about "the frozen hold / Flocked with the sheep white smoke of the farm house cowl," there is a little too much winsomeness about the oddity of "hold" where we might expect "fold"; and there is a little too much self-regard about the submerged pun on the word "flocked" which has the sense of white fluff as well as a herd of sheep. All the more so because the adjective "sheep white," with its own double-take on "snow white" comes along immediately in the same line:

> and the frozen hold
> Flocked with the sheep white smoke of the farm house cowl
> In river wended vales.

It may be a bit smart-assed to see this more as a case of "vended Wales" than "wended vales," but the poet's own verbal opportunism encourages the reader to indulge in this kind of nifty put-down. Indeed, I have the impression that negative criticism of Dylan Thomas's work is more righteous and more intoned with this kind of punitive impulse than is commonly the case. Even a nickname like "The Ugly Suckling" has an unusually cutting edge. It often seems less a matter of his being criticized than of his being got back at, and my guess is that on these occasions the reader's older self is punishing the younger one who hearkened to Thomas's oceanic music and credited its promise to bring the world and the self into cosmic harmony.

I count myself to some extent among this disappointed group—but not always. Not, for example, when I re-encounter a poem like "Do Not Go Gentle Into That Good Night," which fulfills its promise precisely because its craft has not lost touch with a suffered world. The villanelle form, turning upon itself, advancing and retiring to and from a resolution, is not just a line-by-line virtuoso performance. Through its repetitions, the father's remoteness—and the remoteness of all fathers—is insistently proclaimed, yet we can also hear, in an almost sobbing counterpoint, the protest of the poet's child-self against the separation:

> Do not go gentle into that good night,
> Old age should burn and rave at close of day;
> Rage, rage against the dying of the light.

Though wise men at their end know dark is right,
Because their words had forked no lightning they
Do not go gentle into that good night.

Good men, the last wave by, crying how bright
Their frail deeds might have danced in a green bay,
Rage, rage against the dying of the light.

Wild men who caught and sang the sun in flight
And learn, too late, they grieved it on its way,
Do not go gentle into that good night.

Grave men, near death, who see with blinding sight
Blind eyes could blaze like meteors and be gay,
Rage, rage against the dying of the light.

And you, my father, there on the sad height,
Curse, bless, me now with your fierce tears, I pray.
Do not go gentle into that good night.
Rage, rage against the dying of the light.

This poem was written at a late moment in Thomas's life, when he was thirty-seven, almost twenty years after "Before I Knocked." The year before, in 1950, he had worked on the too deliberate raptures of "In the White Giant's Thigh" and the never-to-be-completed "In Country Heaven." And on and off, he was all the while fiddling with the genial dreamscape of *Under Milk Wood*. But now, in 1951, at a time when his father was dying from cancer and his relationship with his wife Caitlin was in a kind of deep freeze because of his affair with the American woman whom biographers call "Sarah," now Thomas came through with a poem in a single, unfumbled movement, one with all the confidence of a necessary thing, one in which again at last the fantasy and extravagance of imagery and diction did not dissipate themselves or his theme. Words "forking lightning," frail deeds dancing "in a green bay," blind eyes blazing "like meteors"—these defiant and lavishly affirmative phrases could conceivably have appeared in a windier ambience such as "Lament," a male chauvinist tirade written at the same time, but within the genuinely desperate rhetoric of the villanelle itself they are informed with an urgency which guarantees their immunity from the virus of rant and posturing.

This is obviously a threshold poem about death, concerned with the other side of the mortal coin which obsessed him in "Before I Knocked." In that earlier poem, the body was about to begin what Thomas calls elsewhere its "sensual strut"; here the return journey out of mortality into ghosthood is about to be made, so in fact the recurrent rhymes of the villanelle could as well have been "breath" and "death" or "womb" and "tomb"—but what we have instead are "night" and "light." And the night is a "good night," but for once, a characteristic verbal tic has become an imaginative strength instead of a clever surface irritation. "Good night" is a pun which risks breaking the decorum of the utterance but instead it finally exemplifies its complexity and strength. The mixture of salutation and farewell in the phrase is a perfect equivalent for the balance between natural grief and the recognition of necessity which pervades the poem as a whole.

This is a son comforting a father; yet it is also, conceivably, the child poet in Thomas himself comforting the old ham he had become; the neophyte in him addressing the legend; the green fuse addressing the burnt-out case. The reflexiveness of the form is the right correlative for the reflexiveness of the feeling. As the poem proceeds, exhortation becomes self-lamentation; the son's instruction to the disappointed father to curse and bless him collapses the distance between the sad height of age and physical decay in the parent and the equally sad eminence of poetic reputation and failing powers in the child. "Do Not Go Gentle" is a lament for the maker in Thomas himself as well as a farewell to his proud and distant schoolteacher father. The shade of the young man who once expressed a fear that he was not a poet, just a freak user of words, pleads for help and reassurance from the older, sadder literary lion who apparently has the world at his feet.

Not that Thomas intended this meaning, of course. One of the poem's strengths is its outwardly directed gaze, its breakout from emotional claustrophobia through a powerfully capable engage-

ment with the specifically technical challenges of the villanelle. Yet
that form is so much a matter of crossing and substitutions, of
back-tracks and double-takes, turns and returns, that it is a vivid
figure of the union of opposites, of the father in the son, the son in
the father, of life in death and death in life. The villanelle, in fact,
both participates in the flux of natural existence and scans and
abstracts existence in order to register its pattern. It is a living cross-
section, a simultaneously open and closed form, one in which the
cycles of youth and age, of rise and fall, growth and decay find
their analogues in the fixed cycle of rhymes and repetitions.

Indeed, there is something Rilkean in the tendency of "Do
Not Go Gentle," for we are here in the presence of knowledge
transformed into poetic action, and the extreme claims that Rilke
made for poetry are well enough matched by Thomas on this
occasion. The following, which comes from a Rilke letter about
his *Duino Elegies*, seems relevant and worth quoting:

> Death is a *side of life* that is turned away from us . . .
> the true figure of life extends through both domains,
> the blood of the mightiest circulation drives through
> *both: there is neither a here nor a beyond, but a great*
> *unity*, in which those creatures that surpass us, the
> "angels," are at home.

In its canvassing of the idea of a great unity and its employment
of the bodily image of circulating blood, this statement by Rilke is
reminiscent of the murkier, more biological statements of the young
Thomas. Yet in "Do Not Go Gentle" I would suggest that the old
murkiness has been worked through and a new set of angelic rather
than Egyptian words has been worked toward. I would also suggest
that the mighty vaunt of "A Refusal to Mourn the Death by Fire of
a Child in London" has now been made good, and its operatic,
death-defying strains have modulated into something even more
emotionally persuasive. In fact, in the light of Rilke's statement we
can begin to discern the mistake which Thomas made during his
twenties and thirties when he confined himself to the repetition of
his own early procedures and convictions as a poet.

Eliot once diagnosed the problem of a younger contemporary as being a case of technical development proceeding ahead of spiritual development. It is a suggestive observation and what it suggests is that there should be a correspondence between the maturation of a sensibility and its methods of expression at different stages. Thomas's methods as a teenager, bogged in his masturbatory claustrophobia, desperately seeking in language the fulfillment of clandestine sexual needs, the kind of thing that the old Yeats mysteriously called "the touch through the curtain"—those teenage methods were suited to the phallocentric, percussive, short-circuited poetry proper to his situation then, but they were not what he needed later as a sexually mature, world-scarred and world-skilled outsider at the literary center. Thomas's anti–intellectualism, for example, is a bad boy's habit wastefully prolonged and this doctrinaire immaturity, which was at once tedious and entertaining in life, was finally retrograde for his art. But "Do Not Go Gentle" is a positively magnificent achievement. This poem does not "begin with words," as the young Thomas too simply insisted that poetry should, but it "moves towards them." And it is exactly the sensation of language on the move toward a destination in knowledge which imbues "Do Not Go Gentle" with a refreshing maturity. "The Force that through the Green Fuse drives the Flower" gained its power from a language entrapped and certified by its obsessions, and was the kind of poem that an eighteen-year-old of genius could properly and prodigiously deliver. But as long as he kept too rigidly to those bodily, earthy, Egyptian imperatives, it was not possible for Thomas to admit into his poetry the presence of that which Rilke calls the angels. The jurisdiction of the bone-bound island, to which he had pledged his loyalty, forbade the necessary widening of scope. The poems of his twenties and thirties pursued a rhetorical magnificence that was in excess of and posthumous to its original, vindicating impulse. They mostly stand like elaborately crenellated fabrications, great gazebos built to the extravagant but finally exhibitionist specifications of their inventor.

Thomas did recognize the need to open and seek what Rilke

calls "that great unity which is neither here nor beyond," but when he does so time and again what fails him is the tone. The suffered world peels away from the proffered idiom. The great first gift, which enabled him to work instinctively at the deep sound-face and produce a poetry where the back of the throat and the back of the mind answered and supported each other, this did, alas, weaken. His original ability to discover a path for the poem's progress by means of a sixth sense—what he called "creative destruction, destructive creation"—began to atrophy: the enigmas of "Altarwise by Owl-Light" seem to be forced rather than discovered. "After the Funeral" even goes so far as to diagnose the problem and to suggest a way out of it by admitting into the high-pressure conditions of the poem the sweet, uninflated particulars of the world such as "a stuffed fox and a stale fern" and fern seeds "on the black sill." But the problem of harmonizing rhetorical pitch and emotional content remained and was only overcome when Thomas opened the texture of his language and allowed the affirmative strains of "Poem in October" and "Fern Hill" to rise into the higher, less bodily and more "angelic" registers:

> And honoured among foxes and pheasants by the gay house
> Under the new made clouds and happy as the heart was long,
> In the sun born over and over,
> I ran my heedless ways,
> My wishes raced through the house high hay
> And nothing I cared, at my sky blue trades, that time allows
> In all his tuneful turning so few and such morning songs
> Before the children green and golden
> Follow him out of grace.
>
> Nothing I cared, in the lamb white days, that time would take me
> Up to the swallow thronged loft by the shadow of my hand,
> In the moon that is always rising,
> Nor that riding to sleep
> I should hear him fly with the high fields
> And wake to the farm forever fled from the childless land.
> Oh as I was young and easy in the mercy of his means,

> Time held me green and dying
> Though I sang in my chains like the sea.

"Fern Hill" is buoyant upon memories of a sensuously appre-
hended world and suffused by them. Its poetry is admirably and
bewitchingly candid, held out at an unclammy distance between
poet and reader. It is far from Egyptian. Its green singing spaces
are swept by less breathy airs than the too artfully pleasing spaces
of "A Winter's Tale" and one has the gratifying sense of poet
completely absorbed in his very own subject. Yet its dimensions as
a poem of loss become plainer if we set it beside Wordsworth's
"Immortality Ode." It is unfair, of course, to do this, but it makes
clear that what "Fern Hill" lacks is the intonation arising from the
"years that bring the philosophic mind"; it is more intent upon
overwhelming its sorrows in a tidal wave of recollection than facing what Rilke calls "a side of life that is turned away from us." It
is as if Orpheus, grown older, reneged on his larger task, that of
testing the power of his lyre against the gods of the underworld
and wresting life back out of death, and went back instead to his
younger, happier, but less world-saving task of casting musical
spells upon the whole of nature.

My questions from Rilke are taken from a study of the myth of
Orpheus by the distinguished classicist Charles Segal, and I want to
conclude by considering both the excitements and limitations of
Dylan Thomas's poetry in the light of Segal's reading of that particular myth. According to his understanding, Orpheus, in his early
manifestations within Greek culture, is "the oral poet par excellence. He sings outside, under an open sky, accompanying himself
on his famous lyre. His fabled effect upon wild beasts, stones and
trees generalizes to the animal world that mimetic response that an
oral audience feels in the situation of the performance. . . . This
compulsive, incantatory power of oral song . . . the animal magnet-
ism with which it holds its hearers spellbound, all find mythical
embodiment in Orpheus." And so, in turn, I would want to find
in the undiminished incantatory power of early Dylan Thomas
poems on the page, and in the spellbinding memory of his oral

performance of poems from all periods of his career, I would want to find in all of those things a continuing aspect of the Orphic principle, and an example of the survival of rhapsodic poetry of the most ancient kind.

Yet this is the kind of poetry which Plato describes and disavows in his *Ion*. He suspects it in much the same way as critics have suspected Dylan Thomas, and he is against what Segal calls its "magical, quasi-hypnotic effect, emotional response, power to move and compel large audiences." As far as Plato is concerned, the way in which this poetry works bodily, through the agency of the senses, is a limitation. He underrates it because it is powerless to know reality through the intellect. In the *Symposium*, for example, he tells a version of the story of Orpheus which is clearly meant to indicate that Orphic power operates only in the realm of illusion. According to Plato, when Orpheus goes to the underworld and sues for the return of Eurydice, he is given only a phasma, a wraith or shadow, a phantom woman.

But this pejorative version of Orpheus as an energy absorbed in the unconscious flux of nature and exemplifying a process which it cannot know—this is only a beginning. Subsequent poets, from Virgil to Rilke, seek to outflank Plato's objections by developing and extending other parts of the myth besides the musical, spellbinding gift of the singer. Their treatments emphasize the truth-to-life-and-death in the story and they abstract meanings that are variously sombre or symbolic from the drama of Eurydice. Thus, from one perspective, Orpheus's trip to the land of the dead and his initially successful bid to have Eurydice released from the underworld can represent the ability of art—poetry, music, language—to triumph over death; yet from another perspective, Orpheus' fatal backward look must equally represent "the failure of art before the ultimate reality of death"—or, to put it in Charles Segal's more drastic formulation, the loss of Eurydice expresses "the intransigence of reality before the plasticity of language."

To make the final application of all this, then, to Dylan Thomas: we can say that he continued to place a too unenlightened trust in the plasticity of language, that he emphasized unduly the romantic, positive side of the story and overrated the lyre's ability to stay or reverse the course of nature. The backward look of "Poem in October" and "Fern Hill," however radiant and understandable, becomes in this reading like the backward look of Orpheus himself. They avert the eyes from the prospect of necessity. "Do Not Go Gentle Into That Good Night," on the other hand, keeps its gaze firmly fixed on the upward path, and works against the gradient of relapse. Its verbal elaborateness is neither otiose nor merely ornamental. On the contrary, its art is as straightforward and homely as Caedmon's, and as extremely engaged as that of Orpheus in the underworld. In the telling of its rhymes and repetitions, the litany of Dylan the Durable will always be credible and continuing.

(1992)

What Henry James Knew

Cynthia Ozick

The Horrible Hours

As modernism sinks in, or fades out—as it recedes into a kind of latter-day archaism, Cubism turned antiquated, the old literary avant-garde looking convincingly moth-eaten—certain writers become easier to live with. It is not only that they seem more accessible, less impenetrable, simpler to engage with, after decades of familiarity: the quality of mystery has (mysteriously) been drained out of them. Joyce, Proust, Woolf, surely Pound and Eliot—from all of these, and from others as well, the veil draws back. One might almost say, as the twentieth century shuts down, that they are objectively less "modern" than they once were. Their techniques have been absorbed for generations. Their idiosyncrasies may not pall, but neither do they startle. Their pleasures and their stings, while far from humdrum, nevertheless open out into psychological references that are largely recognizable. What used to be revelation (Proust's madeleine, the world that ends not with a bang but a whimper) is reduced to reflex. One reads these masters now with satisfaction—they have been ingested—but without the fury of early avarice.

Yet one of the great avatars of modernism remains immune to this curious attrition: in the ripened Henry James, and in him almost alone, the sensation of mysteriousness does not attenuate; it thickens. As the years accumulate, James becomes, more and more compellingly, our contemporary, our urgency.

The author of *Daisy Miller* (1878), and of *Washington Square* (1880), and even of *The Portrait of a Lady* (1881), was a nineteenth-century writer of felicitous nuance and breadth. The earlier stories and novels are meant to be rooms with a view, thrown open to the light. If mysteries are gathered there, they are gathered to be dispelled. The entanglements of human nature, buffeted by accident, contingency, mistaken judgment, the jarrings of the social web, the devisings of the sly or the cruel, are in any event finally transparent, rational. Isabel Archer's long meditation, in *The Portrait of a Lady*, on her marriage to Gilbert Osmond leads her to the unraveling— the clarification—of her predicament. "They were strangely married," she perceives, "and it was a horrible life"—directly seen, understood, stated, in the manner of the fiction of realism. Like Catherine Sloper, the heroine of *Washington Square*, Isabel has known too little and now knows more. For the James of this mainly realist period, it is almost never a case of knowing too much.

After 1895, the veil thickens. Probably the most celebrated example of a darkening texture is the interpretive history of "The Turn of the Screw" (1898); what was once read wholly in the light of its surfaces can no longer sustain the innocence, or the obtuseness, of its original environment. The tale's first readers, and James himself, regarded this narrative of a frightened governess and her unusual young charges as primarily a ghost story, suitably shadowed in eerie riddle. In his Notebook sketch of 1895, James speaks of "apparitions," of "evil presences," of hauntings and their "strangely gruesome effect." In the Preface to "The Turn of the Screw" for the 1906 New York edition of his work, he appears light-handedly to toss out the most conventional of these rumblings. "I cast my lot with pure romance," he insists, and calls "this so full-blown flower of high fancy" a "fairy-tale pure and simple." But also, and contradictorily, he assigns his apparitions "the dire duty of causing the situation to reek with the air of Evil," the specifications of which James admits he has left it to the reader to supply. "Make him *think* the evil, make him think it for himself," he asserts.

Since then, under the tutelage of Freud, later readers *have* thought it for themselves, and have named, on James's behalf, a type of horror he could not or would not have brought to his lips. What was implicit in James became overt in Freud. With time, and with renewed critical speculation, James's ghosts in "The Turn of the Screw" have swollen into the even more hideous menace of eros corrupted, including the forbidden, or hidden, sexuality of children. Whether James might have conceived explicitly of these images and hints of molestation is beside the point. There is, he contends in the Preface, "from beginning to end of the matter not an inch of expatiation," and evil's particulars are, on purpose, "positively all blanks," the better to delegate the imagination of terror to anyone but the author himself. Still, is it likely that the privacy of James's own imagination can be said to hold positively all blanks? Imagination works through exactitudes of detail, not through the abdication of its own authority. Whatever it was James thought, he thought *some* thing. Or, rather, he felt something: that gauzy wing that brushes the very pit of the mind even as the mind declares nothing is there. James is one of that handful of literary proto-inventors—ingenious intuiters—of the unconscious; it is the chief reason we count him among the imperial moderns.

The pivotal truth about the later Henry James is not that he chooses to tell too little—that now and then he deliberately fires blanks—but that he knows too much, and much more than we, or he, can possibly take in. It is as if the inklings, inferences, and mystifications he releases in his maturest fictions (little by little, like those medicinal pellets that themselves contain tinier pellets) await an undiscovered science to meet and articulate them. The Freud we already have may be insufficient to the James who, after 1895, became the recondite conjurer whom the author of *Daisy Miller* might not have recognized as himself.

In the fiction of realism—in the Jamesian tale before the 1895 crux—knowledge is the measure of what can be rationally ascertained, and it is almost never a case of knowing too much—i.e., of a knowledge beyond the reach not only of a narrative's dramatis personae but also of the author himself. The masterworks of modernism, however, nearly always point to something far more subterranean than simple ascertainment. *The Castle*, for example, appears to know more than Kafka himself knows—more about its own matter and mood, more about its remonstrances and motives, more about the thread of Kafka's mind. In the same way, "The

Turn of the Screw" and other Jamesian works of this period and afterward—*The Awkward Age* above all, as we shall see—vibrate with cognitions that are ultimately not submissive to their creator. It is as if from this time forward, James will write nothing but ghost stories—with the ghosts, those shadows of the unconscious, at the controls. Joyce in particular sought to delineate whatever demons beat below, to bring them into the light of day—to explain them by playing them out, to incarnate them in recognizable forms, or (as in *Finnegans Wake*) to re-incubate them in the cauldron of language. This was what the modernists did, and it is because they succeeded so well in teaching us about the presence of the unconscious that we find them more and more accessible today. But the later James—like Kafka, a writer seemingly as different from James as it is possible to be—is overridden by a strangeness that is beyond his capacity to domesticate or explicate. James, like Kafka, enters mazes and penetrates into the vortex of spirals; and, again like Kafka, the ghost in the vortex sometimes wears his own face.

The 1895 crux, as I have called it, was James's descent into failure and public humiliation. The story of that humiliation—a type of exposure that damaged James perhaps lastingly, and certainly darkened his perspectives—is brilliantly told in Leon Edel's consummate biography: a biography so psychologically discriminating that it has drawn generations of its readers into a powerful but curious sympathy with James. Curious, because an admirable genius is not nearly the same as a sympathetic one, an instruction James himself gives us in, to choose only two, Hugh Vereker and Henry St. George, the literary luminaries of a pair of tales ("The Figure in the Carpet," "The Lesson of the Master") bent on revealing the arrogance of art. Yet to approach James through Edel is, if not practically to fall in love with James, to feel the exhilarations of genius virtually without flaw. James, for Edel, is sympathetic and more; he is unfailingly and heroically civilized, selfless for art, gifted with an acuity of insight bordering on omniscience. He is—in James's own celebrated words—one of those upon whom nothing is lost. Edel's is a portrait that breaks through the frame of immaculate scholarship into generous devotion, a devotion that in the end turns on a poignant theory of James's fragility of temperament—and never so much as on the night of January 5, 1895, when James's play, *Guy Domville*, opening that evening, was jeered at and its author hissed.

Too nervous to sit through the rise of the curtain, James had gone down the street to attend Oscar Wilde's new work, *An Ideal Husband*. When it was over, scorning Wilde as puerile even as he made his way out through a wash of delighted applause, he returned to *Guy Domville* just as the closing lines were being spoken. Though the clapping that followed was perilously mixed with catcalls, the theater manager, misjudging, brought James out on the stage. "All the forces of civilization in the house," James described it afterward, "waged a battle of the most gallant, prolonged and sustained applause with the hoots and jeers and catcalls of the roughs, whose roars (like those of a cage of beasts at some infernal zoo) were only exacerbated by the conflict." George Bernard Shaw, who was in the audience as a reviewer, wrote of the "handful of rowdies" and "dunces" who sent out "a derisive howl from the gallery." James stumbled off the stage and walked home alone, brooding on "the most horrible hours of my life." The catastrophe of public rejection, James's biographer concludes, "struck at the very heart of his self-esteem, his pride and sovereignty as an artist."

It *had* been a sovereignty. In fact, it had been an impregnability. He would not have been so damaged had he not had so far to fall. Literary embarrassment, to be sure, was familiar enough to James; it depressed him, as he grew older, that his novels were no longer widely read, and that his sales were often distressingly puny. But the assault on *amour-propre* that rocked James in the wake of his theater debacle was something else. It was a vulnerability as unprecedented as it was real—feelings of jeopardy, the first faint cracks of existential dread, the self's enfeeblement. He was unused to any of that; he had never been fragile, he had never been without the confidence of the self-assured artist, he had never been mistrustful. What he had been all along was magisterial. Admirers of

Leon Edel's James may be misled by Edel's tenderness into imagining that some psychological frailty in James himself is what solicits that tenderness—but sovereign writers are not commonly both artistically vulnerable *and* sovereign.

And James's record of sovereignty—of tough impregnability—was long. He was fifty-two when the rowdies hissed him; he was twenty-one when he began publishing his Olympian reviews. To read these early essays is to dispel any notion of endemic hesitancy or perplexity. In 1866, at twenty-three, reviewing a translation of Epictetus, he speculates on the character of this philosopher of Stoicism with oracular force: "He must have been a wholesome spectacle in that diseased age, this free-thinking, plain-speaking old man, a slave and a cripple, sturdily scornful of idleness, luxury, timidity, false philosophy, and all power and pride of place, and sternly reverent of purity, temperance, and piety,—one of the few upright figures in the general decline." This has the tone not simply of a prodigy of letters, but of large command, of one who knows the completeness of his powers. If anything can be said to be implicit in such a voice, it is the certainty of success; success on its own terms—those terms being the highest imaginable exchange between an elite artist and his elite readership. And the earlier these strenuous yet ultimately serene expectations can be established, the stronger the shield against vulnerability; mastery in youth arms one for life.

Or nearly so. On the night of January 5, 1895, when the virtuoso's offering was received like a fizzled vaudeville turn, the progress of unquestioned fame came to a halt. What was delicacy, what was wit, what was ardor, what was scrupulous insight? What, in brief, was the struggle for art if its object could be so readily blown away and trodden on? James might wrestle with these terrors till dawn, like that other Jacob, but his antagonist was more likely a messenger from Beelzebub than an angel of the Lord. Failure was an ambush, and the shock of it led him into an inescapable darkness.

He emerged from it—if he ever emerged from it at all—a different kind of writer. Defensively, he began to see in doubles. There was drama, and there was theater. And by venturing into the theater, he had to live up to—or down to—the theater's standards and assumptions. "I may have been meant for the Drama—God knows!—but I certainly wasn't meant for the Theater," he complained. And another time: "Forget not that you write for the stupid—that is, that your maximum of refinement must meet the minimum of intelligence of the audience—the intelligence, in other words, of the biggest ass it may contain. It is a most unholy trade!" Yet in 1875, twenty years before the *Guy Domville* calamity, he exalted what had then seemed the holiest of trades, one that "makes a demand upon an artist's rarest gifts." "To work successfully beneath a few grave, rigid laws," he reflected, "is always a strong man's highest ideal of success." In 1881 he confided to his journal that "beginning to work for the stage" was "the most cherished of my projects."

The drama's attraction—its seductiveness—had its origin in childhood theater-going; the James children were introduced first to the New York stage, and then to the playhouses of London and Paris, of which they became habitués. But the idea of the *scene*—a passion for structure, trajectory, and revelation that possessed James all his life—broke on him from still another early source: the transforming ecstasy of a single word. On a summer night in 1854, in the young Henry's presence, a small cousin his own age (he was then eleven) was admonished by her father that it was time to go to bed, and ran crying to her mother for a reprieve. "Come now, my dear; don't make a scene—I *insist* on your not making a scene," the mother reproved, and at that moment James, rapturously taking in the sweep of the phrase, fell irrevocably in love with the "witchcraft," as he called it, of the scene's plenitude and allure. "The expression, so vivid, so portentous," he said in old age, "was one I had never heard—it had never been addressed to us at home. . . . Life at these intensities clearly became 'scenes'; but the great thing, the immense illumination, was that we could make them or not as we chose."

That, however, was the illumination of drama, not the actuality of theater managers, actors, audiences. The ideal of the stage—as a making, a kneading, a medium wholly subject to the artist's will— had become infected by its exterior mechanisms. "The dramatic form," he wrote in 1882, "seems to me the most beautiful thing possible; the misery of the thing is that the baseness of the English-speaking stage affords no setting for it." By 1886 he was driven to confess that the "very dear dream . . . had faded away," and that he now thought "less highly of the drama, as a form, a vehicle, than I did—compared with the novel which can do and say so much more." In James's novel of the theater, *The Tragic Muse*, begun in 1888, a character bursts out, "What crudity compared to what the novelist does!" And in 1894, in a letter to his brother William, James speculated that "unless the victory and the spoils have not . . . become more proportionate than hitherto to the humiliations and vulgarities and disgusts, all the dishonor and chronic insult," he intended "to 'chuck' the whole intolerable experiment and return to more elevated and independent courses. I have come to *hate* the whole theatrical subject."

It was a gradual but steady repudiation, repeatedly contradicted by James's continuing and zigzag pursuit of managers and productions. In the end, the theater repudiated *him*; but the distinction he insisted on between theater, that low endeavor, and drama, that "highest ideal," went on to serve him in what would become one of his strangest fictions. After *Guy Domville*, he undertook to imagine a novel which would have all the attributes of a theatrical production. The reader would be supplied with dialogue, sets, grand and ingenious costuming, gestures of the head and hand; there would be entrances and exits; there would be drawing rooms and wit. The "few grave, rigid laws" of the drama would wash away all the expository freedoms and flexibilities of the traditional novel— above all, the chance to explain the action, to comment and interpret, to speak in metaphor. Narrative, and the narrator's guiding hum, would give way to the bareness of talk unaccoutered and unconstrued, talk deprived of authorial amplification; talk as *clue*.

The work that was to carry the burden of this lucidly calculat-
ed experiment was conceived on March 4, 1895, three months
after the failure of *Guy Domville*. On that day James entered into
his Notebook "the idea of the little London girl who grows up to
'sit with' the free-talking modern young mother . . . and, though
the conversation is supposed to be expurgated for her, inevitably
hears, overhears, guesses, follows, takes in, becomes acquainted
with, horrors." The Notebook recorded nothing about any intention to mimic the form of a play. But in his Preface to the New
York edition (1908) of *The Awkward Age*, James stressed that, from
the start, the story and its situation had presented itself to him "on
absolutely scenic lines, and that each of these scenes in itself . . .
abides without a moment's deflexion by the principle of the stage-
play." Speaking of the "technical amusement" and "bitter-sweet-
ness" arising from this principle, he reflected on the rich novelistic
discursiveness he had early determined to do without: "Exhibition
may mean in a 'story' twenty different ways, fifty excursions, alternatives, excrescences, and the novel, as largely practiced in English,
is the perfect paradise of the loose end." The play, by contrast,
"consents to the logic of but one way, mathematically right, and
with the loose end as gross an impertinence on its surface, and as
grave a dishonour, as the dangle of a snippet of silk or wool on the
right side of a tapestry." Moreover, he pointed out, the play is
committed to "objectivity," to the "imposed absence of that 'going
behind,'" to eschewing the "storyteller's great property-shop of
aids to illusion."

In choosing to write a novel confined to dialogue and scene; in
deciding to shape *The Awkward Age* according to self-limiting rules
of suppression and omission; in giving up the brilliant variety of the
English novel's widest and lushest potential, an art of abundance
that he had long ago splendidly perfected—what was James up to?
What system of psychological opposition had he fallen into? On the
one hand, a play in the form of a novel, or a novel in the form of a
play, was a response to "the most horrible hours of my life." What
the stage would not let him do, he would do in any case—on his

own venerable turf, with no possibility of catcalls. An act of triumph, or contempt, or revenge; perhaps a reward for having endured so much shame. And, on the other hand, a kind of penance: he was stripping himself clean, reducing a luxuriant craft to a monkish surrender of its most capacious instruments.

But penance for what? *The Awkward Age* represents an enigma. Though it intends unquestionably to be a comedy—a social comedy, a comedy of manners (as "The Turn of the Screw" unquestionably sets out to be a ghost story)—some enormous grotesquerie, or some grotesque enormity, insinuates itself into this ultimately mysterious work. Having straitjacketed his tale with the "few grave, rigid laws" of the stage, James resolved not to "go behind" its scenes with all those dozens of canny analyses and asides that are possible for the novel; yet on the whole it is as if proscenium and backdrop, and all the accouterments between them, have melted away, and nothing is left but what is "behind"—a "behind" any ordinary novelistic explication would not be equal to and could not touch. Paradoxically, the decision *not* to "go behind" put James squarely backstage, in the dark of the wings, in ill-lit and untidy dressing rooms among the sticky filth of discarded makeup jars—in the very place where there can be no explanation of the world on stage, because the world on stage is an invention and an untruth. James descended, in short, into an interior chaos; or to say it otherwise: with the composition of *The Awkward Age* he became, finally and incontrovertibly, a modernist. Like the modernists, he swept past the outer skin (the theater and its stage, the chatter of counterfeit drawing rooms, the comings and goings of actors and audiences, the coherent conscious machinery of things) to the secret life behind—glimmers of buried truths, the undisclosed drama of hint and inference.

The façade of comedy and the horror behind. And the penalty for "going behind"—while rigging up, via those "few grave, rigid laws," every obstacle to it—was the impenetrable blackness, the blankness, the *nox perpetua*, that gathered there, among the ropes and pulleys, where it is inevitable that one "hears, overhears, guesses, follows, takes in, becomes acquainted with, horrors." (The condition, one might note, of K. in *The Castle*.) And the horrors themselves? They cannot be named. It is their namelessness that defines them as horrors.

Yet James did give them a name—amorphous, suggestive, darkened by its imperial Roman origins, reminiscent of ancient clerical pageantry, more a riddle than a name: "the sacred terror." A translation, or, more likely a transmutation, of *sacro terrore*: the awe one feels in the presence of sacred or exalted personages, pope or emperor, before whom one may not speak; the dread one feels before the divine mysteries, or the head of Medusa. The face of a knowledge that is beyond our knowledge—intimations that cannot be borne. In the Preface to "The Turn of the Screw," James referred (handling it lightly so as not to be burned) to "the dear old sacred terror" as "the withheld glimpse" of "dreadful matter." The glimpse is withheld; to be permitted more than the glimpse would be to know too much. The sacred terror is, in fact, the sensation—not simply fright, but a kind of revulsion—that comes when glimpse perilously lengthens into gaze.

THE SACRED TERROR

In 1894, the year before the idea of *The Awkward Age* materialized in his Notebook, and not long before *Guy Domville* went into rehearsals, two electrifying personal events brought James close to the sacred terror, far closer than he wished to be. In both instances he stopped at glimpse and contrived to shut himself away from gaze. The first event was the suicide, in Italy, of Constance Fenimore Woolson. A relation of James Fenimore Cooper, Fenimore (as she was called) was an American novelist who settled successively in Florence, Venice, and Rome. Bent on homage, she had first approached James in 1880, in Florence, with a letter of introduction from America. James found her intelligent and moderately engaging, and offered his assistance as an acutely sophisticated guide to Florentine art. But what was a cautious friendship on his part became, on hers, a worshipful love. James could not reciprocate. She was middle-aged, unmarried, deaf in one ear—an admirable companion whom he was learning to be wary of. He worried that she might mistake occasional camaraderie for an encouragement of the affections. The news of her death in 1894, after nearly a decade and a half of correspondence (her letters were very long, his very short) bewildered and initially misled him. He had the impression she had died of "pneumonia supervening on influenza," and prepared to journey from London to her funeral in Rome. "Poor isolated and fundamentally tragic being!" he summed her up. "She was intrinsically one of the saddest and least happy natures I have ever met; and when I ask myself what I *feel* about her death the only answer that comes to me is from what I felt about the melancholy, the limitations and the touching loneliness of her life. I was greatly attached to her and valued exceedingly her friendship." All that, however, was glimpse, not gaze. The moment James learned it was suicide that had removed Fenimore—she had leaped from a second-story window—he retreated quickly and decided against attending her burial. Leon Edel speculates that James felt some responsibility for the hopelessness that had led to what James termed her "suicidal mania." Whether that is so or not, it is certainly true that James came to rest in a conventional, and distancing, judgment—"fundamentally tragic being!"—and averted his eyes from any connection he might have had with Fenimore's dread, or her destruction. He would not seek to know too much. He would evade the sacred terror. He would not "go behind": the preparation for going behind—the horrible hours—had not yet occurred.

Two years before Fenimore's death, James's sister Alice died in London. The cause was breast cancer, but she had been strangely invalided since girlhood, and was in the care of a young woman companion, Katharine Loring. Alice had followed James to London, or had at least followed his inclination to extract himself from America. Hers was an activist temperament (she interested herself in the hot politics of Irish Home Rule) that had chosen, for reasons neither her physicians nor her family could fathom, to go to bed for life. An 1889 photograph of her lodgings at Leamington—a health resort outside of London—survives: a capacious sick-room, high-ceilinged, with a single vast window, curtained and draperied; pictures dropped on long wires from the wainscoting; a chandelier sprouting fat globes; a tall carved mirror over a black fireplace; a round table with lamp, vase, flowers, books, magnifying glass. The effect is of Victorian swathing—layers of cloth over every flat and vertical surface: the mantel hung with cloth, the table, the back of a chair. Lamps, jugs, flowers, photos parade across the mantel. The Persian hearthrug smothers still another carpet, splotched with large flowers. Alice James herself seems swathed, almost swaddled, half-erect on a kind of sofa muffled in voluminously sprawling bedclothes, pillows propping her shoulder and neck. Next to her, nearer the window, holding a book, sits Miss Loring, her throat and bosom lost in a flurry of scarves. Both women are severely buttoned to the chin. It is a photograph that incites the lungs to gulp air; if it were possible to step into this scene, though the looking glass is polished and clear, one might feel choked by too many flower-patterns, the mistiness of light incarcerated, the stale smells of unrelieved enclosure.

William James, in his farewell letter to his sister, wrote that "if the tumor should turn out to be cancerous . . . then goodbye to neurasthenia and neuralgia and headache, and weariness and palpitation and disgust all at one stroke." To this physician brother, Alice had all along suffered from "the inscrutable and mysterious character of the doom of nervous weakness which has chained you down for all these years." Alice's illness, in short, was—until the advent of cancer—what we nowadays call "psychological." The genius sister of two genius brothers, she was self-imprisoned, self-restricted. Engulfed by cushions and shawls and wrappings at Leamington, in 1889 she began a diary: "I think that if I get into the habit of writing a bit about what happens, or rather what doesn't happen, I may lose a little of the sense of loneliness and desolation which abides with me."

She had had a history of terrors and nightmares. At twenty she had her first nervous breakdown (if that is what it was), at thirty her second, whereupon she was launched into an infinite series of undiagnosable ailments and their dubious, sometimes bizarre, remedies. She talked of suicide, and kept lists of contemporary suicides. She struggled for intellectual autonomy in an age when young women submitted, through marriage or otherwise, to the limitations of the domestic. Invalidism was, obliquely, one manner of solution: it yielded up an escape from ordinary female roles and contexts. At rest on her sofa, surrounded by heaps of books on every table-top, Alice lived in her head.

In her head she fought for Irish liberation; in her head she fought for her own. A famous sentence in her diary records a passionate revolution, in fantasy, of body and soul against a ruling class of one: "As I used to sit immovable reading in the library with waves of violent inclination suddenly invading my muscles, taking some one of their myriad forms such as throwing myself out of the window or knocking off the head of the benignant pater as he sat with his silver locks, writing at his table, it used to seem to me that the only difference between me and the insane was that I had not only all the horrors and suffering of insanity but the duties of doctor, nurse, and straitjacket upon me too."

In contrast to these dark recollections, Alice's diary offers a mellow view of Henry James, who often came to divert her and Miss Loring, bringing catty news and speculative gossip from his broader social world. "I have given him endless care and anxiety but notwithstanding this and the fantastic nature of my troubles I have never seen an impatient look upon his face or heard an unsympathetic or misunderstanding sound cross his lips. He comes at my slightest sign," she wrote, and spoke of a "pitch of brotherly devotion never before approached by the race." After Alice's death in 1892, Katharine Loring took away with her to Boston an urn containing Alice's ashes, and two thick notebooks; the latter were the pages of the diary. Two years later—in 1894, the year of Fenimore's suicide—Miss Loring arranged for the diary to be privately printed, and dispatched one copy to Henry, and another to

William. Both brothers were impressed. Henry described his sister's literary claim—he recognized that the diary *was* a literary work—as "heroic in its individuality, its independence—its face-to-face with the universe for and by herself," and praised the "beauty and eloquence," the "rich irony and humor," of Alice's pen. William's own high pleasure—"a leaf in the family laurel crown"—was tempered by a graver evaluation: "personal power venting itself on no opportunity," he concluded.

But it was Henry who backed away from the diary—much as he had had second thoughts about going to Fenimore's funeral. To begin with, he insisted that the diary not be published in his lifetime; and then he burned his copy—motivated, he said, by Alice's habit of setting down his sometimes unseemly accounts of friends and acquaintances. (Years later he made a bonfire of all the thousands of letters in his possession, obliterating the revelations of decades.) Amusement had become, in his sister's hands, document. James found himself shaken by "so many names, personalities, hearsays (usually, on Alice's part, through *me!*)"; he informed William that Alice's exposures made him "intensely nervous and almost sick with terror about possible publicity, possible accidents, reverberation etc.," and that he "used to say everything to Alice (on system) that could *égayer* [entertain] her bedside and many things in confidence. I didn't dream she wrote them down. . . . It is a 'surprise' that is too much of a surprise." There was more for James to grapple with, though, than the mortification of stumbling on his own remarks. It might be disconcerting that Alice had mentioned a certain essayist's "self-satisfied smirk." Yet something else lay coiled at the bottom of his sister's diary, and James was unequipped to live with it.

He met there, in fact—side by side with the bits of raillery and the vehement Irish nationalism—terrifying resonances and reminiscent apparitions. After the death of the James paterfamilias at home in Massachusetts, the diary disclosed, Alice, desolate in an empty house, was assaulted by the vibrations of a voice: "In those ghastly days, when I was by myself in the little house on Mt. Vernon

Street, how I longed to flee . . . and escape from the 'Alone, Alone!' that echoed thro' the house, rustled down the stairs, whispered from the walls, and confronted me, like a material presence, as I sat waiting, counting the moments." James himself, five years after the undoing of *Guy Domville*, grieved over "*the essential loneliness of my life*" (the emphasis is his own). "This loneliness," he put it, "what is it still but the deepest thing about one? Deeper, about *me*, at any rate, than anything else; deeper than my 'genius,' deeper than my 'discipline,' deeper than my pride, deeper, above all, than the deep counterminings of art."

Alice James's "Alone!" and Henry James's "deepest thing" had their antecedents in a phantasmagorical visitation endured by their father fifty years before. It was a vision, or a phantom, or an omen, so paralyzing to the spirit, so shocking in its horror, that Henry James Senior was compelled to give it a name (seemingly a fusion of "devastation," "visitation," "vast") out of Swedenborgian metaphysics: *vastation*. One spring day after dinner, he testified, "feeling only the exhilaration incident to a good digestion," he was all at once flooded by panic: "To all appearance it was a perfectly insane and abject terror, without ostensible cause, and only to be accounted for, to my perplexed imagination, by some damned shape squatting invisible to me within the precincts of the room, and raying out from his fetid personality influences fatal to life. The thing had not lasted ten seconds before I felt myself a wreck; that is, reduced from a state of firm, vigorous, joyful manhood to one of almost helpless infancy." And another time he described himself as "inwardly shriveled to a cinder," altered to a "literal nest of hell within my own entrails."

The younger Henry James had turned away from Fenimore's suicide. In nearly the same moment he had turned away from his sister's diary. The suicide intimated influences fatal to life from a fetid personality. The diary was fundamentally a portrait of infantile helplessness, a shriveled soul, hell within the entrails. The elder James, with his damned shape; Fenimore, flinging herself to the pavement; Alice, listening to the ghostly susurrations of her abandonment—each had dared to look into the abyss of knowing-too-much; James would not look with them. It was not until he had himself succumbed to his own vastation—eye to eye with the sacred terror on the stage of the St. James's Theater in 1895—that he was ready to exchange glimpse for gaze. The brawling pandemonium (it continued, in fact, for fifteen minutes) had not lasted ten seconds before he felt himself a wreck, reduced from a state of firm, vigorous, sovereign artistry to one of almost helpless infancy. Everything he had thought himself to be—a personage of majestic achievement—disintegrated in an instant. He could not go on as he had. Simply, he lost his nerve.

But he found, in the next work he put his hand to, not only a new way of imagining himself, but a new world of art. By paring away narrative rumination and exposition—by treating the novel as if it were as stark as a play-script—he uncovered (or invented) a host of labyrinthine depths and devices that have since been signally associated with literary modernism. For one thing, representation, while seeming to keep to its accustomed forms, took on a surreal quality, inscrutably off-center. For another, intent, or reason, gave way to the inchoate, the inexpressible. The narrative no longer sought to make a case for its characterizations; indirection, deduction, detection, inference, proliferated. An unaccountable presence, wholly unseen, was at last let in, even if kept in the tale's dark cellar: the damned shape, the sacred terror. The tale began to know more than the teller, the dream more than the dreamer; and Henry James began his approach to the Kafkan. In those "most horrible hours of my life" after his inward collapse on the stage of the St. James, the curtain was being raised for *The Awkward Age*.

THE AWKWARD AGE

The Awkward Age is, ostensibly, a comedy of manners, and resembles its populous class in that it concerns itself with the marriageability of a young woman. Nearly a hundred years after James wrote, no theme may appear so moribund, so obsolete, as the notion of "marrying off" a daughter. Contemporary daughters (and contemporary wives) enter the professions or have jobs, and do not sit on sofas, month after month, to be inspected by possibly suitable young men who are themselves to be inspected for their incomes. The difference between late Victorian mores and our own lies in female opportunity and female initiative, with freedom of dress and education not far behind. Yet the similarities may be stronger than the differences. It is still true that the term of marital eligibility for young women is restricted to a clearly specified span of years; it is still true that a now-or-never mentality prevails, and that young women (and often their mothers) continue to be stung by the risks of time. The gloves, parasols, boas, corsets, feathered hats, and floor-sweeping hems have vanished; the anxiety remains. A century ago, getting one's daughter appropriately married was a central social preoccupation, and, though marriage is nowadays not a young woman's only prescribed course in life, it is as much a gnawing preoccupation as it ever was. In this respect, no one can call the conditions of *The Awkward Age* dated.

In respect of sexual activity, those conditions are equally "modern." If sexual activity, in habit and prospect, defines manners, then—as a comedy of manners—*The Awkward Age* is plainly not a period piece. To be sure, society no longer pretends, as the Victorians did, to an ideal of young virgins kept from all normal understanding until the postnuptial deflowering; but in *The Awkward Age*, which depicts a public standard of ineffable purity not our own, that standard is mocked with bawdy zest. (Henry James bawdy? Consider the scuffle during which little Aggie sets her bottom firmly down upon a salacious French novel.) *The Awkward Age*, as a matter of fact, teems with adultery and emblems of incest; what appears to be wholesome finally suggests the soiled and the despoiled.

Still, it is not sexual standards and their flouting that move this novel from its opening lightness toward the shadowed distortions that are its destination. Rather, it is the unpredictable allegiances of probity. Probity arrives in the shape of Mr. Longdon, who "would never again see fifty-five" but is rendered as an aged, even antedilu-

vian, gentleman, complete with pince-nez, old-fashioned reti-
cences, and touchy memories of his prime. In his prime, in a moral
atmosphere he judges to be superior to that of the present, he (long
ago) loved and lost Lady Julia. He has never married, and for years
has lived away from London, in the country, in a house poignantly
similar to James's own Lamb House in Rye. He is a meticulous
watcher and silent critic, sensitive, upright, certainly elderly in his
perception of himself; a man of the past. One might imagine at first
that Mr. Longdon (he is always called "Mr.") is yet another incarnation of James's eager old gentlemen—the life-seeker Strether
who, in *The Ambassadors*, opens himself to the seductions of Paris,
or the thrill-thirsty John Marcher of "The Beast in the Jungle,"
who waits for some grand sensation or happening to befall him.
Mr. Longdon, by contrast, is a backward-looker. Lady Julia was his
Eden, and the world will never again be so bright or so right. "The
more one thinks of it," he remarks, "the more one seems to see
that society . . . can never have been anything but increasingly vulgar. The point is that in the twilight of time—and I belong, you
see, to the twilight—it had made out much less how vulgar it *could*
be."

He has come to London, then, as a kind of anthropologist
(though his motives are never clarified), on the trail of Lady Julia's
descendants, and is welcomed into the culture of the natives: the
chief of the natives being Mrs. Brookenham, Lady Julia's daughter,
who is at the hub of a fevered salon. All roads lead to Mrs. Brook's,
and the travelers are encrusted with bizarre trappings. The
Duchess, a callously opportunistic Englishwoman who is the
widow of a minor Italian aristocrat, is rearing her Neapolitan ward,
Agnesina ("little Aggie"), as a snow-white slate on which "the figures were yet to be written." The hugely rich Mr. Mitchett,
known as Mitchy, rigged out in unmatched merry-andrew gear
and tolerant to the point of nihilism, is the zany but good-hearted
son of a shoemaker become shoe mogul. Vanderbank, or Van—a
handsome, winning, self-protective, evasive young man of thirty-
five, impecunious on a mediocre salary, whom Mr. Longdon

befriends—is Mrs. Brook's (relatively) secret lover. In and out of Mrs. Brook's salon flow schemers, snobs, faithless wives and husbands, jesters, idlers, fantastic gossips; even a petty thief, who happens to be Mrs. Brook's own son, Harold. And at the tea table in the center of it all sits (now and then) her daughter, Lady Julia's granddaughter, Fernanda—Nanda—who smokes, runs around London "squeezing up and down no matter whose staircase," and chooses as an intimate a married woman with an absent husband.

Nanda is fully aware of the corrupted lives of her mother's circle. Her father is indifferent, negligent, a cipher; her brother sponges on everyone who enters the house, and on every house he enters; her parents live enormously beyond their means; all relationships are measured by what can be gotten out of them. "Edward and I," Mrs. Brook declares to the Duchess, "work it out between us to show off as tender parents and yet to get from you everything you'll give. I do the sentimental and he the practical." With her "lovely, silly eyes," Mrs. Brook at forty-one is youthfully attractive, but cuts two years off her daughter's age in order to snip two years from her own. There is no shame, no guilt, no conscience; the intrinsic has no value.

All these people (but for the blunt Duchess, who is plain Jane) have names that are cursory, like their lives: Mrs. Brook, Van, Mitchy, Aggie, Tishy, Carrie, even Nanda; it is as if only Mr. Longdon troubles to take a long breath. "I've been seeing, feeling, thinking," he admits. He understands himself to be "a man of imagination," an observer, with a "habit of not privately depreciating those to whom he was publicly civil." (A habit that James himself, on the evidence of the embarrassments of Alice's diary, did not always live up to.) Mrs. Brook's salon, by contrast, feeds on conspiracy, on sublimely clever talk, on plots and outrageous calculations, on malice and manipulation, on exploitation, on matchmaking both licit and illicit; everyone is weighed for cash worth. Mitchy rates high on the money scale, low on social background. Vanderbank, with his beauty and cultivated charm, is the reverse. Mr. Longdon has money, judiciousness, and an unappeased and unfinished love for Lady Julia, whose memory serves as a standard for fastidious decorum and civilized reciprocity—none of it to be found in present-day London, least of all in Mrs. Brook's drawing room. Mr. Longdon despises Mrs. Brook and is almost preternaturally drawn to Nanda. Though Lady Julia was beautiful and Nanda is not, he is overcome by what he takes to be a magical likeness. In Nanda, Lady Julia is nearly restored for him—except that Nanda is a modern young woman with access to the great world; she knows what Lady Julia in her girlhood would never have been permitted (or perhaps would never have wished) to know.

The ground on which *The Awkward Age* is spread—and woven, and bound, and mercilessly knotted—is precisely this: what a young woman ought or ought not to know, in a new London that "doesn't love the latent or the lurking, has neither time nor sense for anything less discernible than the red flag in front of the steam-roller" as Vanderbank cautions Mr. Longdon. "It wants cash over the counter and letters ten feet high. Therefore you see it's all as yet rather a dark question for poor Nanda—a question that in a way quite occupies the foreground of her mother's earnest little life. How *will* she look, what will be thought of her and what will she be able to do for herself?" Nanda at eighteen, having come of age (Mrs. Brook, for all her shaving of years, can no longer suppress this news), is ready to be brought down—from the schoolroom, so to speak—to mingle among the denizens and fumes of Mrs. Brook's nether realm. "I seem to see," James complained in his Notebook, ". . . English society before one's eyes—the great modern collapse of all the forms and 'superstitions' and respects, good and bad, and restraints and mysteries . . . decadences and vulgarities and confusions and masculinizations and femininizations—the materializations and abdications and intrusions, and Americanizations, the lost sense, the brutalized manner . . . the general revolution, the failure of fastidiousness." And he mourned the forfeiture "of nobleness, of delicacy, of the exquisite"—losses he connected with "the non-marrying of girls, the desperation of mothers, the whole alteration of manners . . .

and tone, while our theory of the participation, the *presence* of the young, remains unaffected by it."

Nanda, in brief, still unmarried at twenty, becomes, by virtue (or, one might say, by vice) of her saturation in her mother's circle, unmarriageable. The Duchess has reared little Aggie on a different scheme—the strict continental preservation of her purity, mental and other. Little Aggie is consequently a marvel of protected innocence and ignorance, decorative and inutile, "like some wonderful piece of stitching." She is "really the sort of creature," Vanderbank offers, that Nanda "would have liked to be able to be." And Mrs. Brook lightly yet chillingly notes, "She couldn't possibly have been able . . . with so loose—or, rather, to express it more properly, so perverse—a mother."

Nanda's mother's looseness and perverseness is pointed enough: she knows her daughter is in love with Vanderbank, but means to keep hold of him for herself. Vanderbank, in any event, is useless as a potential husband—he has no money. Mitchy has both money and hope, and is perpetually in pursuit of Nanda. But fond though she is of him, Mitchy—a free balloon, a whimsical cynic, dotingly unconcerned, endlessly kind, all without being rooted in serious discrimination—is for Nanda literally untouchable. She will not so much as allow him to kiss her hand. Mitchy, she tells Mr. Longdon, is "impossible." Who, then, will Nanda marry? In surroundings thickened by innuendo and conspiracy, Mr. Longdon, man of probity, himself descends to insinuation and plot—though he might think of these as inference and discretion. In combination with the Duchess, he cooks up the idea of inducing Vanderbank to marry Nanda. Despite the delicacy that veils his intent, it crudely comes down to money: Mr. Longdon will make it worth Vanderbank's while to propose to Nanda. After which, hearing of Mr. Longdon's scheme, Mitchy will relinquish Nanda (Nanda has herself urged Mitchy on Aggie), and the Duchess, finally, will have a clear field to sweep him up for her immaculate little ward. Shoemaker's offspring or no, Mitchy is a prize promising strings of pearls.

Aggie, wed to Mitchy, turns instantly wild. What was yesterday a *tabula rasa* grows hectic overnight with prurient scribblings. But under Mrs. Brook's reign (and London practice), a sullied Aggie is acceptable, predictable, even conventional. The Duchess is not simply calm. She is smug. Aggie, married, is promptly expected to know whatever there is to know of sexual heat, deceit, the denigration of husbands, the taking of lovers, the scufflings of wives. There is no surprise in any of it. English rules apply: abdications and intrusions, revolution and the failure of fastidiousness—as long as the wedding is past. Postnuptial contamination troubles no one.

Nanda's is a different case. She is tainted and unmarried. "If Nanda doesn't get a husband early in the business," the Duchess advises Mr. Longdon, "she won't get one at all. One, I mean, of the kind she'll take. She'll have been in it over-long for *their* taste." "Been in what?" Mr. Longdon asks. "Why in the air they themselves have infected for her!" the Duchess retorts. The infection is carried by the clever young men who, "with intellectual elbow-room, with freedom of talk," hang about Mrs. Brook's drawing room, putting their hostess "in a prodigious fix—she must sacrifice either her daughter or . . . her intellectual habits." And the Duchess crows: "You'll tell me we go farther in Italy, and I won't deny it, but in Italy we have the common sense not to have little girls in the room." Yet Nanda is far from being a little girl. "Of course she's supposedly young," the Duchess pursues, "but she's really any age you like: your London world so fearfully batters and bruises them."

In the end Vanderbank declines to marry Nanda, not even for profit. She delights him; he admires her; he may even adore her; and he is certainly not in love with her mother. Nanda, on her side, seemingly ignorant of Mr. Longdon's bribe (though she is ignorant of nothing else), longs for Vanderbank's proposal. On a lyrical summer afternoon, it appears about to come; finally it does not. Nanda is "infected": she knows too much. Superficially, one may protest fashionable London's double standard—excessive worldliness does not interfere, after all, with the marital eligibility of young men. And the argument can be made—it *is* made—that, if Vanderbank cannot marry without money, he cannot marry with it either: perhaps he scruples to wed on means not his own. But it is not Mr. Longdon's bribe that Vanderbank finds impossible. It is Nanda herself, Nanda in her contamination. Nor is the infection he intuits in her merely social worldliness, however alarming that worldliness may be.

Nanda's infection is more serious than that. Her knowing pestilential things heard and seen in her mother's salon is not the whole source and sum of her malady. What might have stopped at taintedness through oversophistication has, since the arrival of Mr. Longdon—to whom she has passionately attached herself—deepened into another order of contagion. Behind the comedy, a seal lifts from over the void; the sacred terror is seeping into the tale. A gentleman of integrity, universally understood as such, Mr. Longdon begins to draw after him a gradual toxicity, screened by benevolence. Nanda speaks affectionately of his "curious infatuation." She is herself curiously infatuated: "I set him off—what do you call it?—I show him off," she tells Vanderbank, "by his going round and round as the acrobat on the horse in the circle goes round the clown." And she acknowledges that her conversations with Mr. Longdon explore "as far as a man and a woman can together." To her mother she explains, "I really think we're good friends enough for anything." "What do you call that then," Mrs. Brook inquires, "but his adopting you?" And another time Mrs. Brook wonders whether this "little fussy ancient man" is attempting to "make up to" her daughter.

But the bond between Mr. Longdon and Nanda is more mysterious than any December-May flirtation, and it is assuredly not an adoption. It is true that Mr. Longdon pursues, he courts, he possesses. He takes Nanda away to his country house for a long stay. And finally he takes her to live with him permanently. Still, it is not an adoption, not a liaison, not anything like a marriage. It may be intended as a salvation: Nanda must be removed from Mrs. Brook's polluting household; Nanda, infected, is not marriageable. Mrs.

Brook is privy to the fact of Mr. Longdon's bribe (Vanderbank has tattled to her), and though it may (or may not) portend her losing Vanderbank as lover, nothing could gratify her more. "I can't help feeling," she observes, "that something possibly big will come of Mr. Longdon." "Big" means, in this lexicon, money; and when the bribe to Vanderbank fails, Nanda, for want of an alternative falling under Mr. Longdon's protection, decidedly *does* fall into money.

She also falls into a peculiar aura: the aura of James's post-*Guy Domville* mood. James endowed Mr. Longdon not only with his own house, but with his own age, and with his own intimations of mortality and loss. To Nanda Mr. Longdon bursts out: "Oh, you've got time—you can come round again; you've a margin for accidents, for disappointments and recoveries: you can take one thing with another. But I've only my last little scrap." Mr. Longdon, one surmises, is here a mirror for certain darkening aspects of James himself. And so, interestingly, is Nanda, whose early self-recognition—"I shall never marry"—is a version of James's own youthful announcement: "I am too good a bachelor to spoil." The price of being so good a bachelor was a latterday profundity of loneliness, and in his later years—though there was no Lady Julia in James's past on which to hang a present attachment—there were sentimental yearnings toward a whole series of engaging and gifted young men. The journalist Morton Fuller (who became Edith Wharton's lover for a time) was one of them; Hendrik Andersen, a sculptor, was another. A third, who struck James as especially endearing, was Jonathan Sturges. Sturges, crippled by polio in childhood, was an American residing in England, "full of talk and intelligence, and of the absence of prejudice . . . saturated with London, and with all sorts of contrasted elements in it, to which he has given himself up." This account of Sturges, appearing in one of James's letters, might easily be a portrait of Nanda. During the course of composition of *The Awkward Age*, which James was just then serializing for *Harper's*, Sturges was received with tender hospitality in Lamb House, and remained for many weeks. Nanda's visit to Mr. Longdon in his house in Suffolk (Lamb House is in Sussex) similarly lasts a number of weeks. The charming young men who so much appealed to James in this desolate period may have turned up, in Nanda, as a kind of imagined solution to isolation and despair. In real life, the charming young men came and went. In the novel, Nanda will move in and stay forever.

But *The Awkward Age* offers no solution after all. Nanda's ultimately going to live with Mr. Longdon is—for James's time and for our own—a serious anomaly. Nanda has twice been the subject of a bribe—once with Vanderbank, and again with her parents, who are only too glad to see that Mr. Longdon, by taking her in, really is doing something "big" for her. There is nothing honorable in Vanderbank's refusal of Mr. Longdon's bribe, and there is nothing straightforward in that refusal, which is never directly spoken. Vanderbank, pleasing everyone and no one, simply drifts away. He has the carelessness of consummate indifference; what is too tangled, or too demanding, can have no claim on him. He will never come through. "There are things I ought to have done that I haven't," he reluctantly tells Nanda in their brief last meeting. "I've been a brute and I didn't mean it and I couldn't help it." Moments before this admission, he sums it all up: "The thing is, you see, that I haven't a conscience. I only want my fun."

Mr. Longdon himself, presumably a man of acute conscience, does not escape corruption. Entering a corrupt community—a bribable community—he uncovers in himself an inclination to offer bribes. For Nanda's parents, the thing is more flagrant than a bribe. Mrs. Brook has, beyond question, sold her daughter to a rich man who will undoubtedly make her his heir. Mrs. Brook's acquiescence in Nanda's removal confirms the smell of the marketplace: plainly she would have declared against Nanda's going off with a "little fussy ancient man" who was poor. Mr. Longdon, in consequence, has succeeded in buying for his empty house a young woman nearly a third his age—and no matter how benign, or rescuing, or salvational this arrangement may appear to him, it is at bottom a purchase transaction, intended to assuage his lonely need. The young woman he purposes to protect will be sequestered from society on the premise that she is anyhow unmarriageable; on his account (even if he supposes it to be on *her* account) she will be foreclosed from the turnings and chances of a life beyond his own elderly precincts.

But Nanda has been brought to Mr. Longdon's house for still another reason: the revenge of love and the revenge of hate. Love of Lady Julia, hatred of Mrs. Brook. If Lady Julia in all her loveliness once passed him by, two generations afterward he is in possession of her grandchild. "I'm a hater," he says bluntly, reflecting on the decline of the standard that once made a "lady." In secluding Nanda from her mother's reach, he is trumpeting his contempt for Mrs. Brook: private hatred becomes public scorn. Nanda, for her part, goes with him willingly. She is complicit in the anomaly of their connection; she is the instrument of her own retreat. It is not the money—the being provided for—that lures Nanda; it is the strangeness, and, above all, the surrender.

For Nanda, Mr. Longdon's house holds out a suicidal peace: renunciation, a radical swerving from hope. Agreeing to enter that house of relinquishment (and moribund refinement)—this time never again to leave it—she is hurtled into a final storm of grief. Long ago, Mr. Longdon lost Lady Julia. Now Nanda has lost Vanderbank. They are matched in desolation.

> It burst from her, flaring up in a queer quaver that ended in something queerer still—in her abrupt collapse, on the spot, into the nearest chair, where she choked with a torrent of tears. Her buried face could only after a moment give way to the flood, and she sobbed in a passion as sharp and brief as the flurry of a wild thing for an instant uncaged; her old friend meantime keeping his place in the silence broken by her sound and distantly—across the room— closing his eyes to his helplessness and her shame. Thus they sat together while their trouble both conjoined and divided them.

Here James, in suddenly "going behind," momentarily abandons his "few grave, rigid laws" of dramatic restraint. It is as if, in this outburst of bereavement, the idea of helplessness and shame cannot be prevented from pressing forward, willy-nilly, from the cobwebbed backstage dark. The sacred terror is at last flung straight in the face of the tale. Not only helplessness and shame, but corruption; callousness; revenge; sexual displacement. Nanda displaces (or replaces) Lady Julia; beyond the novel's enclosure she may displace—or mask—James's endearing young men who come and go. There are, besides, incestuous hints: the young woman who might have been her protector's grandchild is intimately absorbed into the days and nights of his house. Her parents have abdicated. Her mother has sold her. The man she hoped to marry will not have her, even for a fortune. The man who takes her in, troubled by secret fevers and unthreshed motives, is sunk in a web of confusion; the young woman represents for him half a dozen identities, relations, unwholesome resolutions. And she, in joining him, has gone to bed, in effect, for life—as a penalty, or perhaps in penance, for knowing too much.

A panicked scenario. How much of it did James know? Did the teller penetrate to the bowels of the tale? The tale, in any case, penetrates—or decodes—the teller. The mosaic fly-eye of the narrative assembles all the shards and particles of James's chronicle of crisis, glimpse after glimpse, and sweeps them up, and compiles and conflates them into one horrendous *seeing*—James in his aging forlornness, in a house devoid of companionship and echoing with his sister's "Alone!"; Fenimore's wild crash; Alice's burial-in-life; the return of his father's "damned shape" and its fatal influences. And what was that shape if not James himself, at the crest of a life delivered over wholly to art, helpless on the stage on the evening of January 5, 1895, the crown of his genius thrown brutally down? "Thus they sat together while their trouble both conjoined and divided them." Divided, because James in his domicile, unlike Mr. Longdon, is alone, and will always be alone. Conjoined, because James is at once both Mr. Longdon and Nanda. But surely more than either or both. These two have been dropped into a pit. James is the pit's master, its builder and evoker.

After the cataclysmic turning point of *Guy Domville*, hidden knowings are everywhere in James—notably in *What Maisie Knew*

(1897) and "The Turn of the Screw," and culminating in the last
great pair of conspiratorial works, *The Wings of the Dove* (1902)
and *The Golden Bowl* (1904). The recurrence, in his own sensibility, of the paternal vastation, the recognition of an immutable
deprivation (*"the essential loneliness of my life"*), the nearby explo-
sions of suicide and self-immolation, the "horrible hours" themselves—all these pitchforked James out of the Victorian and into
the modern novel. He broke down both social and narrative
forms and plummeted, sans the old fastidiousness (and optimism),
into the smoldering detritus of exhausted ways. It is probable that
The Awkward Age is a novel that knows far more than its author
knew, and holds more secrets of panic, shame, helplessness, and
chaos than James could candidly face. But it was this work that
crucially and decisively pried open the inmost door to the void.
After which, released from glimpse into gaze, James could dare as
Conrad dared, and as Kafka dared.

At the climax of his powers Henry James looked freely into the
Medusan truth, he snared the unconscious. "Make him *think* the
evil," he said, soliciting the unprepared nineteenth-century reader
as the twentieth came near (a century that was to supply unthinkable evil), "make him think it for himself." And in the end—anarchy loosed upon the world, and pitilessness slouching toward
him—James thought it for himself.

(1992)